Hypertext and Hypermedia

Hypertext and Hypermedia

Jakob Nielsen

Technical University of Denmark
Copenhagen, Denmark

ACADEMIC PRESS, INC.

Harcourt Brace Jovanovich, Publishers

Boston San Diego New York
London Sydney Tokyo Toronto

ACADEMIC PRESS, INC.
1250 Sixth Avenue, San Diego, CA 92101

United Kingdom Edition published by
ACADEMIC PRESS LIMITED
24-28 Oval Road, London NW1 7DX

Library of Congress Cataloging-in-Publication Data

Nielsen, Jakob
  Hypertext and hypermedia / Jakob Nielsen.
    p. cm.
    Includes bibliographical references.
    ISBN 0-12-518410-7 (alk. paper)
    1. Hypertext systems. I. Title
  QA76.76.H94N54 1990   90-92
  005.75′4—dc20   CIP

Printed in the United States of America
90 91 92 93   9 8 7 6 5 4 3

Contents

Preface

Why is this a *book*?

Given that I am so enthusiastic about hypertext it might have been reasonable to expect that I would have published my ideas about it in a hypertext form. But there are still so many practical disadvantages connected with electronic publishing that I decided to stay with paper a little longer.

Assume that you were holding a disk in your hand instead of a book. First, you would not be able to read it in bed or on the bus unless you had one of the "SmartBook" readers described in Chapter 7. Second, even if you had a small portable computer, it would probably not be the brand I have used to write the hypertext so you could not read the contents of the disk anyway. Third, you probably would not have been able to get hold of the disk at all since it would not have had access to the regular distribution channels of the book trade.

One of the main advantages of having this book in a hypertext format would be to provide readers with the possibility of linking directly to supplementary reading material for issues of special interest to each individual reader. Unfortunately this would be mostly impossible to do given current copyright restrictions, since the relevant literature on hypertext has so many different copyright holders that nobody could acquire all the relevant permissions.

Instead I have relied on the traditional form of "dead" links in the form of references to the published literature. Appendix B contains an extensive bibliography on hypertext, which is annotated to allow you to determine the relevance of a given reference before you go to the trouble of getting hold of it. References throughout the book point to this bibliography through the standard notation of listing the author's last name and the year of publication in square brackets.

To try to compensate for the lack of a running hypertext, Chapter 2 gives a very detailed case study of one hypertext system and even tells you how to get hold of a free copy of it (if you have the right machine and the right electronic network connections). Chapters 4 and 5 give examples of several additional hypertext systems, and the book is richly illustrated to give you an idea of the variety of ways hypertext can be implemented.

Camera ready copy for the book was completely desktop published with Microsoft Word version 4.0 for the Macintosh (with the exception of rasterized photos). This technique allowed as fast a production schedule as humanly possible in the non-online medium (with a little help from electronic mail, fax machines, and Federal Express), so that we have been able to include developments up until two months before the book was published.

A Multitude of Hypertext

This book is based on many examples of hypertext in both the form of systems and applications. There are now so many different approaches to hypertext that it would be wrong to base a book on a single one.

It would also be wrong for users to base their judgment of hypertext's usefulness for them on the basis of knowing a single example of hypertext. Many people may know a single system because they have seen it reviewed or because it is used by one of their friends. Such first hand information should of course be utilized as *part* of a decision on whether to use hypertext, but it should not be the only input to the decision.

It is important to realize that hypertext is such a broad concept that one hypertext system might well be completely unsuited to a particular application even though the application could be well supported by another hypertext system. Therefore this book aims at providing you with an idea of the multitude of hypertext, so that you will be better able to decide for yourself whether your needs can be served by hypertext and what requirements should be fulfilled to serve these needs *well*.

Acknowledgements

Many people have helped me write this book either directly or through their comments on my various earlier writings in the hypertext area. I would like to thank:

Michael H. Andersen, Technical University of Denmark
Peter Brown, University of Kent at Canterbury, U.K.
Tat-Seng Chua, National University of Singapore
Laura De Young, Price Waterhouse
James D. Foley, George Washington University
Jeffrey A. Fox, The MITRE Corporation
Christian Gram, Technical University of Denmark
Lynda Hardman, Office Workstations Ltd., U.K.
Gordon Howell, Scottish HCI Centre
Hiroshi Ishii, NTT Human Interface Laboratories, Japan
Hannah Kain, Baltica Finans, Copenhagen, Denmark
Andrew E. Kerr, James Hardie Industries, Ltd., Australia
Julie Launhardt, IRIS,[1] Brown University
John J. Leggett, Texas A&M University
Rob Lippincott, Lotus Development Corporation
Anne Loomis, IRIS, Brown University
Uffe Lyngbæk, Technical University of Denmark
Ray McAleese, University of Aberdeen, U.K.
Gary Marchionini, University of Maryland
Terry Mayes, Scottish HCI Centre
Alex Morrison, Cognitive Applications Ltd., Brighton, U.K.
Elli Mylonas, Harvard University
Anne Nicol, Apple Computer, Cupertino, CA
Kurt Nørmark, Aalborg University, Denmark
Annelise Mark Pejtersen, Risø National Research Laboratory, Denmark
Henrik Rasmussen, Contex, Denmark
Mark Sawtelle, IRIS, Brown University
John L. Schnase, Texas A&M University
John Schnizlein, George Washington University
Ben Shneiderman, University of Maryland
Ted Sicker, WGBH Educational Foundation
Malcolm Slaney, Apple Computer, Cupertino, CA
Norbert A. Streitz, Gesellschaft für Mathematik und Datenverarbeitung
    (GMD), West Germany
Frank Wm. Tompa, University of Waterloo, Canada
Janet Walker, Digital Equipment Corporation, Cambridge, MA
John A. Waterworth, National University of Singapore

---

[1] IRIS = Institute for Research in Information and Scholarship.

Patricia Wright, Applied Psychology Unit, Cambridge, U.K.
Nicole Yankelovich, IRIS, Brown University

Also, I owe many thanks to my publisher and copyeditor at Academic Press, Alice Peters and Lucy Ferriss for helping me clean up the manuscript.

My work on this book was partly supported by grant 1221-89-081108 from the Danish Ministry of Culture.

Parts of this book are based on work performed within the SAFE project, partially funded by the Commission of the European Communities under contract number D1014 of the Exploratory Action of the DELTA program.

The views expressed in this book are obviously those of the author, however, and do not necessarily reflect those of the SAFE consortium[2] or the Danish government.

Jakob Nielsen

---

[2] Philips International (prime contractor), Courseware Europe, the Scottish HCI Centre, Ernst Klett Verlag, Educational Computing Consortium, University of Twente, University of Amsterdam, Eindhoven University of Technology, Technologia e Investigacion Ferroviaria Sociedad Anonima, University of Leeds, University of Lancaster, University of Athens, Office Workstations Ltd. (OWL), Uitgeversmaatschappij Argus, Technical University of Denmark, and University College of Galway.

1.   Defining Hypertext and Hypermedia

The simplest way to define hypertext is to contrast it with traditional text like this book. All traditional text, whether in printed form or in computer files, is *sequential*, meaning that there is a single linear sequence defining the order in which the text is to be read. First you read page one. Then you read page two. Then you read page three. And you don't have to be much of a mathematician to generalize the formula which determines what page to read next....

Hypertext is *nonsequential;* There is no single order that determines the sequence in which the text is to be read. Figure 1.1 gives an example. Assume that you start by reading the piece of text marked **A**. Instead of a single next place to go, this hypertext structure has three options for the reader: Go to **B**, **D**, or **E**. Assuming that you decide to go to **B**, you can then decide to go to **C** or to **E**, and from **E** you can go to **D**. Since it was also possible for you to go directly from **A** to **D**, this example shows that there may be several different paths that connect two elements in a hypertext structure.

Hypertext presents several different options to the readers, and the *individual* reader determines which of them to follow *at the time of*

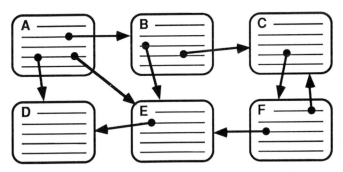

Figure 1.1. *Simplified view of a small hypertext structure having six nodes and nine links.*

1

reading the text. This means that the author of the text has set up a number of alternatives for readers to explore rather than a single stream of information.

The same is true of footnotes in traditional printed texts, since readers have to determine upon reaching the footnote marker whether to continue reading the primary stream of text or to branch off to pursue the footnote. Therefore hypertext is sometimes called the "generalized footnote." Another printed form with access structures similar to hypertext is the encyclopedia with its many cross-references.

As can be seen from Figure 1.1, hypertext consists of interlinked pieces of text (or other information). These pieces are illustrated as computer screens in Figure 1.1, but they can also be scrolling windows, files, or smaller bits of information. Each unit of information is called a *node*. Whatever the grain size of these nodes, each of them may have pointers to other units, and these pointers are called *links*. The number of links is normally not fixed in advance but will depend on the content of each node. Some nodes are related to many others and will therefore have many links, while other nodes serve only as destinations for links but have no outgoing links of their own.

Figure 1.1 also shows that the entire hypertext structure forms a network of nodes and links. Readers move about this network in an activity that is often referred to as browsing or navigating, rather than just "reading," to emphasize that users must actively determine the order in which they read the nodes.

A hypertext link connects two nodes and is normally directed in the sense that it points from one node (called the *anchor* node) to another (called the *destination* node). Hypertext links are frequently associated with specific parts of the nodes they connect rather than with the nodes as a whole. In the example in Figure 1.1, we see that the links are anchored at specific locations in the departure node while their destinations are the entire arrival node. A typical application of this feature is to have a link anchored at a certain word in the departure node and then let the user activate the link by clicking on that word.

When users follow the links around the hypertext network, they will often have a need to return to some previously visited node. Most hypertext systems support this through a *backtrack* facility. Assume that we are currently located in node **D** in Figure 1.1. If we had arrived at this node via the path **A→B→E→D**, then the backtrack command would take us to node **E** the first time it was issued. A second backtrack command would then take us further back along our path to node **B**. If, on the other hand, we had jumped directly from node **A** to node **D**, then issuing the backtrack command at node **D** would take us to node **A** since that would then be where we came from. This example shows that backtracking is just as dependent on the individual user's movement as is the order in which the nodes were visited in the first place.

Narrower Definitions of Hypertext

Since hypertext has become so popular in recent years, much rides on the exact definition of what constitutes hypertext. Many products are advertised as hypertext without being so according to the common definition presented above. Additionally, many products that are hypertext according to this definition lack important features which might be included in a narrower definition of hypertext.

For example, Frank Halasz from Xerox PARC has put forward the view that a true hypertext system should include an explicit representation of the network structure in its user interface. As shown in Figure 1.1, *any* hypertext will form a network of nodes and links, but in most current systems that network is only present inside the computer. At any given time the user sees only the current node and the links leading out from that node; it is up to the user's imagination to picture how the entire network is structured.

Halasz wants to give the user a dynamic overview showing the structure of this network. Very few current hypertext systems provide such diagrams.[1] The reason the overview diagram needs to be dynamic is that it is normally impossible to draw a graphic representation of the entire hypertext on a computer screen since a hypertext typically contains thousands of nodes. Instead the diagram is only displayed in detail for the local neighborhood surrounding the user's current location, which is often highlighted on the diagram. The various ways of providing an overview are discussed in further detail in Chapter 8.

Almost all current hypertext systems are limited to providing one-directional links like the ones shown in Figure 1.1. This means that the system can show the user the links that have the current node as their departure point but not the ones that have it as their arrival point. In

---

[1] Halasz's own system, NoteCards, is one of the few exceptions. It is discussed further in Chapter 5.

other words, the system will tell you where you can go next but not in what alternative ways you might have arrived at where you are now.

K. Eric Drexler has advocated the use of bi-directional links in hypertext, meaning that the system should also be able to display a list of incoming links. From a computer science perspective it would be almost a trivial task to implement such a feature, but almost none of the current hypertext systems do so.[2]

One example comes from Intermedia, which does support bidirectional links. A hypertext structure on Chinese poetry [Kahn 1989b] has links from each poem to the references to those anthologies where it has been reprinted and/or translated. This set-up automatically ensures that each listing for an anthology or a translator has a complete set of links pointing to occurrences of the relevant poems in the Intermedia hypertext.

Drexler has also stated the need for supporting links across various forms of computer network such as Local Area Networks (LANs) and international networks. This step will become necessary if hypertext is ever going to replace the traditional publishing business, since nobody can have all the world's literature stored on their own local computer no matter how big an optical disk they get. Access to remote databases will become a necessity for many future hypertext applications, but almost all current hypertext systems are limited to working with data stored on a single personal computer.

Many non-hypertext computer techniques may at least match various aspects of the definition of hypertext, but true hypertext should also make users *feel* that they can move freely through the information, according to their own needs. This feeling is hard to define precisely but certainly implies small overhead with respect to using the computer. This means short response times so that the text is on the screen as soon as the user asks for it. Small overhead also requires low cognitive load when navigating, so that users do not have to spend their time wondering what the computer will do or how to get it to do what they want.

When asked whether I would view a certain system as hypertext, I would not rely so much on its specific features, command, or data structures, but more on its user interface "look and feel."

---

[2] It would just involve updating two lists instead of one every time a new link was added.

Hypermedia: Multimedia Hypertext

The traditional definition of the term "hypertext" implies that it is a system for dealing with plain text. Since many of the current systems actually also include the possibility for working with graphics and various other media, some people prefer using the term *hypermedia,* to stress the multimedia aspects of their system. Personally, I would like to keep using the traditional term "hypertext" for all systems since there does not seem to be any reason to reserve a special term for text-only systems. Therefore I tend to use the two terms *hypertext* and *hypermedia* interchangeably with a preference to sticking to *hypertext.*

As discussed in the next section, being multimedia is not enough for a program to be hypermedia. But it is possible to use quite extravagant multimedia capabilities to good effect as part of a hypermedia system. For example, the Swedish design company *AVICOM* is designing a hypermedia system for a natural history museum in Stockholm called *Naturens Hus* ("the house of nature"). This system includes the more or less traditional hypermedia linking, e.g. maps of the region with photos of the birds living in various areas with recordings of these birds singing. But the hypermedia system also controls a slide projector projecting an image on the very floor where the user is standing. This technique is used to increase the user's sense of immersion in an environment, for instance by turning the floor blue when the system is discussing a geological period where the entire Stockholm region was under water.

In any case, hypertext is a natural technique for supporting multimedia interfaces since it is based on the interlinking of nodes that may contain different media. Typical media in hypermedia nodes are text, graphics, video, and sound.

Graphics can be either scanned images or object-oriented pictures constructed by some computer graphics algorithm. Graphics can be used purely as illustration or they can be more actively involved with the hypertext aspects of the hypermedia system by also including anchors for hypertext links.

One example of the use of graphics in a hypertext manner is the Drexel Disk from Drexel University in Pennsylvania [Hewett 1987]. Drexel is one of those universities that require all their students to own a Macintosh computer. This policy makes it possible for faculty to develop courseware and to know that all their students will be able to

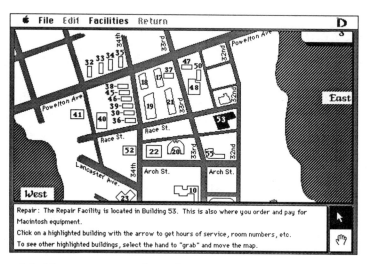

Figure 1.2. *The campus map from the Drexel Disk.* © *1989 by Thomas T. Hewett, reprinted with permission.*

run it. It also makes it possible for the university to supply introductory information for the freshmen in a hypertext format on the so-called Drexel Disk. This disk contains a lot of information about the university which is interlinked in a hypertext manner. One of the nodes of information is the campus map shown in Figure 1.2.

Whenever the rest of the hypertext mentions some university building, the Drexel Disk allows the student to take a hypertext jump to the campus map to see the location of that building. The campus map also includes links from the individual buildings to descriptions of the departments and the other facilities they house.

Various moving images in the form of video or animations are also common data types in hypermedia nodes. Figure 1.3 shows the use of animation to illustrate a movement that might otherwise be very hard to visualize.

One difficulty with representing video in hypertext is the question of how to name links. The most traditional solution has been to use plain text as the hypertext anchor leading to the playing of a piece of video, but that is not a very hyper*media*-like choice.

An alternative solution has been developed at the MIT Media Lab by Hans Peter Brøndmo and Glorianna Davenport [Brøndmo and

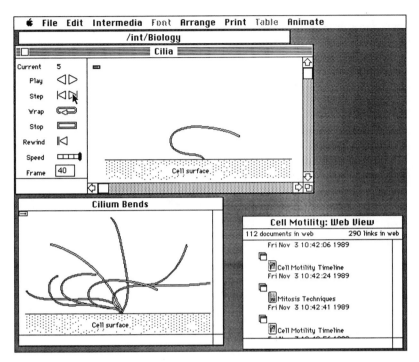

Figure 1.3. *The document "Cilia" (upper left) was created using InterPlay, Intermedia's two-dimensional animation editor. When a link is followed to this document, the animation is automatically triggered to illustrate the movements of the cilia. © 1989 Brown University, reprinted with permission.*

Davenport 1990] for their *Elastic Charles* project.[3] They represent the link to a video clip by a miniaturized version of the clip or a part of it. Thus their anchors are actually small moving images in their own right called *micons* (moving icons), since users are often able to recognize a piece of film by viewing the movements it contains.

The use of sound in hypertext introduces yet another linkage problem [Catlin and Smith 1988]. It is fairly easy to have a sound as the destination for a hypertext link; the sound plays when the anchor is activated. But in many applications one also wants to anchor departure points in the sound itself. For example one sound-based hypermedia system is used for teaching music theory and links various CD records containing famous works of music to texts analyzing details of the

---

[3] The *Elastic Charles* is a hypermedia "magazine" about the Charles River (in Boston/Cambridge); it interconnects several videos about the river filmed by MIT students.

music. Users have to be able to indicate that they are interested in a specific piece of music and want to read the comments for it. It is unfortunately impossible simply to click on the sound in the same way as one can click on a word or a graphic image. Instead one has to provide the user with a *visual surrogate* representation of the sound on which to click. In the case of music an obvious surrogate would be a picture of the notes but for other sounds a less intuitive representation has to be used.

Hypertext and Regular Computer Applications

Upon reading the definition of hypertext in the beginning of this chapter, readers with a training in computer science might have thought, "This is just databases." It is true that hypertext has many similarities to databases, and one does need some form of database at the bottom of a hypertext system actually to store and retrieve the text and other media contained in the nodes.

Hypertext is fundamentally different from traditional databases from a user perspective, however. A normal database such as the database of employees in a company has an extremely regular structure defined by a high-level data definition language. All of the data follow this single structure, so we might have ten thousand employee records all of which have the same fields for name, address, salary, telephone extension, etc.

A hypertext information base has no central definition and no regular structure. We might still have ten thousand nodes in case we have a hypertext for the employees of a company. But now some of the nodes are very extensive, with lots of information, and others are relatively sparse. Some employees may work on projects with co-workers in other divisions, and might therefore have added links from the description of their work to the nodes for those other employees. In general, the structure of a hypertext network is defined as a union of the local decisions made in building each of the individual nodes and links. Each link is put in because it makes sense in terms of the semantic contents of the two nodes it connects and not because of some global decision. This means that a hypertext has great flexibility, which is normally an advantage but can also be a disadvantage.

Another traditional computer application with similarities to hypertext is outliner programs like ThinkTank. Outliners are normally used to construct the outlines of reports or presentations in a

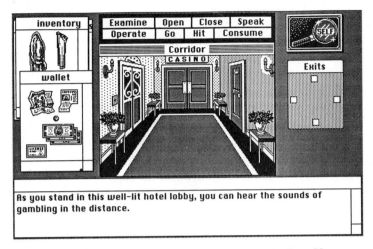

Figure 1.4. *A situation from the* Déjà Vu II: Lost in Las Vegas *graphic adventure game, which is very similar to hypertext in its user interface. Notice how the user can move to other locations in the game by clicking in a first-person navigational view of the corridor (as well as the "Exits" explicit menu of links).* © *1988 by ICOM Simulations, Inc., reprinted with permission.*

hierarchical manner. They are similar to hypertext in that they connect units of text in a user-defined format. But that format is typically restricted to a strict hierarchy. A chapter heading in an outliner can be viewed as having pointers to the section headings it contains, and these section headings again have pointers to the headings of the subsections they contain. But a chapter heading in an outliner cannot have a pointer to a subsection in *another* chapter even though that subsection may be very relevant to its topic. That limitation is why outliners are not hypertext.

In a similar way, a multi-window system is also not necessarily hypertext. In fact, some hypertext systems like HyperCard and KMS are not window-based at all. A traditional multi-window editor may allow users to move among several units of information and compare them on the screen, but the users *themselves* must call up the extra windows. The basic concept of hypertext implies that the computer finds the information for the user.

A class of computer systems that are indeed navigation based are adventure games (see the example in Figure 1.4). They can be viewed as hypertext according to some definitions and in a few cases people have actually implemented an adventure game in a hypertext system. I will not classify adventure games as hypertext because they are fundamentally based on making it difficult for the user to navigate to the desired destination and they often hide the clues for the links to other locations in the information space. This is in complete contrast to the requirement for low cognitive overhead in a hypertext user interface.

As mentioned, even though many hypertext systems are in fact hypermedia systems and include many multimedia effects, the fact that a system is multimedia-based does not make it hypertext. The mixture of text and graphics is not enough in itself. Many multimedia systems are based mostly on displaying various film clips to a passive user who does not get to navigate an information space. Only when users interactively take control of a set of dynamic links among units of information does a system get to be hypertext.

One type of multimedia system that is often confused with hypermedia is interactive video. Again, it is certainly possible to use interactive video effects in a hypermedia interface to good effect, but many so-called interactive video systems are not really interactive enough to classify as hypermedia.

The real issue here is the extent to which the user is allowed to determine the activities of the system. Many interactive video systems reduce the user to the role of a passive television viewer who is only allowed to select video clips from menus. As an example, consider a system installed at the THINK permanent exhibition at the IBM Gallery of Science and Art on Madison Avenue in New York. The system teaches the user about various issues surrounding the U.S. Constitution by showing a long alphabetical menu of the issues. The user is limited to selecting an issue from the list, whereupon the system will play an appropriate video clip. One of the issues is "piracy," which points to a video clip showing, first, traditional pirates from the eighteenth century and then modern aircraft hijackers. The video explains how the language in the Constitution that was originally intended to fight traditional piracy in international waters has been used in recent years to provide the legal underpinning for attempts to prosecute modern terrorists.

The reason this design is not hypertext is that the user has no way to interact with the video clip once it starts playing. In other words, the granularity of the interaction is too coarse to provide the user with the feeling of being in control and able to explore an information space. A true hypertext system would have contained links from the overview video to supporting material about the extent of the piracy problem when the Constitution was framed, how pirates were caught and prosecuted, the growth of modern terrorism, and actual legal actions against those terrorists who have been caught.

Of course it may very well be that the non-hypermedia interactive video interface is the correct solution for a system to teach the U.S. Constitution in a public exhibit space in Manhattan. It is likely that most gallery visitors have a limited interest in the issues and want only to see that an IBM screen can display nice color video under computer control. Allowing users more navigational options would have led to a more complicated interface than simply having users select an issue from a long alphabetical list. So perhaps a plain interactive video system was indeed a better design than a real hypermedia system. Even though hypertext is great, it is not a panacea.

The Hype about Hypertext

There is no doubt that hypertext is being "hyped" to a great extent at the moment. Some of the hype in certain advertisements may be overdone but I personally agree that there are good reasons to believe that hypertext is something special.

One of the most important advantages of hypertext is that it is a method for integrating three technologies and industries that have been separate until recently: publishing, computing, and broadcasting in the form of television and film. There have been a few non-hypertext attempts to mix methods among these three industries such as the "publishing" of some video tapes or the use of computing in the editorial departments of newspapers. But in general, each of the three industries continues with business as usual.

Hypertext, however, provides the opportunity to publish information structures to the general public in much the same way as books or newspapers are currently published. These information structures would be based primarily on moving images, in the tradition of the film and animation industries, and would be under computer control to allow for user interaction.

As an example, consider the NewsPeek system developed at the MIT Media Lab under the direction of Walter Bender. NewsPeek watches the nightly television news for you and records those parts that it knows are of interest to you. You can then browse through the news structures generated by NewsPeek at your convenience.

Systems like NewsPeek can turn the tables of the power structure in journalism. Until now, the general public has been on the bottom of a pyramid populated by journalists and editors who decide what individual readers and viewers should spend their time on. Computer-based news systems put the power in the hands of the individuals. If you watch one hour of television news every night then you will spend more than twenty thousand hours on this one activity over your lifetime. A computer technology that saves you half of this time is equivalent to a medical breakthrough increasing your life expectancy by two years.

NewsPeek-like systems can gather news from many sources such as broadcast and cable television and various newswire services. They can then integrate this news in a hypertext structure with links among detailed news stories downloaded from the *New York Times*, tables from the Dow Jones service, and film clips from the TV. If a newswire service mentions a topic not covered on the TV news, your computer might link to illustrations it generates itself from a stock of illustrations, for instance maps of the world, stored on a CD-ROM.

All of this news is presented in a format edited by your own computer to match exactly your interests and preferences. For example, the computer might know that you were going on a business trip to Brussels because it had taken care of your airline reservations. It would then give news stories from Belgium higher priority than stories from other countries, and it would present a story about, say, a forecast for a snowstorm in the Brussels area as "front page" material on your personal newspaper.

Scenarios like this are an example of another reason many computer scientists are excited about the potential inherent in hypertext. Even more modest applications of hypertext show that hypertext is fundamentally a *computer* phenomenon as observed by Gilbert Cockton from Glasgow University. Hypertext can only be done on a computer, whereas most other current applications of computers might just as well be done by hand. You can only get so excited about designing yet another word processor or accounting program since you are fundamentally doing nothing except making slight improvements to activities that have been conducted almost as well without computers in the past. Hypertext applications, in contrast, only make sense if you have a computer. Except perhaps for presidents, *nobody* gets a personalized newspaper now, but *everybody* will when hypertext gets more established.

The reason people are getting excited about hypertext *now* even though the concept dates back to 1945 is that it can now be implemented with commercially used technology. Some hypertext systems run on small, "plain vanilla" IBM PC clones, while many of the more advanced hypertext systems run on equipment like the Macintosh or IBM PS/2, which exist in millions of installations.

The computer revolution has resulted in an information explosion where managers risk drowning in detailed data and scientists are buried under a mountain of technical reports. The computer might solve these problems by using artificial intelligence (AI) to manage the complexity of modern society and find exactly those pieces of information that its human user needs. The sad truth is that AI does not have anything like the abilities needed to do this well, and hypertext is also exciting because it is an interaction form relying on *natural* intelligence to address these problems.

A hypertext system works in collaboration with the user who has the intelligence to understand the semantic contents of the various nodes and determine which of its outgoing links to follow. As an example, Gerri Peper and colleagues from IBM tried implementing a system to support computer network maintenance in two different versions, an expert system and a hypertext system [Peper et al. 1989]. Their experiments are discussed in further detail in Chapter 9, but briefly the result was that the two systems scored about the same on various measures of efficiency but the hypertext system won in the overall comparison because the operators could easily find out how to update the information it contained. In the expert system, the information was coded in a machine-readable knowledge base and required the assistance of special "knowledge engineers" for updates.

A hypertext is under the control of the user who can customize it by adding links and annotations. Most other computer systems are monolithic and can be modified only by specialists.

Finally, a very important reason for being enthusiastic about hypertext is that it has the potential to save great amounts of money in certain applications. For example, the documentation for an F-18 fighter aircraft is 300,000 pages big [Ventura 1988] and requires 68 cubic feet of storage space when printed on paper. This statistic should be compared with the 0.04 cubic feet the same information takes up when stored on a CD-ROM hypertext.

Not only does hypertext save on the storage space, it also saves on the cost of updating the information. The 300,000 pages of F-18 documentation is not a fixed set of information but changes constantly. Imagine the mailing costs involved in shipping updates to Air Force bases around the world by classified courier service. And imagine the scenes, right out of a slapstick comedy, when every single updated page has to be inserted in the right location in the right binder. Instead one can just press a new CD-ROM and tell people to destroy the old one.

These savings are one important reason many computer manufacturers are now working on shipping technical documentation in hypertext format. Digital Equipment Corporation has been shipping an online documentation system called BookReader with the full documentation set for VAX/VMS on a CD-ROM since 1989 and Hewlett-Packard has a project called LaserROM to convert to a few CD-ROMs the 8,000 *different* documents they ship to their customers every year [Rafeld 1988]. Many of the current CD-ROMs do not offer enough hypertext features but Apple has released a test CD-ROM approaching the hypertext principle.

2. An Example of a Hypertext System

This chapter gives eleven screen shots from a hypertext system I have developed using HyperCard as an implementation tool.[1]

Figure 2.1 is the opening screen of the hypertext system. It includes buttons for getting help and other general information and an option to reset the recorded user history. This screen serves as the "landmark" of the hypertext structure and is accessible from throughout the system by clicking on the "Front cover" icon.

The most prominent graphic on this screen is a picture of a book which is intended to convey a general sense of the nature of the data in this information base. If the user clicks on the name of the author of the book, a new screen will be displayed containing a digitized photo of the author. This facility was of help in the iterative design of this system, since people who had downloaded earlier versions from various computer network services could easily locate the author by sight at conferences to pass on their comments.

The upper right-hand corner of the screen displays a timestamp informing us about the time since we last visited this node in the hypertext system. Since this is the front cover of the book, it thereby also tells us the time since we last used this system.

In this demonstration example, we will assume that we click on the title of the book or on the book cover itself. This action will display Figure 2.2 since the picture of the book itself is the anchor for opening the book. User studies indicate that the use of a book cover and its title as a hypertext anchor is fairly unintuitive for many users. They quickly understand clicking on icons and framed words (like "Quit" in this screen design) but often have to be encouraged to just click on a general

---

[1] This chapter is a modified version of parts of my paper "The art of navigating through hypertext," which appeared in *Communications of the ACM* **33**, 3 (March 1990). © 1990 by the Association for Computing Machinery, reprinted with permission.

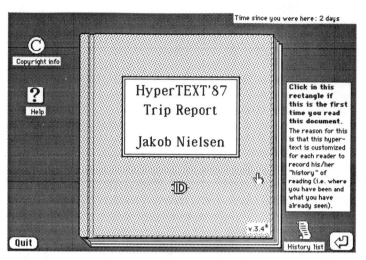

Figure 2.1.

graphics picture having no specific target indicated. In this case, a special problem is that the normal way to open a book cover is to pull it *up* while the mechanics of mouse-operated pointers require a push *down*. Because of this observation, the help screen (not shown here) was changed to state explicitly that the book was opened by clicking on it.

Figure 2.2 is the global overview diagram of the contents of the hypertext structure. It serves as a two-dimensional table of contents. The two-dimensional structure was chosen since there is by definition no linear structure of a hypertext: There is no "first" chapter. The layout of the items is intended to suggest their relation: i.e., "Systems" and "Applications" are related, whereas "Definition of 'hypertext'" is a subissue of "Research issues." "Definition of 'hypertext'" is represented directly on the overview map because it is an especially important node in the hypertext network. Users can access the definition node directly throughout the system since the screens of the main text (Figure 2.4 etc.) include this global overview diagram as an active set of hypertext anchors.

The lines between the items are also intended to give an indication of how they are related since they show that "HyperTEXT'87 Workshop" is the central topic whereas "CSCW'86 Trip Report" is a disconnected topic. In fact, there are hypertext links from some of the nodes in the Hypertext'87 report to some of the nodes in the CSCW'86 report, but these links were judged to be of minor importance and are therefore not represented in this overview diagram.

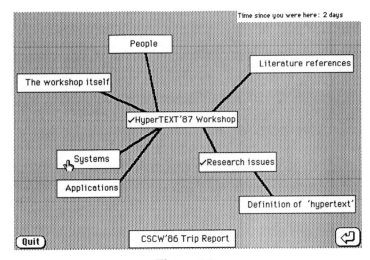

Figure 2.2.

Checkmarks indicate the nodes that we have visited in previous use of the system (in this case "Research issues").

The more fine-grained overview diagram of hypertext nodes in Figure 2.3 is the local diagram associated with the subject "Hypertext systems," which was chosen from the global overview diagram in Figure 2.2. We click on "Classification of hypertext systems" to display Figure 2.4.

We note that the timestamp in the upper right hand corner of the screen states that we have "NEVER" been here before. This timestamp is a general facility of the system intended to help readers recognize information they have already seen without having to wonder whether they actually have seen it before.

The local overview diagrams have a lighter background color than the global diagram in Figure 2.2. Almost no users notice this difference because they do not see the two colors simultaneously, but the same colors are consistently used in the small scale overview diagrams in the main text, as shown in Figure 2.4 where they are more noticeable.

Figure 2.4 is a page showing the standard design of the main text of this hypertext. Since this node has more text than can be seen on this one screen, the system follows a book metaphor in allowing readers to page forward to the remaining text by clicking on the right arrow shown at the lower right corner of the book page. Screens other than the first page of a node will also display a left arrow, which pages backwards.

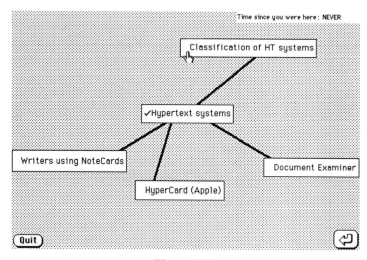

Figure 2.3.

The screen design includes small copies of the overview diagrams. All the screens in the main text part of the hypertext system show the same global diagrams; they then display the appropriate local diagram containing the current node. The overview diagrams are active since both of them highlight the user's current location, and also serve as hypertext anchors. Clicks in the global diagram jump to the corresponding local diagram (e.g. to Figure 2.3 if "Systems" is clicked), and clicks in the local diagram jump directly to the corresponding node.

On this screen it would be a "good thing" to start by reading the definition of the word hypertext, so we click on that button, which displays Figure 2.5. In general, a problem with hypertext is that it destroys the authority of the author to determine which sections readers need to read first, but in this case we have at least hinted at the recommended reading order by making the anchor for the definition especially prominent.

Some people may think that the need to guide the reader on this screen is an indication that the whole notion of nonsequential text is flawed. If one needs to make certain buttons very large and graphically attractive in order to induce readers to select them first, why bother giving any options at all? The reason is that there are several different classes of readers. Some readers may be experts in the domain of the information base and will know how to navigate it to find the information of specific interest to them. They can certainly do so even

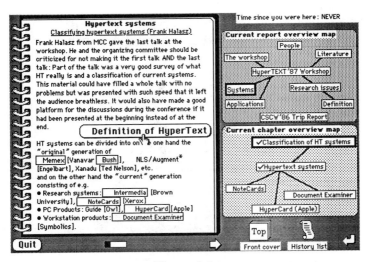

Figure 2.4.

though the author has made certain anchors prominent, since readers retain complete freedom of movement. Other readers, however, may be novices who are more in need of guidance. Instead of forcing people to read in certain ways, our hypertext design allows individual readers to customize their reading to their individual needs and learning styles. But since novices do not yet know the structure of the information space and may have difficulties in understanding the meaning of the terminology, I feel that it is reasonable for the author to provide them with hints.

The graphic design of Figure 2.5 is intended to emphasize its landmark status and to differentiate it from the text of the other nodes. The definition is accessible from all the screens of the main text through its anchor in the global overview diagram.

Just before the screen dump shown here was taken, we clicked on the hypertext anchor "non-textual types" to get the small pop-up annotation giving examples of these types. The pop-up will go away when we click on it or when we leave the screen to go elsewhere. Hypertext anchors for pop-ups are marked on the screen by a raised asterisk, which is intended to invoke the notion of a footnote from traditional books. The asterisk is a different notation from the boxes used for anchors for hypertext links which jump the user to a new screen; the difference helps users predict the actions of the system in response to their clicks. Version 1 and 2 of this system had the same box notation for both kinds of link, and users found it very frustrating

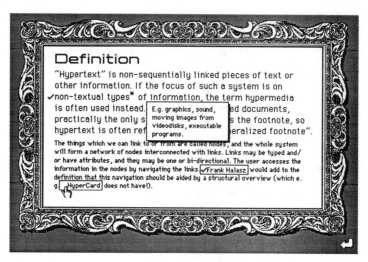

Figure 2.5.

not to know in advance whether a click would just pop up a small annotation or take them to an entirely different context.

After we clicked on the anchor for the pop-up annotation, the system automatically put a checkmark in front of it to help us remember that we have already seen this annotation if we return to this page later. The system has also put in a checkmark at the anchor marked "Frank Halasz," since we have also seen the destination for that link (it is the screen in Figure 2.4). So let us click on "HyperCard" instead to go to Figure 2.6.

When we arrive at this node, the system puts checkmarks at the hypertext anchors for "Frank Halasz" and "Classification of HT systems," since we have visited the destinations for those links already.

That this screen is part of the node describing Apple's HyperCard system can be seen from the highlighting of that node in the local overview diagram and also by the two headings inside the picture of the book page. The boldfaced heading describes the location in the global overview diagram, and the underlined heading describes the location in the local overview diagram. These two headings are automatically concatenated by the system to form a text string referring to a node in the history list shown in Figure 2.10. In a preliminary design of these headings, the picture of the book page was smaller and the headings were placed outside the book page to indicate that the headings were a kind of computer-generated "state information" and not part of the running text. Even though the early design placed the

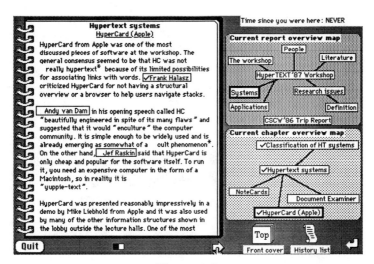

Figure 2.6.

headings in the same physical location on the screen as the current design, test users did not view the text outside the book page as being a label for the contents of the book page. This failure can be explained by the *gestalt* law of closure, which states that things that are within the same closed region are seen as corresponding. The solution was simply to move the headings into the closure of a larger book page.

The little black and white boxes below the book page form a scroll bar that indicates two things: Our relative location within the current node and the size of the node. The length of the scroll bar is proportional to the number of pages in the node, so the scroll bar in Figure 2.4 is longer than the scroll bar in this figure because the node visited in Figure 2.4 is bigger than the node we are visiting here. Proportional scroll bars make it possible always to have the "thumb" of the scroll bar (the black box) be the same size, corresponding to the fact that the book pages have a fixed size. The relative size of the thumb compared to the entire scroll bar indicates the proportion of the total text that the user is currently seeing.

The black box indicates our relative position within the node in an analog format. An alternative would have been a digital format (e.g. "page 1 of 2"), but the scroll bar design can also be used as an anchor for direct hypertext jumps to the other pages within the node: When the user clicks in the scroll bar, the system jumps to the page in the node that has the relative location corresponding to the click.

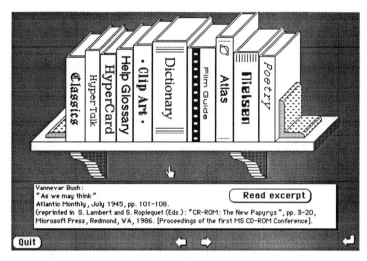

Figure 2.7.

Here, we see that the current node is quite small and that we are on its first page, so we might decide to look at the rest of the node by clicking on the "right arrow" button. The next page looks similar to this one except that it has a "left arrow" button instead of a "right arrow" button, so it is not shown here. The next page has a hypertext reference to "Vannevar Bush," which we follow to get a reference to this famous author.

As indicated by the drastically different graphic design, the screen in Figure 2.7 is part of the literature reference section of the information space. The left and right arrows are for moving alphabetically through the reference list. The alphabetical order of authors' last names is an access mechanism with very low semantic meaning, so to utilize hypertext principles, the books on the bookshelf have been designed as hypertext anchors to help users discover literature references. For instance, by clicking on the book marked "Poetry" we can jump to a literature reference about the use of hypertext for teaching poetry.

Some of the book buttons are linked to multiple destinations, one of which is chosen by random. For example, the book marked "Classics" will jump to one of the references considered to be classics in the hypertext field. This randomness was inspired by the "Something Else" feature in the Drexel Disk [Hewett 1987] and should only be used in situations where users are exploring the information space in a browsing mode. In most situations, predictability would of course be the preferred interaction characteristic, and I actually had one user

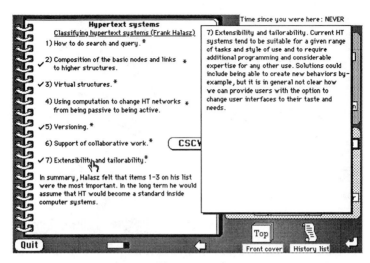

Figure 2.8.

complain that he had spent almost an hour experimenting with the book buttons in a vain attempt to discover the algorithm used to select their destination. This user was a computer scientist, however, and it is likely that more ordinary users would ascribe the system's behavior to "magic" and not worry too much about it. I do not have enough evidence from my usability studies to decide this design issue for certain; a more detailed study of the effects of randomness in user interfaces would be required. My intuition based on this limited experience suggests that it would actually be better to employ a predictable design. One way of doing so would be to use the Intermedia [Yankelovich et al. 1988] technique of popping up a menu listing the possible destinations whenever the user activated an anchor linked to multiple destinations.

From the screen in this figure we could click on the "Read excerpt" button to see some quotes from the original article by Vannevar Bush. Following automated cross reference to other articles is one of the great benefits of hypertext, but we will not do so in this example for copyright reasons. The copyright problem is exactly one of the worst socioeconomic barriers to realizing the full potential of hypertext. Instead we click several times on the backtrack ("return") arrow in the lower right corner of the screen, backtracking through the intervening screens until we return to the screen shown in Figure 2.4.

We have backtracked to the screen shown in Figure 2.4 and from there we have read through the rest of the node, ending up on the

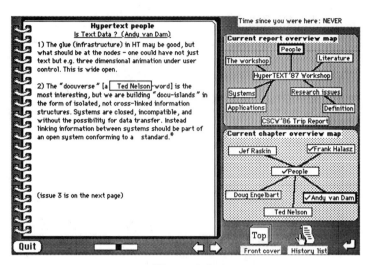

Figure 2.9.

screen shown in Figure 2.8. This part of the text contains a list of seven issues that are hypertext anchors for pop-up windows. We have already seen issues 2, 3, and 5 (as indicated by the checkmarks put in by the system) and here we have just clicked on the anchor for issue 7.

We can now read the full text describing issue 7 while still being able to see the list outlining the full set of issues. Because of the small screen, the pop-up unfortunately obscures the overview diagrams, but we can always click on it to make it go away.

To get from Figure 2.8 to Figure 2.9 we have wandered a little bit around the hyperspace and finally happened to click on "People" in the global overview diagram and then on "Andy van Dam" in the local overview diagram that resulted from that action. We have then read through some of the pages in the node until we came to this list of hypertext research issues.

This design has some problems with context-in-the-small" since not all the issues can be listed on the same screen. All the text for issue 3 had to be moved to the next page to avoid breaking it up and getting even worse context-in-the-small problems. Originally this screen did not have the extra line "(issue 3 is on the next page)" but usability testing indicated the need for this continuation notice, as many users would otherwise transfer their intuitions from printed books and assume that a screen with a blank bottom half was the end of the current chapter.

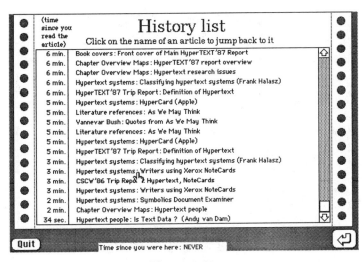

Figure 2.10.

From this screen we decide that we do not want to read about Andy van Dam any more but want to return to one of the earlier nodes which we happened upon in our earlier browsing. To do so, we click on the "History list" button.

The history list in Figure 2.10 is a sequential listing of all the nodes we have visited in the hypertext. Each node we have visited is represented on the list, once for every time we have visited it, thus making the list a truly linear mapping of our path through the nodes. For each visit to a node, the history list also indicates the time since that visit, because our understanding of different parts of the list will depend quite a lot on whether it shows nodes we have just visited, nodes we visited a few hours ago, or nodes we visited some days (or perhaps years) ago.

Here we could click on the line listing a node to return to it, but we will not do so since this figure concludes the demonstration guided tour of the system.

The first version of this hypertext system allowed readers to add their own annotations to the primary text. Figure 2.11 shows how these annotation pages looked. The graphic design is intended to convey the impression that this is some short added material separate from the main report. A different typeface is used to indicate that the annotations normally will have been written by people other than the author of the main hypertext.

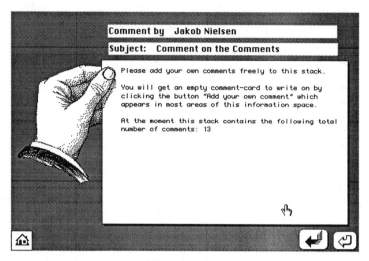

Figure 2.11.

Since a single node in the hypertext could have several associated annotations, a user asking to read annotations would first be taken to a screen showing a menu of the annotations for the current node (not shown here). The user could then choose to read an annotation based on the menu's listing of the authors and subjects.

This screen design has two backtrack arrows, since there are presumably two different ways the user might want to return. (This node has no further hypertext jumps available because the system does not provide a facility for adding annotations to the comments themselves.) The standard return arrow performs the standard backtrack function of returning the user to the departure point for the previous hypertext jump, which in this case is the menu of annotations. An extra arrow to the left of the standard return arrow is an "express return," which returns readers directly to the location from which they jumped to the annotation menu, thus providing a shortcut through the straight backtrack path. In tests, however, almost no test users understood this facility.

How to Get Your Own Copy

Version 1 of the hypertext system described in this chapter is available on a Macintosh format CD-ROM on the *BMUG PD-ROM vol. 1* (1988) [path Stacks: Hyper Media: HyperText Stacks Folder:

HyperTEXT'87 Trip Report], published by Discovery Systems, 7001 Discovery Blvd., Dublin, Ohio 43017, USA.

People with electronic mail access can download[2] Version 3 of the system (the version described in this chapter) from the *Info-Mac* archives as `c ard/hypertext-report-part1.hqx` and `..part2.hqx`. (The Info-Mac archives are available by using FTP [account *anonymous,* any password] in the `info-mac` directory on sumex-aim.stanford.edu [36.44.0.6].) One can also get a copy by sending electronic mail to `listserv@ricevm1.rice.edu` or `listserv@ricevm1.bitnet` with the following two lines in the body of the message:

```
$MACARCH GET CARD/HYPERTEXT-REPORT-PART1.HQX
$MACARCH GET CARD/HYPERTEXT-REPORT-PART2.HQX
```

These two files should be concatenated and converted by the *StuffIt* utility, which is available in many shareware collections.

---

[2] Note that the instructions for downloading have changed slightly since the first printing of this book. This very change is a typical indication of the current difficulties associated with the publishing of electronic documents (discussed further in Chapter 12).

3.   The History of Hypertext

Hypertext has a surprisingly rich history compared to most phenomena in the personal computer industry, especially considering that most people had not heard of it until recently. Table 3.1 gives an overview of the history of hypertext; the major events are discussed in more detail in this chapter.

Memex (1945)

Vannevar Bush (1890–1974) is normally considered the "grandfather" of hypertext, since he proposed a system we would now describe as a hypertext system as long ago as 1945. This system, the Memex ("memory extender") was never implemented, however, but was only described in theory in Bush's papers.

Bush actually developed some of his ideas for the Memex in 1932 and 1933 and finally wrote a draft paper on it in 1939. For various reasons [Nyce and Kahn 1989] this manuscript was not published until

1945	Vannevar Bush proposes Memex
1965	Ted Nelson coins the word "hypertext"
1967	The Hypertext Editing System and FRESS Brown University, Andy van Dam et al.
1968	Doug Engelbart demo of NLS system at FJCC
1975	ZOG (now KMS): CMU
1978	Aspen Movie Map, first hypermedia videodisk Andy Lippman, MIT Architecture Machine Group
1984	Filevision from Telos; limited hypermedia database widely available for the Macintosh
1985	Symbolics Document Examiner, Janet Walker
1985	Intermedia, Brown University, Norman Meyrowitz
1986	OWL introduces Guide, first widely available hypertext
1987	Apple introduces HyperCard, Bill Atkinson
1987	Hypertext'87 Workshop, North Carolina

Table 3.1. *Overview of the history of hypertext*

1945, when it appeared in the *Atlantic Monthly* under the title "As We May Think."

Bush described the Memex as "a sort of mechanized private file and library" and as "a device in which an individual stores his books, records, and communications, and which is mechanized so that it may be consulted with exceeding speed and flexibility." The Memex would store this information on microfilm, which would be kept in the user's desk. This desk was intended to have several microfilm projection positions to enable the user to compare different microfilms, in a manner very similar to the windows that have only recently become popular on personal computers.

The Memex would have a scanner to enable the user to input new material, and it would also allow the user to make handwritten marginal notes and comments. But Bush envisaged that

> most of the Memex contents are purchased on microfilm ready for insertion. Books of all sorts, pictures, current periodicals, newspapers, are thus obtained and dropped into place. Business correspondence takes the same path.

Actually we have not yet reached the state of hypertext development where there is a significant amount of preprocessed information for sale that can be integrated with a user's existing hypertext structure.

The main reason Vannevar Bush developed his proposal for the Memex was that he was worried about the explosion of scientific information which made it impossible even for specialists to follow developments in a discipline. Of course this situation is much worse now, but even in 1945 Bush discussed the need to allow people to find information more easily than was possible on paper. After having described his various ideas for microfilm and projection equipment, he stated that

> All this is conventional, except for the projection forward of present-day mechanisms and gadgetry. It affords an immediate step, however, to associative indexing, the basic idea of which is a provision whereby any item may be caused at will to select immediately and automatically another. This is the essential feature of the memex.[1] The process of tying two items together is the important thing.

Hypertext, in other words!

---

[1] Bush wrote "memex" with a lower case m, but since it is now considered the name of a hypertext system, I will write "Memex" with an upper case M.

In addition to the establishment of individual links, Bush also wanted the Memex to support the building of trails through the material in the form of a set of links that would combine information of relevance for a specific perspective on a specific topic. He even forecast the establishment of a new profession of "trail blazers,""who find delight in the task of establishing useful trails through the enormous mass of the common record." In current terminology, these trail blazers would be people who add value to published collections of text and other information by providing a web of hypertext links to supplement the basic information. But since we do not even have a market for basic hypertexts yet, we unfortunately have to do without special trail blazers.

The building of trails would also be an activity for the ordinary Memex user, and using his microfilm ideas, Bush assumed that such a user might want to photograph a whole trail for friends to put in their Memexes. Again we should note that current technology is not up to Bush's vision, since it is almost impossible to transfer selected subsets of a hypertext structure to another hypertext, especially if the two hypertexts are based on different systems.

Vannevar Bush was a famous scientist in his days and was the science advisor to President Roosevelt during the Second World War when science-based issues like inventing nuclear weapons were of great importance. After "As We May Think" ran in the *Atlantic Monthly*, it caused considerable discussion, and both *Time* and *Life* ran stories on the Memex. *Life* even had an artist draw up illustrations of how the Memex would look and a scenario of its projection positions as the user was completing a link. Doug Engelbart, who later became a pioneer in the development of interactive computing and invented the mouse got part of his inspiration by reading Bush's article while waiting for a ship home from the Philippines in 1945.

In spite of all this early interest surrounding the Memex it never got built. As hinted above, our current computer technology is still not able to support Bush's vision in its entirety. We do have computers with most of the Memex functionality but they are based on a completely different technology from the microfilm discussed by Bush.

It is interesting to recall that Bush was one of the pioneering scientists in the development of computer hardware and was famous for such inventions as the MIT Differential Analyzer in 1931. Alan Kay from Apple has suggested that the areas about which we know most may be those where we are most *in*accurate in predicting the future, since we see all the problems inherent in them. Therefore Bush could gladly dream about impossible advances in microfilm technology but he would have been reluctant to publish an article about personal computing since he "knew" that computers were huge things costing millions of dollars.

Augment/NLS (1962–1976)

After Bush's article from 1945, nothing much happened in the hypertext field for twenty years. People were busy improving computers to the point where it would be feasible to use them interactively, but they were so expensive that most funding agencies viewed as completely irresponsible the suggestion that computer resources should be wasted on nonnumeric tasks such as text processing.

In spite of this attitude, Doug Engelbart started work in 1962 on his Augment project, developing computer tools to augment human capabilities and productivity. This project was the first major work in areas like office automation and text processing; in fact the entire project was much more ambitious and broad in scope than the productivity tools we currently enjoy in the professional work environment. The project was conducted at SRI (Stanford Research Institute) with a staff that grew to 45 people.

One part of the Augment project was NLS (for oN-Line System[2]), which had several hypertext features even though it was not developed as a hypertext system. During the Augment project, the researchers stored all their papers, reports, and memos in a shared "journal" facility that enabled them to include cross-references to other work in their own writings. This journal grew to over 100,000 items and is still unique as a hypertext structure for support of real work over an extended time.

In 1968 Engelbart gave a demo of NLS at a special session of the 1968 Fall Joint Computer Conference. Giving this first public demo of many of the basic ideas in interactive computing was something of gamble for the group. Engelbart had to use much of his grant money to obtain special video projectors, run microwave transmission lines

---

[2] The reason for the strange acronym was to distinguish the name from that of the oFf-Line System, FLS.

between his lab and the conference center, and get other kinds of specialized hardware built, and he would have been in big trouble if the demo had failed. But it worked, and in retrospect spending the money was the right decision; many people have said that it was that demo that got them fired up about inventing interactive computing.

In spite of the successful demo, the government dropped its research support of Engelbart in 1975 at a time when he had more or less invented half the concepts of modern computing.[3] Augment continued as an office automation service but was not really developed further. Engelbart himself is still pushing his original augmentation ideas and has recently started the "Bootstrap Project," located at Stanford University.

Xanadu (1965)

The actual word "hypertext" was coined by Ted Nelson in 1965. Nelson was an early hypertext pioneer with his Xanadu system, which he has been developing ever since. Parts of Xanadu do work and have been a product from the Xanadu Operating Company since 1990.

The Xanadu *vision* has never been implemented, however, and probably never will be (at least not in the foreseeable future). The basic Xanadu idea is that of a repository for *everything* that anybody has ever written and thereby of a truly universal hypertext. Nelson views hypertext as a literary medium[4] and he believes that "everything is deeply intertwingled" and therefore has to be online together. Robert Glushko [1989b], in contrast, believes that multi-document hypertext is only called for in comparatively few cases where users have explicit tasks that require the combination of information.

If Nelson's vision of having all the world's literature in a single hypertext system is to be fulfilled, it will obviously be impossible to rely on local storage of information in the user's own personal computer. Indeed, Nelson's Xanadu design is based on a combination of back end and local databases, which would enable fast response for most hypertext access since the information used the most by

---

[3] After the Augment project was as good as terminated, several people from Engelbart's staff went on to Xerox PARC and helped invent many of the second half of the concepts of modern computing.

[4] Nelson's main book on hypertext is actually entitled *Literary Machines* (see the section on classics in the bibliography).

individual users would still be stored on their local computers. Whenever the user activates a link to more exotic information, the front end computer transparently links to the back end repository through the network and retrieves the information.

In Xanadu it is possible to address any substring of any document from any other document. In combination with the distributed storage of information, this capability means that Xanadu includes a scheme for giving a unique address to every single byte in the world if there should be a need for it.

Furthermore, the full Xanadu system will never delete any text, not even when new versions are added to the system, because other readers may have added links to the previous version of the text. This permanent record of all versions makes it possible for other documents to link either with the current version of a document or with a specific version. Frequently one will want to link with the most up-to-date material, as when referring to census statistics or weather forecasts, but in more polemic documents one may want to ensure a reference to a specific version of a position one is arguing against.

The reader of a document linked to a specific version of another document will always have the option of asking the system to display the most current version. This "temporal scrolling" can also be used to show how documents have looked in previous versions and can be useful, for instance for version management of software development.

Nelson does realize that this scheme means that billions of new bytes will have to be added to Xanadu every day without the hope of freeing storage by deleting old documents. His comment is, "So what...?" and a reference to the fact that the current load on the telephone system would have been impossible under the traditional technology of human operators connecting every call. The history of computer technology until now does give reason for some optimism with respect to being able to support the Xanadu vision some time in the future.

When everything is online in a single system and when everybody may link with everybody else, there will be tremendous copyright problems if the traditional view of copyright is maintained. Nelson's answer is to abolish the traditional copyright to the extent that information placed in Xanadu will always be available to everybody. This principle may be feasible; the system would still keep track of original authorship and provide royalties to the original author based on the number of bytes seen by each reader.

Publishing an anthology would be a simple matter of creating a new document with some explanatory and combining text and with links to the original documents by other authors who would not need to be contacted for permission. Because of the royalty, everybody would be financially motivated to allow other people to link with their work, since it will be through the links that readers discover material worth reading. Even so, some authors might fear being quoted out of context or having their work misrepresented by other authors. This problem is taken care of in theory in Xanadu because the reader always has the option of asking for the complete text of any document being quoted by a link. In practice, many readers will probably not bother looking at the full text of linked documents, so one might need a mechanism for allowing authors to flag links to their work with an attribute indicating that they believe that the link is misleading.

During some of his early work on Xanadu, Ted Nelson was associated with Brown University (Providence, RI). Since then he has mostly been an independent visionary and author, and he is now a fellow at Autodesk, Inc.

Hypertext Editing System (1967) and FRESS (1968)

Even though Xanadu was not even partly implemented until recently, hypertext systems were built at Brown University in the 1960s under the leadership of Andries van Dam. The Hypertext Editing System built in 1967 was the world's first working hypertext system. It ran in a 128K memory partition on a small IBM/360 mainframe and was funded by an IBM research contract.

After the Hypertext Editing System was finished as a research project at Brown University, IBM sold it to the Houston Manned Spacecraft Center where it was actually used to produce documentation for the Apollo missions.

The second hypertext system was FRESS (File Retrieval and Editing System), which was done at Brown University in 1968 as a follow-up to the Hypertext Editing System and was also implemented on an IBM mainframe. Because of this extremely stable platform, it was actually possible to run a demonstration of this code, more than twenty years old, at the 1989 ACM Hypertext conference.

Both these early hypertext systems had the basic hypertext functionality of linking and jumping to other documents, but most of their user interface was text-based and required indirect user specification of the jumps.

Brown University has been a major player in the hypertext field ever since, with its most prominent effort being the development of the Intermedia system (discussed further in Chapter 5).

Aspen Movie Map (1978)

Probably the first hyper*media* system was the *Aspen Movie Map* developed by Andrew Lippman and colleagues at the MIT Architecture Machine Group (which has now merged with other MIT groups to form the Media Lab). Aspen was a surrogate travel application that allowed the user to take a simulated "drive" through the city of Aspen on a computer screen.

The Aspen system was implemented with a set of videodisks containing photographs of all the streets of the city of Aspen, Colorado. Filming was done by mounting four cameras aimed at 90° intervals on a truck that was driven through all the city streets, each camera taking a frame every ten feet (three meters). The hypermedia aspects of the system come from accessing these pictures not as a traditional database ("show me 149 Main Street") but as a linked set of information.

Each photograph was linked to the other relevant photographs a person would see by continuing straight ahead, backing up, or moving to the left or to the right. The user navigated the information space by using a joystick to indicate the desired direction of movement, and the system retrieved the relevant next picture. The resulting feeling was that of driving through the city and being able to turn at will at any intersection. The videodisk player could in theory display the photos as quickly as one frame per 33 millisecond, which would correspond to driving through the streets at 200 mph (330 km/h). To achieve a better simulation of driving, the actual system was slowed down to display successive photos with a speed depending on the user's wishes, but no faster than two frames/sec., corresponding to a speed of 68 mph (110 km/h).

It was also possible for the user to stop in front of a building and "walk" inside, since many of the buildings in Aspen had been filmed for the videodisk. As a final control, the user could select the time of year for the drive by a "season knob," since the entire town was recorded in both fall and winter.[5]

The Aspen system used two monitors for its interface, but in a more natural way than the traditional two-screen solution discussed in Chapter 7. One monitor was a regular vertical screen and showed the street images filmed from the truck. This provided users with an *immersive* view of the city and made them feel as if they had entered into the environment. The second screen was horizontal and placed in front of the immersive screen. Used to show a street map, it provided the user with an *overview* of the environment. The user could point to a spot on the map and jump directly to it instead of having to navigate through the streets. The overview map also provided "landmarks" by highlighting the two main streets of the city. This two-screen solution allowed users easily to understand their position relative to these two main streets.

One reason for the availability of funding to build surrogate travel applications in the late 1970s was the successful liberation of hostages from the Entebbe airport by Israeli troops. Even though these soldiers had never been to Uganda before, they were able to carry through their mission extremely well because they had practiced in a full-scale mockup of the airport that had been built in Israel. Computerized surrogate travel systems might make it possible to train for similar missions in the future without actually having to build entire mockup cities.

It is also possible to imagine that surrogate travel systems like Aspen might be used on a routine basis in the future not just by commando soldiers training for a mission but also by tourists planning their vacations. In the near future, however, the main use of surrogate travel will probably be for educational use; the Palenque system described further in Chapter 4 is a good example.

The Aspen system itself was not really an "application" in the sense that it actually helped anybody accomplish anything. But it was far ahead of its time and of great historical significance in showing the way for future applications. Even now, more than a decade after the

---

[5] This concept is somewhat related to the "temporal scrolling" in the Xanadu system described above. But the Aspen season knob is probably easier to understand for users because it relates directly to a well-known concept from the real world even though it provides a functionality that would be impossible in the real world.

Aspen project was completed, it still stands as one of the more sophisticated hypermedia systems ever built.

As a follow-up to Aspen, the MIT Architecture Machine Group built a more practically oriented system using hypermedia technology to integrate video and computer data. This project was called the *Movie Manual* and involved car and bicycle repair manuals. It is discussed further in Chapter 4.

The *Movie Manual* could use either a regular touch-sensitive computer display or it could project its image on an entire wall in a media room. It had a picture of a car as the table of contents and allowed the user to point to the area that needed repair. The *Movie Manual* would then show its instructions in a mixture of video, annotated images, and ordinary text, allowing the user to customize the screen layout by making the video window larger or smaller. The user could stop the video or play it faster, slower, or backwards.

Symbolics Document Examiner (1985)

The early hypertext systems can best be classified as proof-of-concept systems showing that hypertext was not just a wild idea but could actually be implemented on computers. Even though some systems, like Engelbart's NLS and the early Brown University systems, were used for real work, that use was mostly in-house at the same institutions where the systems were designed.

In contrast, the Symbolics Document Examiner [Walker 1987] was designed as a real product for users of the Symbolics workstations. The project started in 1982 and shipped in 1985, making it the first hypertext system to see real-world use. The Document Examiner was a hypertext interface to the online documentation for the Symbolics workstation, and people got it and used it because it was the best way to get information about the Symbolics, not because it was a hypertext system as such.

The Symbolics manual also existed in an 8,000-page printed version. This information was represented in a 10,000 nodes hypertext with 23,000 links taking up a total of ten megabytes storage space. This hypertext would still be considered large today and was only possible in 1985 because the Symbolics workstation was a very powerful personal computer. To produce all this hypertext, the technical writers at Symbolics used a special writing interface called Concordia, which is discussed further in Chapter 10.

The information in the 8,000-page manual was modularized according to an analysis of the users' probable information needs. The basic principle was to have a node for any piece of information that a user might want.

Furthermore, the design goal for the user interface was to be as simple as possible and not scare users off. Since hypertext was not yet a popular concept in 1985, this goal meant using a book metaphor for the interface instead of trying to get users to use network based navigation principles. The information was divided into "chapters" and "sections" and had a table of contents. Furthermore, users could insert "bookmarks" at nodes they wanted to return to later.

To assess the usability of the Symbolics Document Examiner, the designers conducted a survey of 24 users. Two of them did prefer the printed version of the manual, but half used only the hypertext version and many had not even taken off the shrinkwrap of the printed manual. These users were engineers and they were using advanced artificial intelligence workstations, so they might have been more motivated to use high technology solutions than ordinary users are.

Hypertext Grows Up

Symbolics Document Examiner was an example of hypertext meeting the real world since it saw real use by real customers. But the Symbolics is a fairly specialized artificial intelligence workstation and was very expensive when the Document Examiner was first introduced. So even though it counts as the first real world use of hypertext, it was not a widely distributed and known system.

Several hypertext systems were announced in 1985 and have since seen widespread use, including NoteCards from Xerox and Intermedia from Brown University.

These systems are discussed in further detail in Chapter 5. When they were started in 1985, they were still in the nature of research projects that were kept internal to their respective institutions even though they did receive quite a bit of publicity in the scientific literature. Only in recent years have these systems become commercially available for everybody to buy.

In contrast, when Office Workstations Limited (OWL) introduced Guide in 1986, it was as a commercial product. Guide was the first widely available hypertext to run on ordinary personal computers of the type people have in their homes or offices. At first Guide ran on the

Macintosh; later versions also run on the IBM PC. Guide is also discussed further in Chapter 5. To some extent the release of Guide could be said to mark the transition of hypertext from an exotic research concept to a "real world" computer technique for use in actual applications.

The final step to "realworldness" came when Apple introduced HyperCard in 1987. A nice product in its own right, its real significance was to be found in the marketing concept of giving away the program for free with every Macintosh sold after 1987.[6] This approach has ensured that every Macintosh user has HyperCard, whether they have shown an active interest in buying it or not. The "H"-word was on everybody's lips in 1987. When HyperCard came out, it immediately became the latest craze to produce "stacks" (documents and/or applications) for it. That this stackware, the latest craze in 1987, is *still* the latest craze may be the true proof of genius. Most stackware is bad, but there is so much of it that there are a lot of gems also. HyperCard is also discussed in further detail in Chapter 5.

An event that really marked the graduation of hypertext from a pet project of a few fanatics to widespread popularity was the first ACM[7] conference on hypertext, Hypertext'87, held at the University of North Carolina on November 13–15, 1987. Almost everybody who had been active in the hypertext field was there, all the way from the original pioneers (except Vannevar Bush) to this author. Unfortunately the conference organizers had completely underestimated the growing interest in hypertext and had to turn away about half of the 500 people who wanted to attend the conference. Even so, we were crammed into two auditoriums that were connected by video transmission, and people had to sit on the floor. For those people who were lucky enough to get in, this was a great conference with plenty of opportunity to meet everybody in the field and to see the richness of ongoing hypertext research and development.

History repeated itself when the first open conference on hypertext in Europe was held in 1989. This was the Hypertext'2 conference in York in the U.K. on June 29–30, 1989. The reason this conference was

---

[6] Of course some people claim that Apple more than makes up for the lost income from HyperCard by selling the extra computer memory and larger hard disks needed to support HyperCard applications.

[7] ACM = Association for Computing Machinery, the oldest and probably most prestigious organization for computer professionals in the world.

called Hypertext'2 was that there had been a first, closed conference in Aberdeen the year before. Again the organizers had underestimated the growth of the field and had facilities to accommodate only 250 people. But 500 wanted to come, so half had to be turned away.

The year 1989 also saw the birth of the first scientific journal devoted to hypertext, *Hypermedia,* published by Taylor Graham. It is discussed further in the bibliography.

In conclusion, we can say that hypertext was conceived in 1945, born in the 1960s, and slowly nurtured in the 1970s, and finally entered the real world in the 1980s with an especially rapid growth after 1985, culminating in a fully established field during 1989. We now have several real-world systems that anybody can buy in their local computer store (or get for free bundled with their computer); we have successful conferences and a journal; and most important of all, we have many examples of actual use of hypertext for real projects. These examples are the subject of the next chapter.

4. Applications of Hypertext

As Pat Wright [1989] observes, the variety of hypertext is similar to the diversity of printed material. To use her example, children's pop-up books, railway timetables, and the instructions for operating a washing machine are all very different types of print. Different applications call for different kinds of hypertext support, and this chapter reviews some of the current applications of hypertext.

Not all applications should be done in hypertext. To determine whether an application is suited for hypertext, Ben Shneiderman [1989] has proposed what he calls the **three golden rules** of hypertext:
- A large body of information is organized into numerous fragments.
- The fragments relate to each other.
- The user needs only a small fraction at any time.

Computer Applications

Since hypertext is a computer medium, it is natural to use it in connection with computer-oriented applications. The fourth golden rule of hypertext might be stated "do *not* use hypertext if the application requires the user to be away from the computer." Using hypertext for computer applications completely eliminates any conflict with this rule since the user will already be at the screen anyway.

Besides the actual applications of hypertext discussed below, hypertext can also be used to prototype the user interface for almost any other computer program [Nielsen 1989a], because most initial prototyping consists of linking together screen designs and presenting them to the user in an order determined by simple user actions. Extremely simple prototypes can be constructed in any hypertext system just linking together screen designs in the appropriate order. As the prototyping work advances beyond the storyboard stage, the need for more application functionality increases, but computational hypertext systems with access to a programming language can still be of use in many cases. HyperCard has been used frequently for this purpose.

Online Documentation

Online documentation may be the most natural of all hypertext applications; it was the purpose of the first real world hypertext application, the Symbolics Document Examiner (see Chapter 3).

"Nielsen's first law of computer manuals" states that users do not read manuals, period. The second law is that when a user wants to read the manual anyway, then one can be sure that the user is in big trouble. Because of the first law, users will often not be able to find the manual when they finally need it, since somebody else may have borrowed the manual or it may have become lost in general. This situation does not happen with an online manual, which is always present on the computer. Rob Lippincott from Lotus Development Corp. talks about the need for "just-in-time learning" that allows users to learn *what* they need *when* they want to.

Since no user wants to read the entire manual anyway, users also require good access tools to help them retrieve the sections of the manual that are relevant to their current needs. Hypertext is the obvious method for helping users in this situation, and many recent software packages have been delivered with online manuals or online help systems in hypertext form.

User Assistance

Users need more information than can be found in manuals. In fact, a study by Robert L. Mack of the IBM User Interface Institute and myself showed that business professionals rated traditional reference manuals as the second worst out of twelve methods for initial learning about computer systems.[1]

Hypertext provides a mechanism for integrating several forms of user assistance, including the online manual, an introductory tutorial, an online help system, and even the error messages. Because users only get error messages when they are in some kind of trouble, the error

---

[1] R.L. Mack and J. Nielsen: "Software integration in the professional work environment: Observations on requirements, usage, and interface issues," *Technical Report* **RC-12677**, IBM T.J. Watson Research Center, Yorktown Heights, NY 10598, April 1987.

Figure 4.1. *A screen from the Lotus Multimedia Release 3.0 Demo CD where two users are shown solving a spreadsheet problem in Lotus 1-2-3 Release 3. Note that the screen contains options for linking to related material. The user can also continue and see the actual 1-2-3 screen containing the solution.* © 1989 by Robert M. Lippincott, reprinted with permission.

messages are a prime candidate for providing users with assistance. The traditional perspective implicit in such classic error messages as ILLEGAL COMMAND - JOB ABORTED was that the user must have been criminally stupid to make a mistake, but luckily that perspective has mostly been abandoned in modern user interfaces.

In an integrated user-assistance facility based on hypertext, it would be possible for the user to link from an error message to the location in the help system that gives further assistance on the problem. If the user's difficulty was not the error situation in general but a single incomprehensible word in the message, it would be possible to link from that word to the location in the online manual where it was defined. And if the user wanted further assistance than could be provided by the help system or the manual, it would be possible to link further, to the appropriate location in the tutorial component, to get a computer aided instruction lesson.

This type of integrated user assistance does not exist in current computer systems, but we are seeing hypertext applied to individual components in the user-assistance field. For example, the Sun386i workstation has its online help system implemented as a hypertext [Campagnoni and Ehrlich 1989].

Figure 4.1 shows a screen from the Multimedia Release 3.0 Demo CD from Lotus Development Corporation, which is an introductory tutorial explaining the operation of Lotus 1-2-3 release 3.0 by a multimedia scenario [Eisenhart 1989]. The same amount of plain information might have been given in a traditional printed user's guide, but people are likely to remember the material much better when they can relate it to a concrete usage scenario and when they can become active participants in the tutorial rather than passive readers of static material.

Software Engineering

During the software development lifecycle, a large number of specification and implementation documents are produced, and hypertext has great potential for providing links among them. For example, it would be possible to start from a requirements document and link to that part of the design specification that meets a given requirement. One could then link from the design specification to the actual code to see how that design is implemented; or one could follow the links in the reverse direction, starting from the source code to see what customer requirements lay behind a certain code element.

To benefit fully from this form of hypertext links among the various documents in the software lifecycle, a development organization would need to follow a software engineering methodology supported by an integrated set of computerized tools in a complete CASE (Computer Aided Software Engineering) environment. One such system is the Dynamic Design project at Tektronix [Bigelow 1988], which supports version control for various reports, documents, and code objects by using the Neptune hypertext abstract machine [Delisle and Schwartz 1987].

It is also possible to use hypertext in a less lifecycle-oriented approach by including linking facilities in structure-oriented editors for program code. For example, it is possible to click on a variable to get to see its definition and associated comments, or to link from a procedure

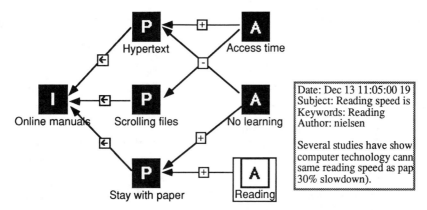

Figure 4.2. *An issue network similar to those used in gIBIS. The "issue" is how to do online manuals, and there are three positions: Use hypertext, use a traditional scrolling text file, and avoid online manuals completely by staying with paper. Several arguments have been posted, and the user has selected the "Reading" argument, which brings its full text up in the text window. The real gIBIS screen is in color and has much larger windows both for the diagram and for the text window. Note that the links are typed as indicated by the small icons showing, for example, that the reading speed argument supports the position of staying with paper.*

call to opening a window with the text of the procedure. The Smalltalk code browser links related pieces of code in somewhat this manner.

Since much of the software engineering process is spent on designing systems rather than simply hacking code, there is also interest in specialized tools to support the design phase of the lifecycle. One interesting system is gIBIS (graphical Issue Based Information System) from MCC (Microelectronics and Computer Technology Corporation) in Austin, TX [Conklin and Begeman 1988]. gIBIS is part of the Design Journal project, which aims to capture the rationale for a software design.

Since software design is usually a collaborative process involving many people, gIBIS is a multi-user hypertext system. It is based on a theoretical model of the design process as a conversation among "stakeholders" who bring their respective expertise and viewpoints to bear on a number of design issues. The participants in the design process argue about these issues by suggesting positions (ways to resolve the issue) and arguments for and against those positions. All of this is represented in a hypertext structure with three types of nodes: issues, positions, and arguments. The "g" in gIBIS comes from the graphic representation of the hypertext network as shown in Figure 4.2. The overview diagram gives the user an idea of the design rationale at a glance and also provides access to the underlying full text.

Originally, gIBIS was designed for use on Sun workstations with color screens and it therefore uses color to indicate the types of nodes and links in the network overview diagram. At first, users were allowed to customize the assignment of colors, but later versions of gIBIS have been based on standardized use of color, making it possible for users to learn quickly the type mappings for the most commonly used nodes and links. Type identification then becomes a rapid, unconscious activity. gIBIS also runs on monochrome displays and then uses the iconic representation of types shown in Figure 4.2.

Operating Systems

Finally, hypertext has the potential for revolutionizing the user interface to personal computers in general in order to arrive at a task-integrated working environment. Current personal computers are fundamentally based on a file paradigm, where the user manipulates discrete (but large) units of information in the form of files. Each file can typically be found only in a single location in the file system, and it is typically best suited for use by a single application program.

This model had a good fit with early personal computers, which were rather small and limited in many ways. They operated only on a few data types (often text and numbers); each user used only a small number of applications because they were difficult to learn; and the file storage was limited by the capacity of small hard disks. Modern personal computers like the IBM PS/2 and Macintosh II families are intended for multimedia data, and they support sufficiently user friendly interfaces to allow users to learn and use many different applications.[2] Furthermore, they are often connected to large hard disks (I have a 140 MB disk myself), optical disks, or network-based servers, and therefore have to access a large number of files.

Most current file systems organize files in a hierarchy and require the user to navigate through multiple levels of nested subdirectories to

---

[2] One reason users are now able to use more applications is that the user interfaces are getting consistent. Users can transfer their skills from one program to the next, which therefore becomes easier to learn. See J. Nielsen (ed.): "Coordinating User Interfaces for Consistency," Academic Press 1989.

reach the relevant files. Users often forget where they have stored a certain piece of information and are restricted mostly to searches based on filenames. Some add-on products like Lotus Magellan do exist and can help users find files on the basis of a full text search, but they are still fairly primitive compared with the navigation facilities offered by the best hypertext systems.

It would be possible to extend future operating systems with a system-based hypertext service somewhat like the Sun Link Service now offered by Sun [Pearl 1989]. This extension would allow different applications to link transparently to information generated by other applications and stored elsewhere on the computer. Users would need to establish the connection between two work items only once and would then be freed from having to navigate manually. Hypertext links would take the user from one piece of information to the next, thereby avoiding the need for the user to drop into the file system. Users could concentrate on their tasks and have the computer integrate its applications and data to fit those tasks.

Business Applications

This section concentrates on "mainstream business," but quite frankly there are not yet all that many business applications of hypertext in place to be used every day for real profit. But there are potential applications that are currently being investigated by several companies, and there are also some systems in real use. Also, many of the applications mentioned under other headings are "real business" examples; the software and entertainment industries, for example, are just as dependent on profits as everybody else.

Repair and Other Manuals

The MIT *Movie Manual* discussed in Chapter 3 is an example of a repair manual done in hypertext. It contains descriptions of how to repair cars and bicycles linked to video clips of mechanics performing the various operations and even to video segments showing typical mistakes and what could go wrong during certain operations.

One memorable sequence, which I still recall from seeing it in 1983, is a video clip showing what would happen if certain nuts were loosened too rapidly. The film shows the oil pan slipping and discharging its contents all over the head of the poor mechanic. After having seen this sequence, you use your wrench cautiously for a long time.

The *Movie Manual* was suited for both experienced and novice mechanics. One facility for the novice was an explanation of the tools used in the repair procedure. Each time a tool was mentioned there was a hypertext link to a picture of the tool and a description of how the tool was used. A true novice could even watch a film of an experienced mechanic using the tool to observe how the expert would handle the tool. Of course these links would never be followed by experienced mechanics, but they were very useful for do-it-yourself people.

The IGD (Interactive Graphical Documents) System [Feiner et al. 1982] is an early hypertext manual for repair of electronic equipment produced at Brown University with support from the U.S. Navy. It is highly based on graphically *showing* the technicians how to repair things, rather than on describing the same material in textual form.

These early repair manuals include some options for having the system model the user as being, for instance, a novice or an expert repair technician. It would also be possible to have the hypertext links depend on information about the outside world. In a system like IGD for repair of electronic equipment on warships, there might be some cases where a given piece of equipment could be repaired in two different ways: a careful and generally recommended way, and a quick-and-dirty way. The link that displayed a description of the repair procedure would then depend on the system's knowledge of the status of the ship. If it was in no particular danger, then the careful repair procedure would be accessed, but if the ship was under attack, the system would naturally display the fastest possible repair procedure. This dynamic reconfiguration of a repair manual is one of the great advantages of hypertext compared to traditional printed works, which would have to display every single option to the technician, and would thereby be more complex and require increased user literacy.

We are currently seeing a trend for many car companies to supply instructions to mechanics in hypertext form (often on CD-ROM), because there are so many different models and spare parts that the distribution of complete sets of regular manuals is becoming infeasible.

Dictionaries and Reference Books

Several dictionaries and large reference works have been converted from a traditional paper form to a hypertext format but so

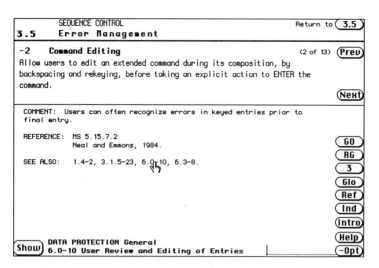

Figure 4.3. *A screen from the DRUID (Dynamic Rules for User Interface Design) hypertext version of a major compendium of user interface design guidelines. © 1989 The MITRE Corporation, reprinted with permission.*

far we have seen no major project trying to generate a hypertext dictionary from scratch. Two of these conversion projects (the *Manual of Medical Therapeutics* and the *Oxford English Dictionary*) are described in further detail in Chapter 11.

Figure 4.3 shows a hypertext version of a famous reference work in the user interface field: the design guidelines collected by Sid L. Smith and Jane N. Mosier from the MITRE Corporation. This single reference work has actually been converted into several other hypertext forms, including one commercial product for the IBM PC called NaviText SAM [Perlman 1989] and a Japanese translation implemented in a fourth-generation language by a group coordinated by Hiroshi Tamura of the Kyoto Institute for Technology. Unfortunately, so far nobody has conducted a comparative experiment to assess the usability of these different conversions of the same underlying text.

The DRUID system shown here is currently only a prototype of a fairly ambitious design that will include support for many steps in the usability engineering lifecycle. For example the system is intended to provide support for using the hypertext as a checklist for design and evaluation. DRUID allows users to select and weight the importance of relevant guidelines for a system design, and also allows users to rate the compliance with those selected guidelines.

Even the prototype DRUID system includes all the guidelines of the printed report with the appropriate hypertext links. It turns out that user interface design guidelines are heavily interlinked because they often complement (or even contradict) one another. In Figure 4.3 we are reading about the need to allow users to edit a command before they have submitted it for execution. This guideline is linked to four other relevant guidelines, and we have here clicked on the reference to guideline 6.0–10, resulting in a preview of that guideline on the bottom line of the screen. If we wanted to study the guideline on "user review and editing of entries" we could click on the "show" button to follow that link to its destination. The guideline on user review and editing further states that in the case of error, the user should be allowed to fix the problem by editing the erroneous input instead of being required to reenter everything (which might introduce new errors). It is obviously relevant for any system designer who is reading about command editing also to know what to do in the case of an error, so this hypertext link is very well placed.

The guideline in Figure 4.3 also has literature references to a U.S. military standard (MS) and to a scientific paper from the journal *Human Factors*. These links are unfortunately not all that useful in the current version of the hypertext since they take the user only to the relevant bibliographic reference. In the next version of DRUID, the links to the military standard will be made "live" and actually take the user to the full text of the relevant sections of MIL-STD-1472D. Such "multi-document hypertext" [Glushko 1989b] can significantly increase the utility of hypertext. For the foreseeable future users will probably have to acquire the rest of the references from their library in the traditional way.

The Electronic Whole Earth Catalog is a CD-ROM version of the printed *Whole Earth Catalog* which has been updated to early 1989. The main difference between the printed and CD-ROM versions is that the CD-ROM contains a large number of digitized sound clips of the various records reviewed in the catalog. The CD-ROM seems to contain the same illustrations as the printed version, albeit using the somewhat poorer resolution of scanned Macintosh screen images.

The sound clips are a major advantage of the electronic version, but it also has better search options than the printed book. For example, when I was interested in buying a quotation dictionary, I wanted to read reviews of this kind of book and so tried to look up "quotation" in the index of the latest printed Whole Earth volume, *Signal*. That word was not in the index, but using the full text search capabilities of the electronic version, I found a review of "Bartlett's Familiar Quotations," which had been listed under **B** in the printed index.

The Electronic Whole Earth Catalog is a fairly big hypertext compared to most current projects with its 9,742 nodes taking up a total of 413 megabytes. Most of this storage space is used for the sounds, however, with only 34 megabytes needed to store the main parts of the hypertext. A hypertext using all the storage space on the CD-ROM for text would be a much larger and more complex work, like the *Crompton's Encyclopedia* (released by Encyclopaedia Britannica), which takes up 26 volumes in its printed form. Even that work has only 31,200 entries and spends a lot of room on about 15,000 illustrations, 45 animation sequences, and one hour of digitized audio.

Clearly one of the biggest advantages of hypertext encyclopedias and dictionaries, compared to a printed work, is that they can show moving images and play sound. For example, Highlighted Data has released a version of *Webster's Dictionary* on CD-ROM with sound recordings of how the 160,000 words actually are pronounced.

Auditing

Auditing is another natural application for hypertext because it is based on relating information from various sources and checking for consistentcy. The audit task includes gathering and producing large numbers of documents and linking them together to substantiate the accuracy of the information they contain. A huge amount of information gets distilled into a single financial statement, so links are needed between the conclusions and the source data. Furthermore, the audit of an international company involves a large audit team distributed over several countries, leading to several advantages for various forms of computer support like electronic mail and hypertext links among documents produced in different areas of the world.

Studies conducted by the Price Waterhouse Audit Research and Technology Group indicate that approximately 30% of the time spent on an audit is dedicated to producing, relating, and reviewing "Audit Working Papers." This figure does not even take into account the time spent obtaining the information. Therefore a good hypertext system for auditing support has the potential to reduce the time needed to conduct an effective audit, and Figures 4.4 and 4.5 illustrate a prototyping effort

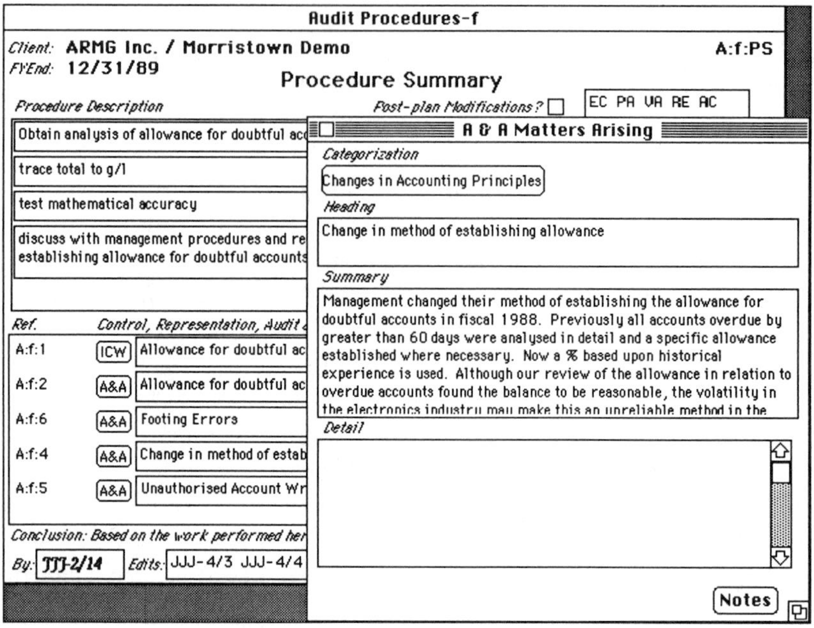

Figure 4.4. *A Procedure Summary Form has fields for the most important information for the audit procedure. The list of potential issues has links to supporting evidence (on the left) and to windows with room for further detail (here the user has clicked on "Change in methods of establishing allowance" to see its description window). The description window provides further detail and also shows that this auditing issue has been categorized under "Changes in Accounting Principles." This classification makes it possible to construct summary reports elsewhere in the system and thus show all the issues in a category. This figure illustrates a prototyping effort, which does not necessarily reflect current or future audit methodology or practice. © 1989 by Price Waterhouse Technology Centre, reprinted with permission.*

that the Price Waterhouse Technology Centre in Menlo Park has started to investigate these possibilities [De Young 1989].

The hypertext system links the information produced during the audit process and makes it possible to track information from, say, a final financial statement back to where it originated. It is possible to scan original documents from the client, and it might conceivably be possible in the future to link directly into the client's own computer system. Since the linking structure is so important for the issues raised during the audit process, the auditors need to take personal responsibility for the establishment of links. In a traditional, paper-

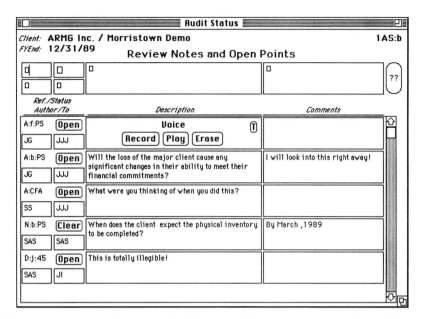

Figure 4.5. *Review Notes can help large audit teams manage and coordinate activities by providing the ability to view the same information from several perspectives. This window gives an overview of issues that remain to be resolved and has hypertext links to the underlying documents. This figure illustrates a prototyping effort which does not necessarily reflect current or future audit methodology or practice. © 1989 by Price Waterhouse Technology Centre, reprinted with permission.*

based audit this responsibility is sometimes noted manually by adding initials to references to other documents, but the hypertext system can automatically timestamp every new or changed link and record the name of the user.

One difference between auditing and many other hypertext applications is that the presentation of the information used in auditing has been fairly standardized over a long period of time. Because less flexibility is needed in an auditing hypertext, the form filling paradigm is a natural user interface as shown by the figures.

The well-structured nature of the auditing hypertext makes it possible for the system to provide automatic access to higher-level reports computed on the basis of the hypertext network. The system can automatically construct lists of all issues of a certain type or all issues handled by a certain auditor. As an example of another coordination tool, Figure 4.5 shows a management report for keeping track of the status of the work in large teams of auditors.

A high degree of standardization can be observed not just in the structure of auditing procedures and reports but also in the very language of the reports. Therefore there are substantial advantages in being able to *reuse* portions of the language in reports from previous audits of the same client or of another client with a similar type of business. A hypertext system would facilitate such reuse by making the appropriate earlier documents easily available in online versions for copying and editing.

Trade Shows, Product Catalogs, and Advertising

Many kinds of advertising and communication to customers can be improved by hypertext. Right now hypertext has a novelty value, which is an advantage in itself in some types of advertising. For example you can attract attention at trade shows by having a computer with hypertext information about your products.

Hypertext can also be used to provide information about an entire trade show and help people find those exhibitors that would interest them, as has been done at some MacWorld exhibits.

In the long term, the novelty value of hypertext will of course disappear and one will have to rely on the intrinsic advantages of hypertext in an advertising context. One of these advantages is the general ability of hypertext to provide access to large amounts of information but to show the user only those small parts that interest him or her. This property of hypertext is important for applications like product catalogs. A hypertext product catalog can reduce the complexity of choosing among a large number of options by showing only those that are relevant for the individual customer. It can also offer help in placing the order and might even place it by an online connection to the vendor. A hypertext catalog could also include an option to remember what products the user ordered the previous time, thus making them especially easy to reorder.

Having a hypertext product catalog could be a tremendous asset for direct marketing people if they could gain access to data about how customers have used the hypertext.[3] For example the system could

---

[3] In some countries it may be illegal to collect such data without the user's knowledge.

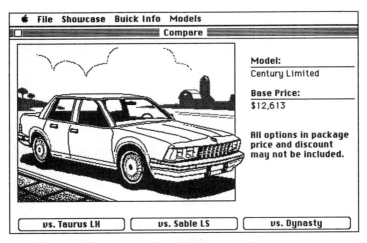

Figure 4.6. *A screen from a 1988 SoftAd for Buick. © 1988 by The SoftAd Group, Inc., reprinted with permission.*

record how many times a specific user clicked on links related to the price of products and special savings options as compared to how many times the same user clicked on links related to advanced features of the product or descriptions of luxury options. This somewhat simpleminded example shows how the hypertext system could provide the basis for a market segmentation down to the level of the individual customer. The next hypertext catalog sent to the customer could be tailored to have more prominent links of the type that customer had shown an interest for.

Hypertext advertising can also benefit from other properties of the computer medium. For example, Buick has released their car catalog in hypertext form for several years now and has included driving simulations and other games to attract attention. Figure 4.6 shows a screen from this so-called SoftAd. In a hypertext form for comparative advertising, this screen allows the user to compare the Buick cars with several competing alternatives. Users can click on the one other car they might consider buying instead and then see a detailed comparison like that in Figure 4.7. This example again uses hypertext to manage complexity. A printed catalog would have had to compare all the cars in a single confusing table.

In the marketing field, the bottom line is considerably more interesting than theoretical speculations about information complexity. And hypertext does sell. The manager of Buick Motor Division's electronic product information department, Nancy J. Newell, was

File   Showcase   Buick Info   Models

Century Limited vs. Dodge Dynasty Premium

Equipment	Century Limited	Dynasty
Base Price	$12,613	$12,275
Destination Charge	$425	$445
Air Conditioning/Tilt Steering	package	package
Delay Wiper/Side Molding	package	standard
Cruise Control	package	package
AM/FM Radio w/Cassette	package	$494
Carpet Savers/Power Antenna	package	package
Power Windows/Locks	package	package
Wire Wheel Covers	package	$231
6-Way Power Driver Seat	package	$248
Rear Defogger/Side Mirrors	package	standard
Package Price	$2,072	$1,893
Package Discount	($500)	($276)
Price As Equipped	$14,610	$15,310

Figure 4.7. *A comparison screen from the 1988 Buick SoftAd generated by clicking on the "vs. Dynasty" button in Figure 4.6. © 1988 by The SoftAd Group, Inc., reprinted with permission.*

quoted in *Business Week* on October 9, 1989 as saying that 12% of those who bought cars after receiving the Buick disk ended up picking a Buick. This rate is about double their usual market share.

Intellectual Applications

I do not want to imply that business and education are not intellectual activities, but there seems to be a third category of applications that are less immediate in nature and more oriented towards the scholarly approach. In fact, many of these "intellectual" applications are actually used quite a lot in business.

Idea Organization and Brainstorm Support

Some hypertext enthusiasts claim that hypertext is the most natural way to organize human ideas because its semantic network-like structure matches the human brain. That may or may not be true, but even if hypertext should not be the optimal way to organize human thoughts it is still much better than the linear text format used by word processors. The one way humans certainly do *not* work when they are, say, writing a book is to start by getting the idea for what to write on page one, then moving on to getting the idea for page two, and going on like that until they finally end by getting the idea for the last page.

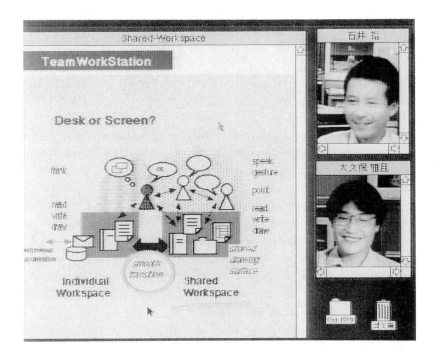

Figure 4.8. *A session with two users cooperating on the NTT TeamWorkStation. The screen shows video images of both users and also has a shared workspace where both users can point at the same time (note the two cursors—one at the top of the window and one at the bottom). The real screen is in color and has better resolution than is reproduced here. © 1990 by NTT Human Interface Laboratories, reprinted with permission.*

We have already discussed gIBIS as a tool for organizing the discussions of software designers (see Figure 4.2). NoteCards from Xerox [Halasz et al. 1987] is another famous hypertext system built mainly to be used as an idea organizer. It will be discussed further in Chapter 5.

Because hypertext allows the coordination of many disparate pieces of text, it can also be used to organize the ideas of groups of people. Doing so was part of the basic design of gIBIS but was originally not possible in NoteCards. More recent versions of NoteCards do include support for cooperative work. Besides regular multi-author support, hypertext can also help coordinate ideas by its basic capability for having any user add new annotations and links to any node. For example, the Intermedia InterNote service shown in

Figure 6.2 allows an author to make a hypertext available to a larger group and to collect their comments as annotations.

Collaboration can also take place via electronic mail or computer conferences which can be enhanced by hypertext mechanisms. Figure 4.8 shows an advanced Japanese research prototype by Hiroshi Ishii from the NTT (Nippon Telegraph and Telephone Corporation) Human Interface Laboratories. The TeamWorkStation allows several users to interact with the same multimedia workspace at the same time; but most computer conferences are run in asynchronous time, meaning that users don't have to be present on the system simultaneously.

Even though there are obviously some advantages to the TeamWorkStation approach of allowing users to talk and to see each other while they annotate the shared workspace, there are also advantages to the systems where users work at different times. Asynchronous communication is very practical for collaboration across time zones, as in the auditing example discussed above. An audit of a company with subsidiaries in Australia, the U.S., and Europe will never see all the auditors awake at the same time.

The basic principle of computer conferences and most electronic mail is that several participants write messages with comments on previous messages by other participants. The HyperNews system from the Technical University of Denmark (see Figure 8.10) is a hypertext interface for such a conferencing environment. Hypertext links connect a message both forwards and backwards in time with all those other messages in the same stream of comments.

Journalism

In addition to the long term possibility of having newspapers and television news in an integrated hypermedia system (see Chapter 1), it is also possible to use hypertext in the current way of doing journalism. Much of a journalist's work is of course plain gathering of information and writing of stories, and the hypertext mechanisms for idea organization discussed above should be able to help.

For the collection of information it would also be possible to use large hypertext collections of previously published news material. Newspapers like the *New York Times* already provide information services with online access to databases with "old news," but the information is currently not in hypertext form. Many other newspapers still use traditional files of paper clippings and good journalists are able to flip through such files at an amazing speed. They have learned to recognize cues from the typography and layout of the clippings and are able to classify an article without having to read it. For example, a certain layout and typography would be recognized as being from the London *Times* while another would be recognizably from the *National Enquirer*. The same size letters in a headline might be used in one publication to signal the start of the Third World War while it could mean that a movie star has knocked down a police officer in another. This type of quickly recognizable signal to support a journalist's skill-based behavior needs to be included in a hypertext news retrieval system if it is to compete with a simple pile of press clippings.

Radio or television reporters can also use hypertext to provide background information during a broadcast. For example, ABC produced a hypertext with about 10,000 nodes for its coverage of the U.S. presidential election in 1988 to allow its anchor Peter Jennings fast access to relevant information. Having a well-linked hypertext instead of traditional cueing cards allows a broadcast commentator to have more "that reminds me of" remarks.

In an interesting twist, ABC has reused much of their 1988 hypertext material in producing an educational hypertext in 1989 called *The '88 Vote*. In addition to the hypertext material it also contains film clips from the Presidential campaign and key commercials from both candidates. This combined hypermedia package was released by a new division of ABC called ABS News InterActive, which also has other projects underway.

Research

Obviously research to a large extent consists of idea generation and writing, so hypertext tools for supporting those activities can also be used to support researchers. Here I will mention a few examples of applying hypertext to the domains studied by the research.

John L. Schnase from Texas A&M University has written a biology paper in KMS [Schnase and Leggett 1989]. The paper describes an individual energetics model for Cassin's Sparrow (*Aimophila cassinii*), which is a common bird in the west Texas mesquite-grasslands. The goal of the research was to account for the energy expenditure of individual birds over 24-hour periods.

The hypertext structure developed for the research contains all the raw data collected from field observations of the activities of male and female Cassin's Sparrows. It also contains the programs necessary to perform various simulations on the basis of the data. The program to simulate the male birds was written within the KMS action language, which made it possible to run the simulation entirely within KMS. Unfortunately the version of KMS used (6B1) had very poor support for arithmetic expressions and also ran very slowly.[4] Therefore the program to simulate female birds was written in the traditional C programming language.

The C program was still kept within the hypertext structure, so that it was possible to have it cross-referenced with the main paper. When a simulation was to be performed, the KMS action language was utilized to write the C program and the raw data to Unix files and to start the calculations in Unix. The output from the C program was then reimported into KMS by action language statements, so that the user never had to leave the hypertext structure. Because of this use of computational hypertext, it was possible to have a single integrated personal environment for scientific knowledge work that simplified the personal information management problem for the researcher.

Another advantage of having the paper in hypertext format is that it was possible to send it to other biologists by electronic mail and thereby bypass the delay of two to three years posed by a traditional journal. Unfortunately this distribution mechanism does not reach all biologists, so the paper was still submitted to a traditional biology journal. This goal made it necessary to use the system to produce a linearized version of the paper, but the project showed that the hypertext system could support the entire traditional scientific process from the storage and collection of field data over the formulation of models and theories to the production of a camera-ready report. The only research step that had to be done without hypertext support was the collection of field data in the Texas grasslands since KMS does not run on any kind of portable computer.

Another example of using hypertext for the presentation of scientific research is the "notebook" in the Mathematica system about Lyon's cochlear model of signal processing in the ear by Malcolm Slaney [1990]. The table of contents of Slaney's notebook is shown in Figure 8.4. The electronic notebook contains both a traditional paper about the model and the model's mathematical formulas and various

---

[4] The current version of KMS has solved many of these problems.

diagrams calculated from these formulas.[5] This combination makes it possible for readers to enhance their understanding of the model and the formulas by varying the parameters and observing the changes in the figures. Even though this effect might in theory have been achieved by giving the reader access to the source code of a traditional program, there is no doubt that most readers would never have been able (or motivated) to penetrate such a program sufficiently to make intelligent changes.

Slaney's Mathematica notebook is a "literate program" [Knuth 1984] that intertwines the descriptive text of the paper and the active formulas in a single hypertext representation. This approach enables the reader to better understand the individual formulas and provides inspiration for experimenting with certain formulas. Furthermore there is a dialectical relationship between the text and the diagrams: Reading the text influences the reader's understanding of the diagrams, and changing the diagrams by varying parameters or modifying formulas influences the reader's understanding of the text.

In addition to these attempts to construct scientific communicative material entirely in hypertext, there is also the possibility of converting traditional journal articles to hypertext. One such experiment was the "Hypertext on Hypertext" project from the Association for Computing Machinery, which converted one issue of the *Communications of the ACM* journal to hypertext in several different formats [Alschuler 1989]. A more ambitious project is underway at Loughborough University in the United Kingdom to convert eight volumes of the journal *Behaviour and Information Technology* into Guide [McKnight et al. 1990] for possible later publication as a CD-ROM. This larger project takes advantage of the tendency for papers in a given scientific journal to contain many references to other papers in earlier issues in the same journal, by converting these references to hypertext links. Its goal is to make reading the hypertext journal a much more dynamic experience and to increase the likelihood that readers will actually check the references.

Projects to convert traditional journal papers to hypertext might miss some of the opportunities for taking advantage of the new

---

[5] The electronic notebook is available on a Macintosh disk as part of Apple Computer Technical Report # 13 (M. Slaney: "Lyon's Cochlear Model") from the Apple Corporate Library, 20525 Mariani Avenue, Cupertino, CA 95014, USA.

medium. Except for automated references and better search mechanisms, a hypertext version of a traditional paper would not really offer any advantages over a printed version and would suffer the disadvantages associated with forcing users to read large amounts of text from computer screens.

It is likely that the main advantage of hypertext will come from constructing new types of scientific communications which could take advantage of the new opportunities. Scientific "papers" in hypertext would come close to the biology and acoustics examples discussed here by including substantial additional detail which would be suppressed by traditional journal publication. Most readers would not bother following the links to those details, but they would be there for those specialists who might need to do so. Research publications in hypertext would present readers with a "virtual laboratory" and access to much richer representations of the original source data.

Yet another kind of research is the linguistic and theological studies of the Bible which are now being made possible by hypertext. The basic research problem is that the Bible exists in many different versions due to changing translation methods and the various scrolls and manuscripts found by archaeologists. Serious study of the Bible therefore requires the reader to compare several different versions of the same text, a task eminently suited for hypertext. OWL has developed a modified version of Guide called CDWord for the Dallas Theological Seminary, which can maintain access to several manuscript versions and scroll them in parallel such that the same part of the text is always displayed in all manuscript versions no matter which of them is used as the basis for jumps or searches.

As a matter of fact, the Bible, Torah, Koran, and other religious manuscripts can be viewed as some of the earliest examples of the hypertext principles. Many medieval manuscripts were heavily annotated by monks, rabbis, and similar people who devoted substantial time to developing linking structures between the basic documents of their respective religions and more or less canonical interpretations and elaborations such as the Talmud.

Educational Applications

Many of the applications discussed in other sections of this chapter actually have an educational slant. This is, for instance, true of the manuals that teach how to repair things and the hypertext versions of journals, dictionaries, etc.

Even so, there have been many hypertext systems produced specifically for educational use. Hypertext is well suited for open learning applications where the student is allowed freedom of action and encouraged to take the initiative. For example, the *Interactive NOVA* hypertext shown on the cover of this book allows the student to browse through a large set of biology information and see those parts that interest the student or make sense in the context of a current assignment. On the other hand, hypertext may be less well suited for the drill-and-practice type learning that is still necessary in some situations.

One specialized educational hypertext is the Palenque system from Bank Street College of Education [Wilson 1988]. The purpose of the Palenque system is to teach Mexican archaeology to children in the eight- to fourteen-year age range by letting them take a tour of the Palenque ruins. The system is implemented in DVI (Digital Video Interactive) on a CD-ROM and allows surrogate travel among the ruins in a practical application of the methods pioneered by the MIT Aspen *Movie Map* project discussed in Chapter 3.

The CD-ROM contains a large number of photographs of the Palenque site, and the user can move among them in the "traditional" surrogate travel style. Because of the digital image processing it is also possible to provide continuous panning around a 360° panoramic view as if the user was turning in a circle. In addition to the simulated visit to the ruins, the Palenque system also includes a museum with "theme rooms" about the Mayas and the rainforest. As users "walk" around the ruins or "visit" the museum, they have a simulated camera and scrapbook available to construct their own personalized record of their experience.

As an example of how a computer system can sometimes provide an experience richer than real life, the Palenque system includes a "magic flashlight" that allows users to dissolve their surrogate travel view of a building to old photographs of how the same ruin looked before it was restored and even to reconstructions of how the building might have looked in the days of the Mayas.

Palenque is intended to teach children, though it has been great fun for adult users also. In contrast, the Shakespeare project at Stanford University [Friedlander 1988] is explicitly aimed at university level students in drama theory. The hypertext contains film clips from plays like *Hamlet* and *Macbeth* and links between corresponding scenes in the different films, to illustrate how the same play has been interpreted by different directors and actors. There are also links between the film clips and hypertext nodes with analyses by various theoreticians of the texts and the performances.

Furthermore, the Shakespeare project includes a simulation facility called TheaterGame where students can stage their own interpretations of the plays from a database of hundreds of costumed actors and props. While they go through the activities in TheaterGame, the students can jump to hypertext tutorials about unfamiliar concepts, or they may browse a library of annotated examples.

A different kind of educational use of hypertext is to support the teacher's side of the process. John Leggett from Texas A&M University experimented with hypertext support for teachers as part of a course he taught on hypertext [Leggett et al. 1989]. This was probably the first university level course on hypertext. Students were asked to turn in their assignments on the KMS hypertext system at Texas A&M and Leggett graded and annotated them on the system. Since KMS is a multi-user system, Leggett could return the reports to the students on the system and include cross references from one student to another: "See how XX did it...."

Foreign Languages

The linking abilities of hypertext are ideal for the learning of foreign languages. Hypertext can provide automatic access to dictionaries through implicit links from any text, as shown in the Intermedia system in Figure 4.9. A student who does not know English very well might still be able to understand material in Intermedia because of its ability to link to an explanation of any word. As further discussed in the following section on the classics, hypertext also enables students to view two parallel versions of the same text: An original version and a translation.

The Encuentros project at Copenhagen University uses a hypertext system to improve the learning of Spanish. One major problem with learning languages from southern Europe is that people from that region tend to speak in a very agitated and fast manner which makes their utterances hard to understand for Scandinavians. But of course the goal of learning Spanish is to understand the way the language is

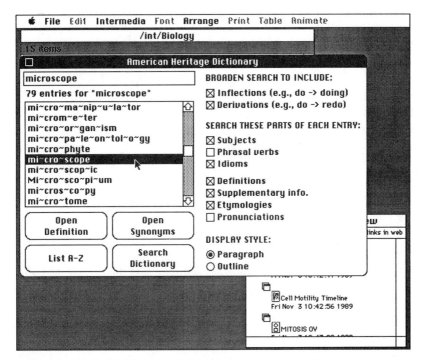

Figure 4.9. *The IRIS InterLex Server, shown here, adds dictionary and thesaurus support to the Intermedia environment. A user may search either Houghton-Mifflin's* American Heritage Dictionary *or Roget's* Thesaurus II *for the definition or synonyms for a specified word. Users can broaden or narrow the scope of the search by turning "inflections" and "derivations" on or off. They can search only the subject fields, or any combination of the other six fields. Both the dictionary and thesaurus lookup are accessible directly from the desktop; the user can just select the word and choose either the "lookup" or "thesaurus" menu command. © 1989 by Brown University, reprinted with permission.*

actually spoken in Spain and not the way a Danish teacher may speak it. Therefore Encuentros shows the student film clips of conversations as they would take place in Spain. If there is a part of a conversation that students do not understand, they can utilize the hypertext facilities and link to a film where the same part of the conversation is spoken more slowly. If they still don't understand it, they can follow a link to a version of the conversation where the actors don't even converse but face the camera and speak their lines v-e-r-y s-l-o-w-l-y and clearly.

À la Recontre de Philippe from MIT's Project Athena [Hodges et al. 1989] teaches French by a role-playing simulation where the student must help a Parisian named Philippe find a new apartment. In one instance they have to relay a message to him from an answering machine. In order to do so, they obviously have to understand the message. In addition to traditional facilities for replaying video sequences, the Philippe system allows students to add subtitles in either French or English if they need them, and it also has hypertext links to a glossary and to cultural notes with backup information about idiomatic expressions or historical locations. The hypertext advantage is that each student can utilize as much of this material as needed or desired by that student.

Classics

Classical Greek literature and culture is a natural application for a CD-ROM, because the chief disadvantage of a read-only device is almost irrelevant. It does not matter so much that the CD-ROM cannot be updated because there is not any new classical Greek literature being written.[6] The Perseus project [Crane 1987; 1988] at Harvard University is a major attempt to provide hypertext support for the study of ancient Greek literature, history, and archaeology. The Perseus CD-ROM gives hypertext access to large amounts of original source text in Greek and also provides several facilities to help students understand the text, including the parallel translation shown in Figure 4.10.

Furthermore, the Perseus disk contains hypertext versions of some scholarly articles and encyclopedia articles that interpret the original Greek sources. These secondary writings often contain extensive references to the primary sources that can be automated as hypertext links. This system has the potential to change completely the way students approach the learning of classical Greek culture. When a textbook may have as many as 25 source references on every page, there is little chance that the student will actually go to a traditional library and find all the dusty volumes on the top shelf. In a hypertext, however, the sources are a single click away, and while students still may not pursue all 25 citations, they will no longer have to accept most

---

[6] Actually, the interpretations and opinions of how Greek literature is read and how exactly the text should appear *do* change. So the read-only nature of the CD-ROM can still be a disadvantage, although it is used in the Perseus project because of its huge storage space.

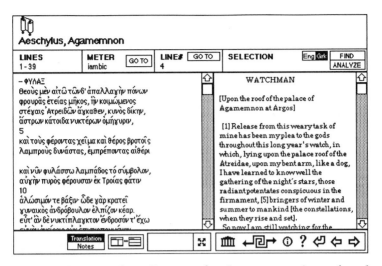

Figure 4.10. *A screen from Perseus showing two versions of a play by Aeschylus. © 1989 by the President and Fellows of Harvard University and the Annenberg/CPB Project, reprinted with permission.*

of the textbook author's statements uncritically. The trend for students to move their focus of attention in the direction of the original Greek sources is also reinforced by translation tools such as automatic morphology analysis[7] and dictionary lookup.

As shown in Figure 4.11, Perseus contains more than text. It has photographs of temples and other architecture and illustrations of archaeological objects. In many cases, one actually gets a better image of the artwork by looking at the photos on the computer than by looking at the original work of art since it may be small or poorly lit in a museum. The hypertext nature of Perseus enables the different parts of the system to enhance one another. For example, the *Bacchae* of Euripides can be appreciated better when one can link to vase paintings of satyrs. Similarly, the histories of Herodotus and Thucydides are clearer when illustrated with maps and photographs of the places they mention.

The current version of Perseus is implemented in HyperCard on Macintosh computers. But classicists have a long-term perspective and are prepared to move on to another platform if a better one becomes available several years from now. A hypertext version of classical

---

[7] Determining the grammatical role of words in a sentence to understand, for instance, which word is the object and which is the subject.

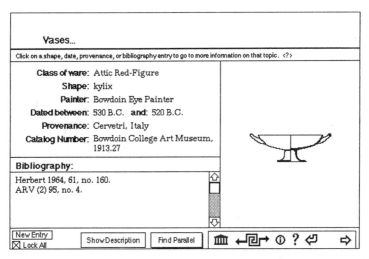

Figure 4.11. *Part of the vase catalog in Perseus. Users will also be able to view enlarged details of the artwork or see color photographs of the vases displayed on a separate monitor. Copyright © 1989 by the President and Fellows of Harvard University and the Annenberg/CPB Project, reprinted with permission.*

Greek literature can be used for many more years than the lifetime of a computer system. Because of this "diachronic" perspective [Crane 1990], all text elements and hypertext links have been coded in a machine-independent format using a set of SGML markup tags. Images are stored in resolution-independent formats like PostScript to allow them to be displayed on other types of computer screens in the future. These standard SGML and PostScript files are then converted once more by an automatic process to a HyperCard format when they are included in the distributed version of Perseus.

The first version of the Perseus disk will appear in the fall of 1990. The Perseus database will grow and change in future releases, since it is being produced in stages. Successive versions of the disk are planned to have more and better information on it.

Museums

A special case of educational hypertext is the museum information system since most people do not go to museums specifically to study. It is impossible to present museum-goers with all the relevant information about the exhibits in a printed form; that would scare them

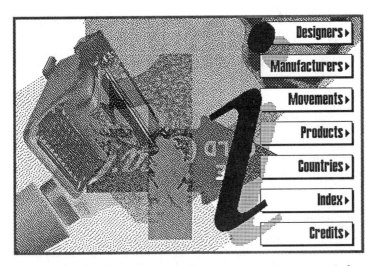

Figure 4.12. *The front screen of the London Design Museum information hypertext. Screen layout © 1989 by Cognitive Applications, contents © 1989 by the Design Museum, reprinted with permission.*

away. The difficulty of knowing the extent of a hypertext information space is actually an advantage in this application.

The Hyperties system (discussed further in Chapter 5) has been used at several museums, including the Smithsonian Institution, for projects providing additional background information about the subjects of exhibitions.

The Getty Museum has produced an electronic version of its illuminated medieval manuscripts to allow their visitors the sense of paging through the books even though the originals are much too fragile to be handled by the public. The traditional way to exhibit medieval manuscripts has been to display a single two-page spread in a glass case, but that method removes the individual illustration from its context as part of the telling of a story. The electronic medium allows the user access to the full sequence of illustrations.

These examples have been minor additions to existing museum resources, but the Design Museum in London, which opened in July 1989, has based its entire information system around a hypertext. Figure 4.12 shows the front screen, which welcomes the user and allows access to various forms of information about modern design. Users can access information about various design movements like Bauhaus or Functionalism or they can access the information starting with countries or manufacturers. They can also look at individual

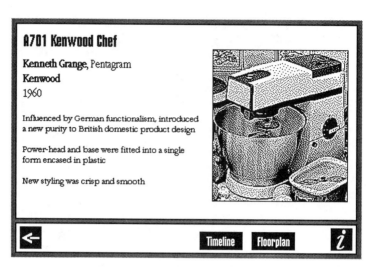

Figure 4.13. *A "product screen" from the London Design Museum. Clicking on "floorplan" takes the user to a screen with the location of the product highlighted. This node also has links to a historical overview ("timeline"), and to information about the manufacturer and designer. Clicking on the "i" will take the user back to the first screen from any other node in the hypertext. Screen layout © 1989 by Cognitive Applications, contents © 1989 by the Design Museum, reprinted with permission.*

designers or products. All of this material is of course connected with hypertext links; visitors who might have started with accessing the screen about the Kenwood Chef in Figure 4.13 because they once owned one themselves could end up reading about other products of the same period and the underlying theoretical design movement defining the look of the 1960s.

Museum systems require "walk-up-and-use" usability in the sense that users will not be willing to go through a special initial period of training to be able to use the system. Simple systems like Hyperties without too many fancy navigational options are suited for this application. The need to pull the museum-goer into the hypertext information space also impels the use of very attractive initial displays like Figure 4.12.

Entertainment and Leisure Applications

Hypertext provides several opportunities for pure enjoyment. Unfortunately there has been very little research conducted in this area, possibly because funding agencies may find it frivolous to study how

Figure 4.14. *The welcome screen for the* Glasgow Online *tourist information system. © 1989 by the University of Strathclyde Department of Information Science, reprinted with permission.*

to have fun. But there has still been some pioneering research as well as the first few commercial examples.

Tourist Guides

Tourist information achieves a good match with the "golden rules" of hypertext since tourists typically want to read only a small part of the information available about a given city or country. Furthermore the information can reasonably easily be divided into nodes for each attraction, tourist service, historical era, or geographical location. The problem with traditional tourist guides is that they need to structure all this information according to a single principle, whereas the tourist has multiple varying needs.

Most tourist guides structure their information according to the type of information and have separate chapters on hotels, restaurants, shopping, and museums and sights. In contrast, ACCESS guides [Wurman 1989] are structured according to the geography of each city and describe everything in a given neighborhood on the same page. The advantage of the ACCESS approach is that it is easy to find a place to eat lunch after a visit to the British Museum, but the disadvantage is that it is hard to find the best place in London to buy science fiction books. I personally often buy both the ACCESS guide to a city and a more traditional guide book.

Glasgow Online [Baird and Percival 1989] is a hypertext tourist guide that combines the best of both types of guide. The front screen of the system (see Figure 4.14) has the traditional subject-oriented view of the city and allows the user to find, say, a hotel in a certain price range. From the description of the hotel, the user can jump to a map of Glasgow with a highlighted icon for the chosen hotel. The user can then click on other icons in the neighborhood to see what other facilities are nearby.

Tourist information systems have the problem that they should be usable by visitors from foreign countries [Baird 1990], who may not speak the local language. The designers of *Glasgow Online* have not completely solved that problem, but they have addressed it by extensive use of icons and graphics and by conducting usability tests with foreign users.

Libraries

Some library applications are for the retrieval of technical or scientific information and are very similar to the applications discussed above under dictionaries or to the information retrieval techniques discussed in Chapter 8. Also, libraries certainly need to include electronic publications like hypertext, if they want to keep up with modern technology. In the future, a "library" might well be a computer network service rather than a building.

The Book House (shown on the cover of this book) is a library system using hypertext techniques to help users find books without the limitations of traditional information retrieval. In contrast to most computer systems for libraries, which are intended for the retrieval of technical literature, the Book House is intended for average citizens who use public libraries to borrow fiction.

The Book House project [Pejtersen 1989] was conducted in cooperation among Risø National Laboratory, Jutland Telephone, RC Computer Inc., the Royal Art Academy, and the Royal School of Librarianship in Denmark under the leadership of Annelise Mark Pejtersen. The system was field tested at the Hjortespring Library with good results.

The user interface of the Book House is based on a building metaphor somewhat like a real library.[8] The first choice upon entering the building is whether to enter a room with books for children, a room with books for adults, or a room with books for everybody. After having made this choice, the user will see the "strategy selection room" shown as the top illustration on the cover of this book. In our illustration we have chosen to search for books for adults, so the people shown looking at the books are adults. The illustrations in the children's section show drawings of children instead.

Because people have many different ways of finding books, the Book House supports four different search strategies, which can be selected in the strategy selection room by clicking on one of the four areas of the room. The simplest strategy is the random browsing used by the man on the right. Users who click at this part of the room are taken directly into the database of books at a random location. The woman in the left part of the room is performing a search by analogy by looking through the shelves for a book similar to one already read. Users who select this strategy will be prompted to select the book they have already read and the system will then present a list of similar books ordered by similarity rating.

The woman looking at a set of pictures is engaged in a browsing strategy whereby she is looking at pictures to find something that may interest her. Users who select this strategy are presented with several screens of icons, each of which represents a set of search terms that can be selected by clicking. This process frees the user from having to generate search terms and may also give rise to potentially new perspectives on perhaps vaguely perceived needs. The search terms associated with each icon have been determined by empirical user testing.

For example, the icon showing a handshake could be viewed as a Dane shaking hand with a foreigner and might therefore represent the abstract concept of aid to developing countries. But it could also be seen as simply representing "friendship." Instead of trying to come up with icons to represent all index terms uniquely, the solution was to assign each icon several meanings and have the 108 icons in the system

---

[8] One indication of the building metaphor is that the icons at the top of each screen for returning to previous states depict the relevant rooms.

cover more than 1000 terms. The exact terms associated with each icon further differ depending on whether the user is a child or an adult.

These icons have been designed for the user's national cultural context. For example, all Danes would recognize the icon for prehistoric settings as a neolithic dolmen. A corresponding British system might have used an image of Stonehenge while other countries would have to use yet other icons.

The man at the desk is performing an analytic search and has access to twelve classification dimensions as represented by the following graphic elements:

- Movie poster: Plot and theme.
- Book cover: Physical appearance of the book (e.g. picture and color of cover).
- Drawers with hearts, weapons, and animals: Genre.
- Busts: Main characters, name and age.
- Globe: Place (geographical environment).
- Landscape through the window: Setting (social, professional, and geographical environment).
- Glasses: Readability of the text.
- Clock: Time period.
- Theater masks: Emotional experience (e.g. exciting or humorous).
- Picture of a writer: The author's intention of cognition/information.
- Index cards: Search by name of author or search by title (two different search dimensions).

By combining several of these classification dimensions, users can find, for instance, romance novels set in seventeenth century France.

In addition to providing several search strategies, the Book House also utilizes hypertext principles to allow users to change strategies by jumping back to the strategy selection room or by linking to books "similar" to the one currently on the screen, no matter how it was retrieved.

From field testing of the Book House it turns out that regular library users do indeed use many different strategies. Using the analytical classifications accounted for 31% of the searches, while picture browsing was second most popular with 27%. Search by analogy accounted for 23% of the searches, and 20% of searches were performed with random browsing. Users liked the system very much: 95% were satisfied with the interface and 84% were satisfied with the search results.

Another example of a library application is providing public access to archives of historical documents. For example, the State Library of New South Wales in Sydney, Australia, contains large amounts of old convict records from the settlement of the colony 200 years ago, and many modern Australians visit the library to discover what crimes their ancestors committed that caused them to be deported. Currently this genealogical search requires people to wade through mounds of old documents and follow the links to past generations by hand. Most of this material would be an obvious candidate for hypertext access, however, since the information is interlinked to a great extent. One problem would be the need to represent the form of the original records and not just their content since they have considerable "romantic" attributes. The right ambience might be created by scanning in images of the original pages and combining them with handwriting recognition to generate a machine readable representation for automatic construction of hypertext links.

Unfortunately current computer technology cannot read the handwriting of eighteenth century Royal Navy officers, and there are several other technical obstacles to implementing a hypertext system for the convict records. These problems will probably be solved in the next ten years or so, and one could well envisage additional library services that would result from having the records on hypertext. For example computer networks would make it possible to bring the library to the users rather than having them come to the library, a feature that would be a considerable advantage in a country as large as Australia. It would likewise be possible to use the original records in teaching the national heritage, even in schools in the outback, and to give all students the feeling of exploring original sources.

Interactive Fiction

As further described in Chapter 9, I got very negative replies when I asked a group of computer science students whether they would like to read fiction online. They only gave online fiction a rating of 0.5 on a scale from zero to four (with two as the neutral point). But that survey asked people who had not had actual experience with reading online fiction and who would therefore have a hard time imagining the potential advantages of *interactive* fiction as opposed to purely *online* traditional fiction.

My personal view is that there is very little to be gained from converting traditional forms of fiction to the online medium. As long as you are just reading a regular novel with a single stream of action, you are much better off reading a printed book. Only when new forms of fiction are invented will we gain any benefit from putting them on hypertext. The reader needs to be able to interact with the fictional universe instead of just being in a page-turning mode.

One possibility for online fiction would be the "shared universe" type of story that has recently become popular in the science fiction genre. The basic idea is that several authors write stories set in the same fictional universe with the same general background and many of the same characters. One could potentially collect several hundred such stories together in a hypertext on a single CD-ROM and let readers pursue the type of plot and character each of them found interesting. Such an online fiction project would fit the three golden rules of having many smaller plot elements that were interlinked and were enjoyable for readers who read only a few such elements.

The commercial feasibility of this type of shared online fiction is problematic, however. Hundreds of authors would need to write stories that would have to be coordinated and interlinked, but buyers would not be willing to pay much more for the CD-ROM than perhaps five times the price of a regular novel, since each of them would only read a small part of the total text. Maybe doing a "shared universe" hypertext CD-ROM would be an idea for a collaborative project for a large group of students taking classes in creative writing?

It is also possible to have interactive fiction in works by a single author [Howell 1990]. The Storyspace system from the University of North Carolina is a hypertext system specifically designed for writing and reading interactive fiction. Probably the most famous work written in the Storyspace system is *Afternoon, A Story* by Michael Joyce (1987). *Afternoon* consists of 539 nodes and 915 links, enough to form a reasonably complex hyperspace for the story. The actual story does not have a traditional plot but is more in the nature of a number of snapshots of an underlying fictional construction, which readers discover as they read more and more snapshots. The *Dictionary of the Khazars: A Lexicon Novel in 100,000 Words* by Milorad Pavic (1988) is an example of this kind of "trackless expanse" [Moulthrop 1989] implemented in a traditional printed book. It is a collection of encyclopedic articles about a Central European people whom the

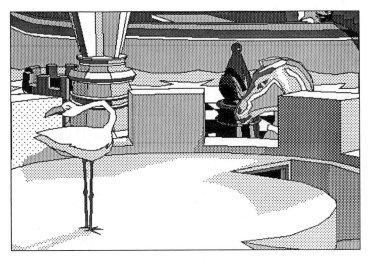

Figure 4.15. *Screen from* The Manhole *showing the user's view after having moved to the top of a tower in the woods. Users will see this screen after having been through some previous screens showing a winding stairway leading to the top of the tower. Because of this movement and the presence of the flamingo on the top of the tower, users initially view the tower as a traditional building, but further movement will reveal something else (see Figure 4.16).* © *1988 by Cyan, reprinted with permission.*

reader gradually gets to know by reading various "dictionary" entries. There is no narrative as such in the book.

Interactive fictions in the form of virtual realities are some of the most popular hypertexts for children. One example is *Inigo Gets Out* (see Figures 8.7 and 8.8), which children find very enjoyable. In a longitudinal study of a single five-year-old boy we have found that he continues viewing/reading/navigating/using/playing with the story even after several months, as well as showing it to other children when they visit. The language does not yet have a single good word for the activity of going through a hypertext like *Inigo Gets Out* since it is completely nonverbal.

A larger nonverbal interactive fiction for children ("of all ages") is *The Manhole* (see Figures 4.15 and 4.16), which contains 753 nodes and takes up 23 megabytes on a CD-ROM. It takes place in a fantasy world with talking animals and dragons where magic bean stalks grow into the sky. The fantasy world is displayed to the user in a first-person perspective (i.e., graphically showing what you would actually see if

Figure 4.16. *Screen from* The Manhole *showing an example of a magical dimension: When users move to the objects seen outside the tower in Figure 4.15, they get to this screen where it is revealed that the tower has been magically transformed to a rook on a chess board (this visual pun is actually better in Danish where a chess rook is called a* tårn *("tower") so that the pun also becomes verbal).* © *1988 by Cyan, reprinted with permission.*

you were positioned at the current location in the world), and users move through the world by clicking on the place they want to go.

Figures 4.15 and 4.16 show an example of navigation that violates traditional expectations. This "magical" movement in the world of an interactive fiction adds spice to the experience of using the system and is probably good in a system having entertainment as its main purpose. It also seems to make it harder to acquire a conceptual model of the navigation space, however, so it would probably not be suited for more work-oriented situations.

The Manhole is not completely nonverbal but contains messages from various characters to the user. These messages are printed on the screen in cartoon-like speech-bubbles and are also read out loud by the system using good quality sound and some interesting voice characterizations. There are four main characters with whom the user interacts: An elephant who paddles the user around in a small boat, a dragon, a walrus, and a rabbit. Each character has a tone of voice consistent with the way it behaves (e.g. the walrus is lazy and the dragon is a hip dude). Other sound effects, including both music and various naturalistic sounds, are also used to good effect so this is a true hypermedia system.

The main experience of viewing/navigating/reading/(whatever we want to call it) *The Manhole* is again not that of following a traditional plot or narrative. Instead the hypertext provides a fictional space in which readers construct their own stories as they move through it. The experience is somewhat like an exploration, but it is distinctly more relaxed than the feeling one gets from exploring adventure games (see the example in Figure 1.4), where the user is set a specific goal and is under continuous pressure to achieve it or "die."

Harry McMahon and Bill O'Neill from the University of Ulster have tried placing a few Macintoshes with sound and image digitizers in an elementary school to get the pupils to create their own interactive fictions. Of course, most of these stories are fairly simple—such as "The teddy bear went for a walk in the forest and met another teddy bear" (a seven-year-old's creation)—and were shown over a sequential series of screens like a cartoon strip.

More advanced designs use a facility called bubbles where the children can first draw their cards and then choose from various shapes of comics-like speech- and thought-balloons to add to the image. The interesting idea is that it is possible to add multiple bubbles to each card whereupon they will be displayed to the reader one at a time. In this way, it is possible for the child to generate a dialogue between characters in the story. It is even possible to contrast what the characters *say* with what they *think*. For example, in a story about a mouse about to be killed, the mouse asked for a last wish: to sing a song. This wish is spoken out loud (placed in a speech-balloon), but the mouse's thought (placed in a thought-balloon) is "I am not as stupid as I look." The next speech-balloon revealed that the mouse had chosen to sing the well-known song about bottles on a wall (falling down one at a time), but starting with, "A thousand million green bottles sitting on a wall...." So this smart mouse will survive for some time to come.

Most of these stories were basically linear in nature and do not really have all that much to do with the concept of hypertext. McMahon and O'Neill have on purpose avoided introducing commercial hyperstories (such as *Inigo Gets Out* or *The Manhole*) to the children in order to be able to observe the natural evolution of their approach to the new medium of interactive fiction. It actually did happen that a few ten-year-olds discovered the hypertext principle on their own. They were creating a story about a person who was visiting an alien world and was captured by the aliens. He was offered a job by the alien boss and thought to himself, "Should I try to escape?" or "Should I take the job?" The reader could click on either of these two thought balloons to proceed with the story. McMahon has remarked that an interesting aspect of this story design was that the pupils had had to change their perspective on writing. Originally they thought of creating a story as they went through it (writing for the writer, as it were), but in this new situation, they had to consider what the reader could do and would want to do, so they had to change their perspective to writing for readers.

5.   Major Current Hypertext Systems

The first hypertext systems like FRESS (see Chapter 3), were mainframe-based, and mainframes certainly *can* support many hypertext features (as further discussed in Chapter 7). Even so, practically all recent systems have been based on personal computers or workstations, and this chapter is limited to these systems. This chapter covers some of the better known general hypertext systems but it is impossible to cover *all* the systems since new ones seem to appear every day.

Which hypertext system should you choose? The simple answer is, "That depends," since there is no single universally best hypertext system no matter what the salespeople might tell you [Nielsen 1989e]. You should consider the size of the information you want to represent in hypertext and whether you want a text-oriented system or a system that is good on graphics. You also have to consider whether your application calls for a multi-user system or whether a single-user system will do. Finally, you have to take usability considerations into account. Some systems are suited for professional users who need a lot of features and who have the time to learn them, whereas other systems are simple enough for naive users. I cannot give you a single recommendation since I use several different systems myself.

Appendix A lists addresses and telephone numbers for the vendors of the hypertext systems discussed in this chapter as well as a few others.

Hypertext on Workstations

Most of the early hypertext systems were based on workstations like Sun, Symbolics, or Xerox Lisp machines; true personal computers have not been powerful enough until recently to be able to support hypertext. Even now, when the most widely used hypertext systems do run on personal computers, there are reasons to prefer workstation-based hypertext for many applications where hardware costs are less crucial. Workstations have big enough screens to show many hypertext windows and overview diagrams at the same time, and they are powerful enough to enable on-the-fly construction of dynamic overview diagrams and computation of complex information retrieval formulas.

NoteCards

NoteCards may be the most famous hypertext system in the research world because its design has been especially well documented [Halasz et al. 1987]. It was designed at Xerox PARC and is now available as a commercial product.

Originally, NoteCards ran only on the Xerox family of D-machines. These computers are fairly specialized Lisp[1] machines and not in very widespread use outside the research world. Therefore NoteCards has recently been made available also for general workstations like the Sun.

One reason for implementing NoteCards on the Xerox Lisp machines was that they provided the powerful InterLisp programming environment. InterLisp made it easy to program a complex system like NoteCards, and it also gave users the option to customize NoteCards to their own special needs since it is fully integrated with the Lisp system. Users who know Lisp can in principle change any aspect of NoteCards and they can implement specialized card types as mentioned below.

NoteCards is built on the four basic kinds of objects shown in Figure 5.1:

• Each node is a single *notecard* that can be opened as a window on the screen. These cards are not really "cards" in the HyperCard sense of having a fixed size but are really standard resizeable windows. Users can have as many notecards open on the screen as they want but quickly risk facing the "messy desktop" problem if they open too many. The notecards can have different types depending on the data they contain. The simplest card types are plain text or graphics but there are at least 50 specialized types of cards for individual applications that need special data structures. For example a legal application might need notecards containing forms for court decisions

---

[1] Lisp is a programming language characterized by having a huge number of parentheses (making it hard to read) and great flexibility (making it one of the preferred languages for artificial intelligence research).

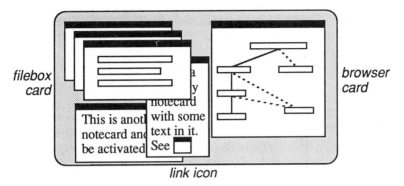

Figure 5.1. *The general layout of a NoteCards screen with the four basic objects: notecards, a link, FileBoxes, and a browser card.*

with fields for the standard units of information (defendant, plaintiff, etc.).

• The *links* are typed connections between cards. Links can be displayed as a small link icon as in Figure 5.1, or they can be shown as a box with the title of their destination card. Users open the destination card in a new window on the screen by clicking on the link icon with the mouse. The link type is a label chosen by the user to specify the relation between the departure card and the destination card for the link. To continue the legal example, lawyers might want one type of link to court decisions supporting their own position and another type of link to decisions that refute their position.

• The third kind of object is the *browser* card, which contains a structural overview diagram of the notecards and links. As shown in Figure 5.1, the different link types are indicated by different line patterns in the browser, thus giving the user an indication of the connection among the nodes. The browser card is an active overview diagram and allows users to edit the underlying hypertext nodes and links by carrying out operations on the boxes and lines in the browser. The user can also go to a card by clicking on the box representing it. The layout of the browser card is computed by system and therefore reflects the changing structure of the hypertext as users add or delete nodes and links.

• The fourth kind of object is the *FileBox*, which is used for hierarchical nesting of notecards. Each notecard is listed in exactly one FileBox. Actually, the FileBox is a special-purpose notecard, so FileBoxes can contain other FileBoxes and it is possible to construct links from other cards to a FileBox.

In one case users customized NoteCards so extensively that the result may be said to be a new system. The Instructional Design Environment (IDE) developed at Xerox PARC [Jordan et al. 1989] is built on top of NoteCards but provides a new user interface to help courseware developers construct hypertext structures semi-automatically. IDE supports structure accelerators that speed up hypertext construction by allowing the user to generate an entire set of nodes and links from a template with a single action.

The standard version of NoteCards has been used for several years both within Xerox and at customer locations. One of the interesting early empirical studies of the actual use of NoteCards was a longitudinal study [Monty and Moran 1986] of a history graduate student who used the system to write a research paper over a period of seven months. This user did not use links across the FileBox hierarchy very much, but that result may not be generalized to other users. The important aspect of the study is that it investigated the behavior of the test subject for an extended period of time and observed the use of the system for a fairly large task.

KMS

KMS probably has the distinction of being the oldest among the currently popular hypertext systems since it is a direct descendant of the ZOG research system developed at Carnegie Mellon University with some development as early as 1972 and as a full scale project from 1975 [Robertson et al. 1981]. The word ZOG does not mean anything but was chosen because it "is short, easily pronounced and easily remembered." At first, ZOG ran on mainframe computers; it was then moved to PERQ workstations, 28 of which were installed on the aircraft carrier USS *Carl Vinson* in 1983 for a field test of such applications as a maintenance manual for weapons elevators.

KMS is an abbreviation for Knowledge Management System and has been a commercial product since 1983. It runs on Sun and Apollo workstations and has been used for a large number of applications. KMS is designed to manage fairly large hypertexts with many tens of thousands of nodes and has been designed from the start to work across local area networks.

In contrast to NoteCards, KMS has a very simple data structure based on a single type of node called the *frame*. A frame can take over the entire workstation screen, but normally the screen is split into two frames, each of which is about as big as a letter-sized page of paper. Users cannot mix small and large nodes and cannot have more than two nodes on the screen at the same time. This might seem limiting at first but proponents of KMS claim that it is much better to use the hypertext navigation mechanism to change the contents of the display than to have to use window management operations to find the desired information among many overlapping windows.

KMS has been optimized for speed of navigation, so the destination frame will normally be displayed "instantaneously" as the user clicks the mouse on an anchor. The time to display a new frame is actually about a half-second, and the designers of KMS claim that there is no real benefit to being faster than that. They tried an experimental system to change the display in 0.05 seconds, but that was so fast that users had trouble noticing whether or not the screen had changed.

If an item on the screen is not linked to another node, then clicking on it will generate an empty frame, making node and link creation seem like a special form of navigation to the user. It is also possible for a click on an item to run a small program written in the special KMS action language. This language is not quite as general as the integrated InterLisp in NoteCards, but it still allows the user to customize KMS for many special applications. See for example the discussion in Chapter 4 of the use of KMS to support the research of a biologist.

KMS does not provide an overview diagram but instead relies on fast navigation and a hierarchical structure of the nodes. Links across the hierarchy are prefixed with an "@" to let users know that they are moving to another part of the information space. Two additional facilities to help users navigate are the landmark status of a special "home" frame, which is directly accessible from any location, and the special ease and global availability of backtracking to the previous node by single-clicking the mouse as long as it points to empty space on the screen.

Hypertext on the IBM PC (and Compatibles)

Many products for the IBM PC claim to be hypertext, but most of them do not really live up to the requirement of letting users feel that they are navigating freely. Even so, there are plenty of true hypertext systems available for the IBM PC. IBM itself has even introduced a product called LinkWay which has certain similarities to HyperCard and is based on linking buttons to cards.

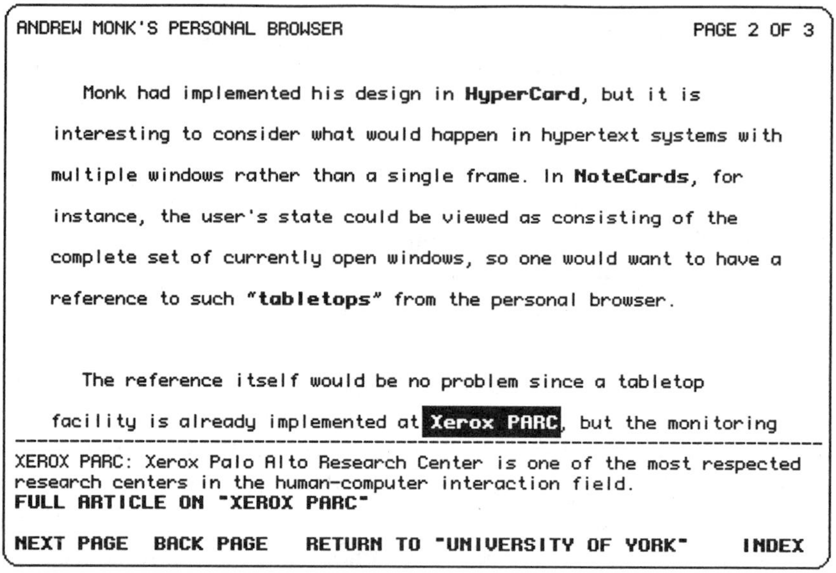

```
ANDREW MONK'S PERSONAL BROWSER                          PAGE 2 OF 3


     Monk had implemented his design in HyperCard, but it is

  interesting to consider what would happen in hypertext systems with

  multiple windows rather than a single frame. In NoteCards, for

  instance, the user's state could be viewed as consisting of the

  complete set of currently open windows, so one would want to have a

  reference to such "tabletops" from the personal browser.


     The reference itself would be no problem since a tabletop

  facility is already implemented at Xerox PARC, but the monitoring
  -----------------------------------------------------------------
  XEROX PARC: Xerox Palo Alto Research Center is one of the most respected
  research centers in the human-computer interaction field.
  FULL ARTICLE ON "XEROX PARC"

  NEXT PAGE   BACK PAGE    RETURN TO "UNIVERSITY OF YORK"        INDEX
```

Figure 5.2. *An example of a Hyperties screen as it typically looks on a text-only screen on a plain vanilla IBM PC.*

Hyperties

Hyperties was started as a research project by Ben Shneiderman [Shneiderman 1987] at the University of Maryland around 1983. It was originally called TIES as an abbreviation for The Electronic Encyclopedia System, but since that name was trademarked by somebody else, the name was changed to Hyperties to indicate the use of hypertext concepts in the system.

Since 1987 Hyperties has been available as a commercial product on standard IBM PCs from Cognetics Corporation. Research continues at the University of Maryland where a workstation version has been implemented on Sun machines under the NeWS window system.

One of the interesting aspects of the commercial version of Hyperties is that it works with the plain text screen shown in Figure 5.2. Hyperties also works with the main graphics formats on IBM PCs and PS/2s and can display color images if the screen can handle them.

The interaction techniques in Hyperties are extremely simple and allow the interface to be operated without a mouse. Some of the text on the screen is highlighted and the user can activate those anchors either by clicking on them with a mouse, touching if a touch screen is available, or simply by using the arrow keys to move the cursor until it is over the text and then hitting ENTER. Hyperties uses the arrow keys in a special manner called "jump keys," which causes the cursor to jump in a single step directly to the next active anchor in the direction of the arrow. This way of using arrow keys has been optimized for hypertext where there are normally only a few areas on the screen that the user can point to and the use of keys has been measured to be slightly faster than the mouse (see Chapter 7).

In the example in Figure 5.2, the user is activating the string "Xerox PARC," which is indicated by inverse video. In the color version of Hyperties it is possible for the user to edit a preference file to determine other types of feedback for selections such as the use of contrasting color.

Instead of taking the user directly to the destination node as almost all other hypertext systems do, Hyperties at first lets the user stay at the same navigational location and displays only a small "definition" at the bottom of the screen. This definition provides the user with a prospective view of what would happen if the link were indeed followed to its destination and it allows the user to see the information in the context of the anchor point. In many cases just seeing the definition is enough. Otherwise the user can of course choose to complete the link.

A Hyperties link points to an entire "article," which may consist of several pages. Users following the link will always be taken to the first page of the article and will have to page through it themselves. This set-up is in contrast to the KMS model, where a link always points to a single page, and to the Intermedia model where a link points to a specific text string within an article. The advantage of the Hyperties model is that authors do not need to specify destinations very precisely. They just indicate the name of the article they want to link to, and the authoring system completes the link.

The same text phrase will always point to the same article in Hyperties, which again simplifies the authoring interface but makes the system less flexible. Many applications call for having different destinations, depending on the context or perhaps on the system's model of the user's level of expertise.

Many of the design choices in Hyperties follow from the original emphasis on applications like museum information systems. These applications need a very simple reading interface without advanced facilities like overview diagrams (which cannot be supported on the plain vanilla PC anyway). Furthermore, the writers of the hypertexts were museum curators and historians who are mostly not very motivated for learning complex high-technology solutions, so the similarity of the Hyperties authoring facilities to traditional text processing was well suited for the initial users. Now Hyperties is being used for a much wider spectrum of applications.

The commercial version of Hyperties uses a full-screen user interface as shown in Figure 5.2, wheras the research system on the Sun uses a two-frame approach similar to that of KMS.

Guide

Guide was the first popular commercial hypertext system [Brown 1987] when it was released for the Macintosh in 1986. Soon thereafter it was also released for the IBM PC, and it is still the only hypertext system that is available on both platforms. The user interface looks exactly the same on the two computers.

Peter Brown started Guide as a research project at the University of Kent in the U.K. in 1982, and he had the first version running on PERQ workstations in 1983. In 1984 the company Office Workstations Ltd. (OWL) got interested in the program and decided to release it as a commercial product. They made several changes to the prototype, including some that were necessary to get the user interface to conform to the Macintosh user interface.

Peter Brown continues to conduct research in hypertext using the Unix version of Guide that is maintained at the university. It is also used for some consulting projects in industry. If nothing else is stated, my use of the term "Guide" will refer to the commercial version on the IBM PC and the Macintosh and not to the Unix workstation version, since there are several differences between them. The IBM PC version of Guide has the advantage of being supplemented by other products from OWL such as IDEX for the conversion of SGML text files to hypertext (see Chapter 11).

Guide is similar to NoteCards in being based on scrolling text windows instead of fixed frames. But whereas the links in NoteCards refer to other cards, links in Guide often just scroll the window to a new position to reveal a destination contained within a single file. Link anchors are associated with text strings and move over the screen as the user scrolls or edits the text. This approach is in contrast to, say,

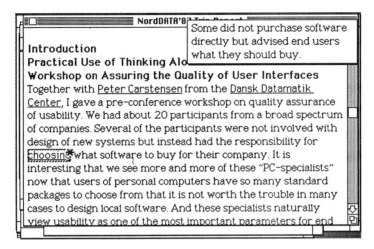

Figure 5.3. *A typical Guide screen where the user is pressing down the mouse button over the anchor for a pop-up note, which is temporarily displayed in the small window at the top right of the screen.*

HyperCard where anchors are fixed graphic regions on the screen. Guide does include support for graphic links, but they seem somewhat less natural to work with in the Guide user interface, and graphics have to be imported from external drawing programs.

Guide supports three different forms for hypertext link: Replacements, pop-ups, and jumps.

The *replacement button* is used for in-line expansion of the text of the anchor to a new and normally larger text in a concept that is sometimes called stretchtext.[2] Replacement buttons form a hierarchical structure of text and are useful to represent text in the manner of a traditional textbook with chapters, sections, and subsections. Typically, the initial display will show all the chapter headings and users will then expand the one chapter in which they are interested by replacing the chapter heading with the list of sections in the chapter. They can then further replace the section that interests them the most with its list of subsections, and so on. While making these replacements, the user continuously has the other chapter headings available (perhaps by scrolling the window a little) and thereby preserves context. The reverse action of a replacement is to close the expanded text and have it re-replaced with the original text.

---

[2] The "stretchtext" term is probably due to Ted Nelson. Similar concepts were found in Augment and several early text editors at Xerox PARC.

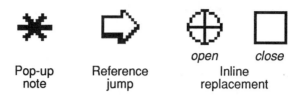

Figure 5.4. *Guide uses varying cursor shapes to indicate the type of hypertext action available to the user.*

The replacement button exists in a variation called *inquiry replacement*, which is used to list several options and have the user choose one. When the user clicks on a replacement button that is part of an inquiry, that button will expand, and the other buttons in the inquiry will be removed from the screen until the user closes the expansion again. This interface is useful for multiple-choice type applications, like a repair manual where the user is asked to click on the type of equipment that needs repair. The explanation for the selected type is expanded and the other, irrelevant types are hidden.

The second type of hypertext is small pop-up windows provided by clicking *note buttons* as shown in Figure 5.3. This facility is useful for footnote-type annotations, which are closely connected to the information in the main window. The pop-up is only displayed as long as the user holds the mouse button down over the note button, implying that the "backtrack" command consists simply of letting the mouse button go. This type of user interface is sometimes called a "spring loaded mode" because users are in the mode only as long as they continue to activate a dialogue element that will revert to normal as soon as it is released. The pop-ups are modes, nevertheless, since they make it impossible for the user to perform other actions (e.g. making a copy of the text in the pop-up window) as long as they are displayed.

The third form for hypertext in Guide is the *reference button*, which is used to jump to another location in the hypertext. To get back to the departure point, users have to click a special backtrack icon.

The three different kinds of hypertext in Guide are revealed to the user by changing the shape of the cursor, as shown in Figure 5.4. One might have imagined that this fairly extensive set of different types of hypertext in a single small system would confuse users, but our field studies [Nielsen and Lyngbæk 1990] showed that users had no problems distinguishing among the three kinds of button.

As further discussed in Chapter 9, we also found that users liked the note button for pop-ups best and that the reference button for jumps got the worst ratings. It is interesting to consider that the reference button is exactly the feature that was not included in the "cleanly designed" research prototype of Guide but was added for the commercial release [Brown 1987]. It is of course impossible to say from our data whether the reference button was rated relatively poorly because it was not integrated nicely into the overall design or because gotos are just harmful in general.

Version 2 of Guide introduced a fourth type of button called the *command button*, which executes a script in the special-purpose Genesis language when clicked. Genesis is not a general programming language like HyperCard's HyperTalk, however, and is typically only used to access a videodisk to play a specified set of frames.

Hypertext on Macintosh

Even though hypertext work started on workstations and much advanced work on systems still takes place there, the Macintosh has become the most widely used platform for hypertext work concentrating on the *content* of the hypertext instead of the features. This development is probably due to Macintosh computers' being much more widely available than the more expensive workstations, leading to an actual market for content-rich hypertexts. In spite of its small size, the Macintosh is good enough to support the basic features needed for the fairly small-complexity hypertext, which it is feasible to construct currently.

HyperCard

It is important to note that the designer of HyperCard, Bill Atkinson, has admitted that it was not really a hypertext product from the beginning. He originally built HyperCard as a graphic programming environment and many of the applications built into HyperCard actually have nothing to do with hypertext. Even so, HyperCard is probably the most famous hypertext product in the world today.

There are several reasons for HyperCard's popularity. A very pragmatic one is that it has been bundled free with every Macintosh sold by Apple since the introduction of HyperCard in 1987. You cannot beat the price, and the fact that it comes automatically with the machine also means that it has been introduced to a large number of people who would otherwise never have dreamt of getting a hypertext system.

The second reason for HyperCard's popularity is that it includes a general programming language called HyperTalk, which is very easy to learn. My experiments indicate that people with some previous programming experience can learn HyperTalk programming in as little as two days. Furthermore, this programming language is quite powerful with respect to prototyping graphic user interfaces. It is not very well suited for implementing larger software systems needing maintenance over periods of several years, however.

HyperCard is a good match for many of the innovative things people want to experiment with in the hypertext field. It is easy to learn, it can produce aesthetically pleasing screen designs, and it allows fast prototyping of new design ideas. My own hypertext system, described in Chapter 2, was implemented in HyperCard. HyperTalk makes HyperCard well suited for experiments with computational hypertext where information is generated at read-time under program control.

As the name implies, HyperCard is strongly based on the card metaphor. It is a frame-based system like KMS but mostly based on a much smaller frame size. Most HyperCard stacks are restricted to the size of the original small Macintosh screen even if the user has a larger screen. This is to make sure that all HyperCard designs will run on all Macintosh machines, thereby ensuring a reasonably wide distribution for HyperCard products. Version 1 of HyperCard enforced the card size restriction without exceptions, but the newer version 2 has made it possible to to take advantage of larger screens.

The basic node object in HyperCard is the card, and a collection of cards is called a *stack*. The main hypertext support is the ability to construct rectangular buttons on the screen and associate a HyperTalk program with them. This program will often just contain a single line of code written by the user in the form of a goto statement to achieve a hypertext jump. Buttons are normally activated when the user clicks on them, but one of the flexible aspects of HyperCard is that it allows actions to be taken also in the case of other events, such as when the cursor enters the rectangular region, or even when a specified time period has passed without any user activity.

The main advantage of the HyperCard approach of implementing hypertext jumps as program language statements is that links do not need to be hardwired. Anything you can compute can be used as the destination for a link.

In addition to the basic jumps to other cards, HyperCard can at least simulate pop-ups like the ones in Guide by the use of special show and hide commands. The designer can determine that a specific text field should normally be hidden from the user but that it will be made visible when the user clicks some button. The end result of these manipulations will be very similar to the Guide pop-ups.

HyperCard does have one serious problem compared to Guide, however, and that is the question of having hypertext anchors associated with text strings. In Guide these "sticky buttons" are the standard, allowing users to edit the text as much as they like and still keep their hypertext links so long as they do not delete the anchor strings. In HyperCard, an anchor is normally associated with a text string by placing the rectangular region of a button at the same location of the screen as the text string. But this anchoring method means big trouble if the user ever edits the text, since it is sure to change the physical location of the anchor string on the screen.

Figure 5.6 gives a simplified view of how I implemented the hypertext design from Figure 5.5 in HyperCard. First the general graphic design of the nodes was drawn as a background object that would be inherited by all the nodes in its class. This design included the picture of a book and the global overview diagram (since it would be unchanged for all nodes). The background design also included an empty placeholder field for the text to be added in the individual nodes.

For each individual node I then added a foreground layer with the text of the node and some graphics. The foreground graphics included the local overview diagram (since it would be different from node to node) and the heavy rectangles used to highlight the current location in the local and global overview diagrams. Since HyperCard displays all the levels as a single image on the screen, following the same principle as when a animation artist photographs a pile of acetates, the user would never know that the visual appearance of the global overview diagram was created by a combination of a fixed background image and a changing foreground rectangle.

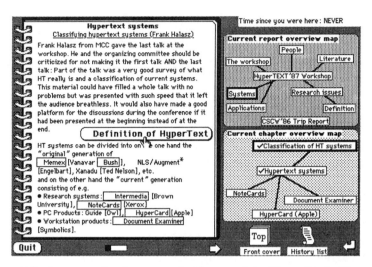

Figure 5.5. *An example of a screen implemented in HyperCard. Figure 5.6 gives a general idea of how this design was implemented.*

Finally, I added a set of buttons to each individual node to achieve the hypertext links. Some of these buttons were for the local overview diagram and were placed over the corresponding graphics, whereas other buttons were anchors associated with text strings in the foreground layer and had to be carefully positioned over the relevant text. Actually, the complete screen contains even more buttons since there are also some global buttons that are common for all nodes and are therefore placed in the background level. They are not shown specifically here.

HyperCard has several competitors, including SuperCard, and Plus. SuperCard has integrated facilities for dealing with color and several variable-sized windows at the same time and also allows object-oriented graphics of non-rectangular shapes to act as buttons. Plus is available both for the Macintosh and for the IBM PC (under Microsoft Windows as well as OS/2), affording cross-platform compatibility of its file format. Several other limitations have not been addressed by these competing products, however.

Some of these unsolved problems are not all that conceptually difficult, and one could imagine that HyperCard would address them in its next version. This is true of the missing sticky buttons and the

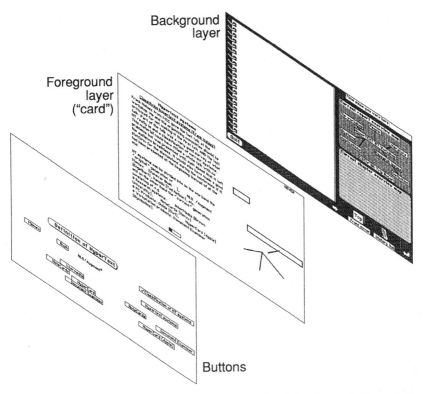

Figure 5.6. *A simplified view of the HyperCard implementation of the hypertext design in Figure 5.5. The background level contains graphics that are common for several nodes, whereas the foreground level contains the text and graphics that are specific for the individual node. Finally, the designer has placed several buttons on top of the text and graphics.*

slow execution speed of HyperTalk programs.[3] Other problems are harder to address since they conflict with the basic nature of HyperCard. These include issues such as changing the programming language to be completely object-oriented and more maintainable and designing advanced hypertext features or multi-user access.

Intermedia

Intermedia is a highly integrated hypertext environment developed at Brown University over several years [Yankelovich et al.

---

[3] Just changing from an interpreted language to a compiled one (as partly done in version 2 of HyperCard) should do the trick.

1988a] and now finally made available for purchase by others. It runs on the Macintosh but unfortunately only under the Unix operating system. Since most Macintosh buyers do not want to touch Unix, that choice of operating system severely restricts the practical utility of Intermedia. We can hope that a new version may come out in the future to allow Intermedia to run under the standard Macintosh operating system.

Intermedia is based on the scrolling window model, like Guide and NoteCards, but otherwise it follows a different philosophy from the other systems discussed in this chapter. The core of Intermedia is a linking protocol defining the way other applications should link to and from Intermedia documents [Meyrowitz 1986]. It is possible to write new specialized hypertext applications and have them integrated into the existing Intermedia framework, since all the existing Intermedia applications would already know how to interact with the new one.

The links in Intermedia are highly based on the idea of connecting two anchors rather than two nodes. The links are bidirectional so that there is no difference between departure anchors and destination anchors. When a user activates a link from one of its anchors, the system will open a window with the document containing the other anchor and scroll that window until the anchor becomes visible. Thus Intermedia authors are encouraged to construct fairly long documents, since they can easily link to specific points in the documents.

There are two kinds of overview diagram in Intermedia as shown in Figure 5.7. One is the *web view*, which is constructed automatically by the system, and the other is an overview documents like the *Mitosis OV* document in the figure. The overview documents are constructed manually by the author using a drawing package and only by convention have a common layout with the name of the topic in the center and related concepts in a circle around it. A typical Intermedia hypertext for a given course would contain many such overview documents, one for each of the central concepts in the course material.

Intermedia was designed for educational use on the university level and has already been used to teach several courses in both humanities and natural sciences. There is no reason why it should not be used for many of the other hypertext applications listed in Chapter 4, but the educational origin has had some impact on the design. For example, the Intermedia model assumes that several users (i.e., students) will access the same set of hypertext documents (i.e., course

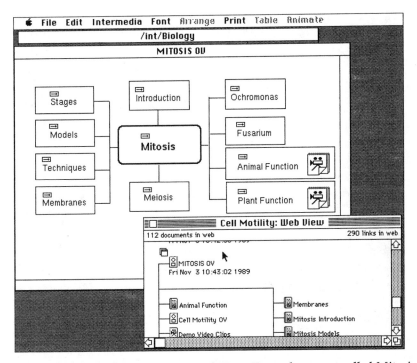

Figure 5.7. *An Intermedia web view. The InterDraw document called Mitosis OV is open. Each arrow icon in the overview diagram indicates the existence of one or more links. These connections are dynamically represented in the "Cell Motility: Web View" document. The web view is individual to each user, and is saved from session to session. One of its functions is to provide the user with a path showing which documents he or she has opened, when they were opened, and how the document was reached (by following a link, opening the document from the desktop, and so on). The figure also illustrates another function of the web view: For the current document (the document most recently activated), the web view provides users with a map of where they can go next, thus allowing them to preview links and follow only those that they want to see. © 1989 by Brown University, reprinted with permission.*

readings) and make their own annotations and new links. Therefore Intermedia stores separate files with links for each user in the form of so-called webs. Figure 5.8 shows the creation of a link in Intermedia. When the user has selected the other anchor for the link (for example the event listed under 1879 in the InterVal timeline) and has activated the "Complete Link" command, the new link will be added to the user's web.

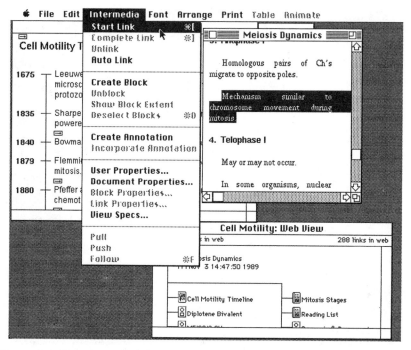

Figure 5.8. *To create a link in Intermedia, the user may select any portion of a document and choose the "Start Link" command. The link creation interface was modelled after the Macintosh cut/copy/paste paradigm; thus, the user may perform any number of intermediate actions and the link will remain pending until the user selects the other anchor for the link and activates the "Complete Link" command.* © 1989 by Brown University, reprinted with permission.

Intermedia is a very well designed hypertext system with a lot of integrated and useful facilities, some of which are discussed in other chapters of this book. See Figures 1.3 (the animation editor InterPlay), 4.9 (the InterLex server for automatic dictionary lookup), 6.2 (the InterNote annotation facility), and 8.9 (full text search).

6. The Architecture of Hypertext Systems

In theory one can distinguish three levels of a hypertext system [Campbell and Goodman 1988]:
- Presentation level: user interface
- Hypertext Abstract Machine (HAM) level: nodes and links
- Database level: storage, shared data, and network access

Actually, no current hypertext systems follow this model in their internal structure; they are a more or less confused mix of features. Even so, the model shows interesting directions for the future and is important for standardization work. The following sections describe each of the levels in further detail, starting at the bottom.

The Database Level

The database level is at the bottom of the three-level model and deals with all the traditional issues of information storage that do not really have anything specifically to do with hypertext. It is necessary to store large amounts of information on various computer storage devices like hard disks, optical disks, etc., and it may be necessary to keep some of the information stored on remote servers accessed through a network. No matter how the information is stored it should be possible to retrieve a specified small chunk of it in a very short time. This sounds very much like a specification for a database, which is what it is.

Furthermore, the database level should handle other traditional database issues, like multi-user access to the information, and various security considerations, including backup. Ultimately it will be the database level's responsibility to enforce the access controls which may be defined at the upper levels of the architecture.

As far as the database level is concerned, the hypertext nodes and links are just data objects with no particular meaning. Each of them forms a unit that only one user can modify at the same time and that takes up so many bits of storage space. In real life, it may be advantageous for the database level to know a little bit more about its data objects in order to enable it to manage its storage space most efficiently and provide faster response. But in any case the hypertext field would do well in taking advantage of the extensive work and experience in the traditional database field for the design and implementation of the database level.

The Hypertext Abstract Machine (HAM) Level

The HAM sits in the middle of the sandwich between the database and user interface levels. This center is where the hypertext system determines the basic nature of its nodes and links and where it maintains the relation among them. See the discussion below about the range of design choices regarding nodes and links. The HAM would have knowledge of the form of the nodes and links and would know what attributes were related to each. For example, a node might have an "owner" attribute that specified the user who created it and who has to authorize updates, or it could have a version number. Links might be typed as in NoteCards, or they might be plain pointers as in Guide.

The HAM is the best candidate for standardization of import-export formats for hypertexts, since the database level has to be heavily machine dependent in its storage format and the user interface level is highly different from one hypertext system to the next. This leaves only the HAM, and since we do need the ability to transfer information from one hypertext system to the other, we have to come up with an interchange format at this level.

Interchanging hypertexts is more difficult than simply interchanging the component data in the nodes, even though there are also problems with the less standardized data formats for non-ASCII information like graphics and video clips. The problem is that hypertext interchange also requires the transfer of linking information. It should be possible to transfer the basic links (i.e., the "A points to B" type information), but large parts of the linking information may be lost.

For example, some hypertext systems like Intermedia have links that point to specific text strings in the destination node, whereas other systems like Hyperties only point to the destination node as a complete entity. A transfer of a hypertext from Intermedia to Hyperties would

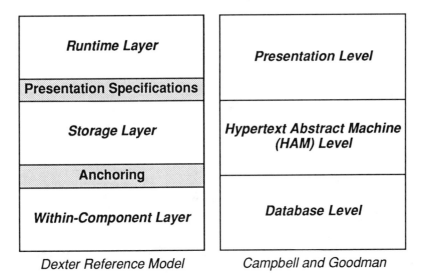

Runtime Layer	Presentation Level
Presentation Specifications	
Storage Layer	Hypertext Abstract Machine (HAM) Level
Anchoring	
Within-Component Layer	Database Level

Dexter Reference Model   Campbell and Goodman

Figure 6.1. *Comparing the Dexter reference model to the three-level model proposed by Campbell and Goodman [1988] and used in this book. There are some terminology differences, such as the use of the word "storage" in the Dexter model to refer to the representation of the abstract hypertext network, but otherwise the main difference is the explicit discussion in the Dexter model of the interfaces between the levels, especially with respect to anchors.*

therefore lose important aspects of the linking information but should still be possible in principle.[1] Of course if the transfer had been from Intermedia to Guide (which does have anchored link destinations), then we would want the transfer to keep the information about the destination substring so that it could be highlighted on arrival. The difficulty is that we would like to achieve both of these results with a single interchange format.

Work on the definition of hypertext interchange formats was initially started through informal meetings of the so-called Dexter Group, consisting of many of the designers of the early hypertext systems.[2] It now continues through more formal activities at the U.S.

---

[1] If we were to transfer a hypertext structure from Hyperties to Intermedia there would be no way to come up with a sensible substring for the destination anchor because the Hyperties author would not have considered that option when writing the hypertext. We would probably have to come up with a dummy anchor in the beginning of the destination node just to keep the Intermedia system happy.

[2] The Dexter Group is named after the inn in New Hampshire where it had its first meeting. The two meetings that resulted in the reference model were organized by

National Institute of Standards and Technology, including a hypertext standardization workshop in January 1990.

This work has resulted in more detailed architectural models than the simple three-level model discussed here [Halasz and Schwartz 1990] and also in some preliminary success in transferring hypertext information from NoteCards to HyperCard. Figure 6.1 shows the relation between the Dexter model and the model used in this book.

The User Interface Level

The user interface deals with the presentation of the information in the HAM, including such issues as what commands should be made available to the user, how to show nodes and links, and whether to include overview diagrams or not.

Let us assume that the HAM level of a hypertext defines the links as being typed. The user interface level might decide not to display that information at all to some novice users and to make typing information available only in an authoring mode. The very distinction between reading and writing is one of the basic user interface issues.

Let us now assume that the user interface level does want to display the link typing to the user. It might want to do so by changing the shape of the cursor, as Guide does (see Figure 5.4), or by having a special notation for various forms for anchors. It could also decide to display typing information in an overview diagram. If it had a color display available, it might choose to show each link type in a different color, whereas on a monochrome display it would have to use different representations, such as different line patterns (like NoteCards), small icons (like gIBIS, see Figure 4.2), or by using words to label the lines.

Actually, this decision cannot be made at the user interface level in isolation without considering the likely form of the data in the HAM. If the hypertext will have only a few link types, then colors or line patterns are suitable choices, but human ability to understand and distinguish such an encoding is limited to about seven different values. Icons could support hypertexts with somewhat more link types, but a hypertext with hundreds of link types would probably require the use of the type names in the interface.

Jan Walker and John Leggett and funded primarily by Digital Equipment Corporation and Texas A&M University.

Nodes

Nodes are the fundamental unit of hypertext, but there is no agreement as to what really constitutes a "node." The main distinction is between frame-based systems and window-based systems.

Frames take up a specific amount of space on the computer screen no matter how much information they contain. Typical examples are the KMS frames and the HyperCard cards. Often the size of the frame is defined as the size of the computer screen, but that determination may not hold in all systems. Since the frame has a fixed size, the user may have to split a given amount of information over several frames if it cannot fit into one. The advantage of frames is that all user navigation takes place using whatever hypertext mechanisms are provided by the system.

In contrast, window-based systems require the user to use a scrolling mechanism in addition to the hypertext mechanisms to get the desired part of the node to show in the window. Because the system can display only a (potentially small) part of the node through the window at any given time, the node may be as large as needed, and the need for potential unnatural distribution of text over several nodes is eliminated. Guide and Intermedia are typical window-based systems.

A great disadvantage of window-based hypertexts is that the hypertext designer has no control over how the node will appear when the user reads it since it can be scrolled in many ways. The advantage is that windows may be of different size depending on the importance and nature of information they hold. One can imagine a window-based system that did away with scrolling and thus kept most of the advantages of both display formats.

The real world is not quite as simple as the clear distinction between frames and windows. HyperCard is mostly frame-based but includes the possibility for having scrolling text fields as part of a card. Hyperties uses a full-screen display without scrolling but instead requires the user to page back and forth through a sequence of screens in case the node is too big to fit on a single screen.

Most current hypertext systems provide fixed information in the nodes as written by the original author. In computational hypertext systems like KMS and HyperCard (with an embedded programming languages) or NoteCards (with an interface to a programming language), it is possible to have *computed nodes* generated for the reader by the system. An example is a node with the current weather forecast retrieved from a videotex system like the American Prodigy or the French Minitel.

A certain amount of information being given, one issue is whether it should be split into many small nodes or kept in a rather small number of larger nodes. Kreitzberg and Shneiderman [1988] report on a small experiment to investigate this issue, wherein they split the same text into either 46 articles of between 4 and 83 lines or 5 articles of between 104 to 150 lines in Hyperties. The result was that users could answer questions significantly faster in the information base with many small nodes (125 sec. vs. 178 sec. per answer). One reason for this result is probably that Hyperties is one of the hypertext systems that links to the beginning of an article and not to the location within an article where the information of interest for the departure point is located. Because of this feature, Hyperties is most easily operated with small, focused nodes dealing with precisely one issue so that there can be no doubt about what part of the node a link points to.

Links

Links are the other fundamental unit of hypertext besides nodes. Links are almost always anchored at their departure point to provide the user with some explicit object to activate in order to follow the link. Most often, this anchoring takes the form of "embedded menus" where part of the primary text or graphics does double duty as being both information in itself and being the link anchor. It is also possible to have the hypertext anchors listed as separate menus, but that somehow seems to reduce the "hypertext feel" of a design. The result of activating the anchor is to follow the link to its destination node.

Most links are explicit in the sense that they have been defined by somebody as connecting the departure node with the destination node. Some systems also provide *implicit* links, which are not defined as such but follow from various properties of the information. A classic example of implicit links is the automatic glossary lookup possible in Intermedia (see Figure 4.9). The InterLex server provides a link from any word in any Intermedia document to the definition of that word in the dictionary, but it would obviously be ridiculous to have to store all these links explicitly. Only when the user requests the definition of a word does the system need to find the destination for the link.

The StrathTutor system [Kibby and Mayes 1989] provides another kind of implicit link. The hypertext author is not expected to provide links between nodes but is instead asked to define a set of relevant attributes for each node and for areas of interest in the node. These attributes are keywords taken from a predefined restricted vocabulary. The areas of interest are called "hotspots" and serve a purpose similar to anchors in other hypertext systems. When the user activates a hotspot, the system will view the user's interests as being defined by the combination of the attributes (keywords) from the current node and the selected hotspot. StrathTutor therefore links to a new node having the highest overlap between its own attributes and this set of attributes. Kibby and Mayes claim that this form for distributed specification of hypertext connections is the only way one can manage the authoring of really big hypertexts.

The StrathTutor links are an example of *computed links* determined by the system while the reader is reading, instead of being statically determined in advance by the author. Another example of computed links is a link from a tourist guide like *Glasgow Online* to the train schedule, where the system could link to the listing for the next train out of Glasgow for each destination.

A hypertext link has two ends. Even if a link is not bidirectional[3] there may still be a need to anchor it explicitly at the destination node. Most frame-based hypertext systems only have links that point to an entire node, but when the destination is large, it is an advantage for the user to have the system point out the relevant information more precisely. See for example how the Drexel Disk highlights Building 53 because the user jumped to the campus map in Figure 1.2 from a description of the repair facility (which is located in that building).

In general, a hypertext design should tell the user *why* the destination for a link was an interesting place to jump to by relating it to the point of departure and following a set of conventions for the "rhetoric of arrival" [Landow 1989a].

Given that the hypertext is based on explicit links, the next issue is whether or not to make the anchors especially prominent on the screen compared with the rest of the node. In a *sparse* hypertext, where maybe less than 10% of the information serves as anchors, it is probably a good idea to visually emphasize the anchors. This is just a special case of the

---

[3] See the discussion of directional versus bidirectional links in Chapter 1.

general user interface guideline of letting the user know what options are available in a dialogue. In a *rich* hypertext, where almost everything is linked to something, the best advice would be to remove any special emphasis on the anchors. After all, if everything is highlighted, then nothing is really highlighted anyway.

It is possible to use the Guide method of providing feedback by changing the shape of the cursor when it is over an anchor (see Figure 5.4). But that method should still be supplemented with some visual indication of the location of the anchors since users will otherwise be reduced to playing mine sweeper with the mouse to discover the active areas of the screen.

Unfortunately the highlighting of anchors conflicts with the use of emphasis in the running text. Traditionally writers have used typographical notation like *italics* or **boldfaced** type to indicate various forms for emphasis or special purpose text like quotations, and we would like to keep these capabilities for hypertext authors. But many current hypertext systems use the same or similar notation to indicate hypertext anchors also. This can unfortunately be very confusing to users unless the author has used a *style guide* to provide consistent notation for anchors and running emphasis. One solution to this problem may be the invention of special typographical cues for hypertext links [Evenson et al. 1989] and the gradual emergence of conventions for hypertext notation.

Most current hypertext systems have plain links, which are just connections between two nodes (and possibly anchors). The advantage of that approach is of course the simplicity of both authoring and reading. There is nothing to do with links except to follow them, and that one action can be achieved by a click of the mouse.

Alternatively, a link can be tagged with keywords or semantic attributes such as the name of the creator or the date it was created. These tags allow one to reduce the complexity of a hypertext through filter queries like, "Show all links created after March 23, 1990" or "Hide all links by so-and-so" (if we think that that person's contributions are rubbish).

Links can also be typed to distinguish among different forms of relationship between nodes. Trigg [1983] presents a very elaborate taxonomy of 75 different link types, including abstraction, example, formalization, application, rewrite, simplification, refutation, support, and data.

In addition to the standard links connecting two nodes, some hypertext systems also have "super-links" to connect a larger number of nodes. There are several possibilities for dealing with having a single anchor connected to several destinations. The two simplest options are either to show a menu of the links or to go to all the destinations at the same time. Intermedia uses the menu option and allows users to choose only a single destination. This approach requires good names for the links or destination nodes in order for users to be able to understand their options. Some users of NoteCards have implemented a "fat link" type that opens windows on the screen for all the destination nodes.

The alternative way to deal with multiple destinations would be to have the system choose for the user in some way. The choice could be based on the system's model of the user's needs or some other estimate of the best destination, or it could simply be random, as in the example discussed towards the end of Chapter 2.

Link anchors present special problems for layered hypertext architectures like the model presented in the beginning of this chapter. In principle, links belong at the hypertext abstract machine level, but the location of the anchor in the node is dependent on the storage structure for the node media. In a text-only node, an anchor position can be described as a substring ("characters 25–37"), whereas an anchor in a film clip needs both substring information ("film frames 517–724") and a graphic location ("the rectangle [(10,10);(20,20)]").[4] Therefore the actual anchoring of the link cannot be handled by the hypertext abstract machine. The solution in the Dexter model [Halasz and Schwartz 1990] is to define an explicit interface between the hypertext abstract machine (called "storage layer" in their model) and the database level (called "within-component layer" in their model) as shown in Figure 6.1. Anchors become indirect pointers and the anchoring interface provides a translation between anchor identifiers in the hypertext abstract machine and actual anchor values in the node data.

Annotations

A special link type is the annotation link to a small, additional amount of information. The reading of an annotation typically takes the

---

[4] Some dynamic anchors may be even harder to specify: Try encoding the anchors in a video of a football game to allow the user to click on a player at any time to link to that player's name and statistics.

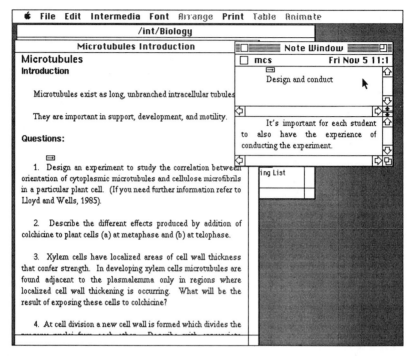

Figure 6.2. *The InterNote service within IRIS Intermedia provides a quick facility for annotating documents of any type. The top frame of the note window (right) contains the annotator's suggestion of a change in wording. The bottom frame explains the reason for the suggestion. The author of the "Microtubules Introduction" document may now choose to incorporate the change by selecting the marker at either end of the link that connects the note to the document and choosing the "Incorporate Annotation" command.* © *1989 by Brown University, reprinted with permission.*

form of a temporary excursion from the primary material to which the reader returns after having finished with the annotation. Annotations are quite similar to footnotes in traditional text and can be implemented, for instance, as Guide pop-up windows that disappear as soon as the user releases the mouse button.

Hypertext writers can use annotations in the same way they would use footnotes in traditional text with the exception that hypertext annotations are less intrusive because they are not shown unless the reader asks for them. The most interesting use of annotations in hypertext is for the readers, however. Many hypertext systems allow readers to add new links to the primary material even if they do not always allow the reader to change the original nodes and links, and readers can use these facilities to customize the information space to their own needs. For example, readers of a hypertext medical handbook [Frisse 1988] might want to supplement the generic description of a drug in the handbook with an annotation stating the brand name normally prescribed at their hospital.

One system that does provide an annotation facility is Intermedia, as shown in Figure 6.2. Other systems like Hyperties do not allow readers to annotate but reserve all options to change the information space for the authors. In the case of Hyperties, one reason for refusing readers the right to add information is that the system was originally designed for museum information systems where one may in fact not want random users to alter the content of the hypertext. Another reason was the desire for an extremely simple user interface to Hyperties: Having a smaller number of options available to the user means that there is less to learn.

Hypertext Engines

All the hypertext systems described in Chapter 5 are really hypertext engines that can display many different hypertext documents. Other hypertext systems are built specifically to display a single document and can therefore provide a much richer interaction with respect to the content of that particular document.

Besides the obvious advantage of not having to program a new application, the use of hypertext engines also has the advantage that they provide a user interface common to many documents. Users who already know how to use Guide, for example, can immediately start to read the next Guide document without any training.

Some hypertext systems like Guide and Hyperties are truly plain engines. The author just pours text into them and they take care of everything else. For example, a pop-up window in Guide *always* appears in the top right corner of the screen. The author does not have to make any user interface decisions except for a few low-level formatting details such as where to break paragraphs. Considering that most people are poor user interface designers, this may well be an advantage.

Other hypertext engines allow the hypertext designer to customize the user interface to a document within a certain framework. HyperCard is a prime example of such a system since it allows the designer to move fields around and add all sorts of background graphics. Even so, the designer is constrained by the basic HyperCard framework of being a frame-based system with a fixed size monochrome card. There are certain user interface facilities available in a kind of construction kit for the designer, but it is not possible to add new interaction techniques.

Actually it *is* possible to extend the framework of HyperCard, but only by leaving its built-in HyperTalk programming language behind and programming so-called external commands (XCMDs) in a traditional programming language like Pascal. NoteCards is extensible because it is integrated with InterLisp, but it also provides several simpler possibilities for hypertext designers to customize their interfaces to the needs of their individual documents [Trigg et al. 1987].

HyperCard not only allows hypertext authors to customize the user interface of their hypertext documents, it *requires* them to do so. HyperCard has no default document design but in principle presents the author with a blank screen where it is necessary to define the placement of text fields before anything can be written.

Finally, some hypertext documents are implemented as specialized applications. These include the Drexel Disk (see Figure 1.2) and Palenque (see Chapter 4). These specialized applications can achieve an exact match between the hypertext system and the needs of the document. For example, for the children exploring the Mexican jungle, Palenque has special features in the form of a filmed television personality who pops up from time to time to introduce new discoveries. The designers of Palenque added this guide character to the interface after having interviewed children about how they would like to explore Maya ruins in the Mexican jungle. And they certainly did not want to do so *alone*.

Integrating Hypertext Ideas into Other Environments

A final architectural observation is that hypertext does not really need to be part of a hypertext system as such. It is possible to utilize ideas from hypertext and integrate them into other computer systems without making them full hypertext systems.

For example, the statistics package Data Desk Professional from Odesta has a facility called HyperView which is shown in Figure 6.3. HyperViews allow the user direct access from one statistical analysis to a small number of other analyses that are relevant given the user's current context. Based on its knowledge of statistics, the program

Aou Table				
Analysis of Variance For	**referen easy**			
Source	**df**	**Sum of Squares**	**Mean Square**	**F-ratio**
Used GUIDE before	1	3.49643	3.49643	2.36

Used other hypertext	Locate Used other hypertext before
Interaction	Bar Chart of Used other hypertext before
Error	Pie Chart of Used other hypertext before
Total	Frequencies of Used other hypertext before
	Dotplot of referen easy by Used other hypertext
	Remove Variable

Figure 6.3. *A HyperView pop-up menu from the statistics program Data Desk Professional. The user is looking at a table containing an analysis of variance and has indicated a special interest in one of the variables. The pop-up menu now allows the user to open windows with additional statistical analyses and graphs that are especially relevant given this context.*

"knows" what other statistical analyses people normally want if they have an interest in the selected variable in the context given by the existing table.

The result of making a choice from the menu in Figure 6.3 is to jump to a new window containing the desired analysis or graph. Of course the system has to calculate the content of that window first so the real result is just to activate the statistics package with a given command and a given set of parameters. But to the user it *feels* like a hypertext-like navigation between connected windows. It is also a great practical advantage of the HyperView facility that it reduces the need for the user to find the correct command among the large set of statistical analyses available in the program and that it automatically specifies the correct parameters.

7. Hardware Support for Hypertext

Hypertext needs to run on a computer and is therefore highly dependent on the available hardware technology. Many of the complaints people have against hypertext applications are not really directed against the very principle of hypertext or the user interfaces of existing hypertext systems but are based on deficiencies in the current generation of computer hardware.

For example, there are many hypertext applications, such as tourist guides, which would only really make sense if hypertext systems could be as portable as a paperback book. One quite good hypertext with travel information, called *Business Class*, got poor reviews in the personal computer magazines exactly because of this problem.

In a field study of hypertext I conducted [Nielsen and Lyngbæk 1990], 33% of the users complained about the very fact that the hardware was not as convenient as paper. Typical comments were "I don't want to have to stay with the computer. I often read reports on the train or at home" or "I have to make a conscious effort to read it and first boot up the Macintosh, while with paper less planning is needed."

Because of this problem, many hypertext researchers dream of the day computers get so small that they are actually as portable as books. Alan Kay discussed this concept several years ago [Kay and Goldberg 1977] and called it the *dynabook* ("dynamic book"). There is actually a commercial product out now called "DynaBook" based on a CD-ROM reader, but it is not nearly what Kay imagined.

One project that has some potential for providing book-like hypertext is the SmartBook, which is being developed by James Hardie Industries in Australia. James Hardie Industries is a large company with annual sales of about 1,000 million Australian dollars, and the SmartBook is just one of their smaller projects. It is a real project, however, and will be for sale soon.

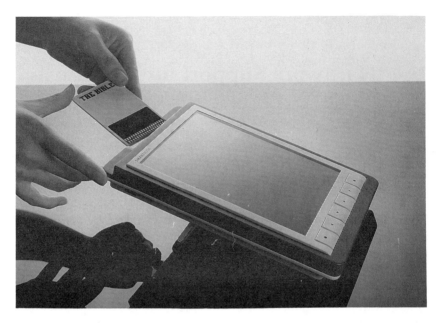

Figure 7.1. *A prototype of the SmartBook. Photo courtesy of James Hardie Industries, Ltd.*

Figure 7.1 shows a prototype of how the SmartBook will look. It is about the same size as a real book and most of its surface is taken over by a display, so it can actually show about the same amount of text as a single page in a book. The user interface has to be extremely simple since the SmartBook is operated by a set of only six keys. Future versions might include a touch sensitive screen and thereby increase the user's options.

The actual text in the SmartBook is taken from a "smartcard" which is a credit card sized piece of plastic containing one megabyte of read only memory in the form of eight one-megabit microchips. Using compression, this storage is enough to hold a book, such as the King James version of the Bible, which will be one of the first SmartBook applications. In the next few years, larger memory chips will become available and it will then be possible to store sets of several books on a single smartcard. Just imagine the practical advantages for travellers of being able to carry a small library of books in your wallet.

The SmartBook is expected to be sold on the consumer market in the mid-1990s for about A$100 plus about A$10 for each smartcard. Initially, the SmartBook will cost about four times as much, however, and sales in 1990 will therefore be to the professional market. One of the initial applications is an Australian tax guide, which takes advantage of the fact that the SmartBook is a computer in disguise and allows users to calculate tax liabilities directly instead of looking them up in huge tables.

Problems with the Computer Screen

One practical problem with many present computer screens is that they cannot show the video images that form an important part of many hypermedia interfaces. This problem is only temporary since add-on video cards have been designed for all the important brands of personal computers to allow them to display live video on the screen integrated with computer generated text and graphics.

Unfortunately these video cards and color screens of sufficiently high quality are still too expensive for many applications, and many systems therefore use the "two-screen solution" exemplified by the *Interactive NOVA* illustrations on the cover of this book. One screen is used to display color video images, while another screen is a standard computer screen showing computer text and graphics and accepting user input via the mouse.

Even though it can be a practical necessity, the two-screen solution is poor from the usability perspective since it requires users to divide their attention between two screens. Also it prevents integration between the computer generated graphics and the video image because they have to be shown on separate screens. The single-screen solution allows better possibilities for dynamically adding annotations and outline drawings to video images and for having users activate image areas by the mouse.

Reading Speed from Screens

The two-screen problem will disappear by itself as the cost of single-screen solutions drops, but hypertext by its very nature needs to be read from a computer screen, and it will therefore always be relevant to consider the actual speed with which people can read from screens. Several scientific studies have compared the reading speed from screens with the reading speed from paper, and they have generally found that screens are about 30% slower. For example, Wright and Lickorish [1983] had users proofread text which appeared

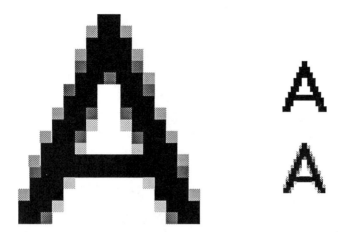

Figure 7.2. *An example of **anti-aliasing**: The "jaggies" in the A have been smoothed over by the use of gray pixels. The two characters on the right show the effect of using anti-aliasing: The top A has not been anti-aliased, while the bottom A uses the gray pixels shown in the left figure.*

on either a traditional computer display or on paper. The time to proofread two texts was quite a lot slower on the screen than on paper (29 min. vs. 21 min.). Gould et al. [1984] got a similar result on a similar test.

Gould et al. [1987] tested a more advanced type of computer display in the form of an IBM 5080 display which had 91 points per inch and displayed anti-aliased fonts. As shown in Figure 7.2, anti-aliasing is a computer graphics technique used to smooth over "jaggies" by the use of grayscales instead of the traditional black-and-white only pixels. Gould et al. had people proofread texts from this advanced screen and from paper and found that they had practically the same reading speed (204 words per minute vs. 206 words per minute) and the same accuracy in finding the spelling errors in the text (79% vs. 81%). The small differences were not statistically significant, so one might interpret the result as showing the same performance on an anti-aliased screen as on paper. Unfortunately, anti-aliasing is not used in the present generation of computer displays, however.

Wilkinson and Robinshaw [1987] tested the error rates of subjects doing proofreading from screens and from paper. During the first ten minutes of the experiment, screens did somewhat worse than paper (error rate 25% vs. 22%) but they did much worse after subjects had been proofreading continuously for 50 minutes (error rates 39% vs.

25%). This difference shows that people get tired more easily when reading from computer screens than when reading from paper.

Because of these results hypertext designers have to take care that users are not required to read too much text on the screen. Even though the plain reading speed is slower from present screens, the overall user performance with a hypertext system can still be better than with paper if the hypertext system allows the user to find the relevant text faster and makes it possible to extract the relevant information without having to read as much.

Screen Size

Bigger screens allow users to see more hypertext material at the same time and allow room for various extra user interface features such as permanently shown overview diagrams. Shneiderman [1987] had users read a hypertext on the Jewish Holocaust in Austria in order to answer questions about it. Users who used a screen displaying 34 lines of hypertext at a time performed slightly faster than users who could only see 18 lines (8.6 min. vs. 9.8 min.), but the difference was not statistically significant, probably because only 12 subjects were used. The 34-line display would correspond to approximately 432 pixels, and 18 lines would correspond to 240 pixels on a graphics display. The same research group also conducted experiments with subjects reading program text from various screen sizes using ordinary text editors [Reisel and Shneiderman 1987]. For a 22-line display (288 pixels), answering the questions took 9.2 min., for a 60-line display (744 pixels), it took 7.9 min., and for a 120-line display (1464 pixels) it took 6.6 min. All these experiments confirm the common belief that bigger is better when it comes to computer screens.

Hansen and Haas [1988] tested the effect of screen size on a more active use of computers in the form of letter-writing. They compared a full-page workstation display, which could hold 47 lines of text, with a small window on the same workstation, which could hold 22 lines of text corresponding to 80 columns of fixed-width characters. Both conditions used proportionally spaced characters. The subjects wrote with about the same writing speed (20 vs. 21 words per min.) but wrote longer letters on the larger screen (353 words vs. 292), and the quality of the letters as rated by an English teacher was higher on the larger screen (11 vs. 8 on a 16-point scale). So people tend to write longer texts when they use bigger screens, but they also write better texts.

Color Coding

Color might be a solution to the problems users have in remembering where in lengthy texts they have previously read something. An experiment conduced by Wright and Lickorish [1988] showed that, when reading one set of printed documents on colored paper, users were able to answer questions about the texts they had read in 51 secs.; but they had to use 60 secs. when using texts printed on single-colored paper. In a follow-up experiment with another set of texts, it turned out that the color-coded paper was slower, and two sets of online text were also found to be slower than monochrome online text. The authors speculate that color might work better as borders or strips or if it was assigned by the readers rather than by the writers (as in highlighting, cf. [Nielsen 1986]).

Pointing Devices

Almost all current hypertext systems are used with a mouse as the pointing device. Several human factors studies of computer interfaces in general have shown that the mouse is a good pointing device, and it has certainly seen wide use in recent years.

Ewing et al. [1986] compared the mouse with a special use of the keyboard arrow keys for activating hypertext anchors in Hyperties. This special use of the arrow keys has them jump the cursor in a single step to the hypertext anchor that is nearest to the previous cursor location in the direction indicated by the arrow key pushed by the user. It turned out that the mouse was somewhat slower than this special use of the arrow keys (3.3 min. vs. 2.8 min. for anchors that are close by and 3.5 min. vs. 3.3 min. for anchors farther away).

For some hypertext applications, such as tourist information systems, the mouse is too fragile to be used. In these situations it is common to use a touch screen as the pointing device instead. Touch screens are not used in the standard protected office environment because having to raise their arms quickly becomes tiresome for users and because the touch screens are normally less precise than the mouse.

The simplest implementations of touch screens emulate the mouse and can therefore be used with any hypertext system without any need to change the software.

Touch screens can, however, be used in several different ways to activate hypertext anchors. Potter et al. [1989] tested several such strategies for activating anchors in Hyperties, including the *land-on* strategy, which activates a point on the screen the moment the user touches that point (similar to a `mouseDown` event in mouse-driven interfaces); and the *take-off* strategy, which activates the point which the user last touched when the hand is taken off the screen (similar to `mouseUp` events). Users performed about the same with these two strategies but had a tendency to be slightly slower with the take-off screens. Error rates were significantly lower with the take-off strategy since users could see what they had selected before lifting their fingers.

Potter et al. also tested a touch screen strategy called *first-contact,* which activates the first selectable area on the screen entered by the user's finger. If the user touches down on a selectable area, the result is the same as the land-on strategy, but if the user touches down on a blank area, nothing is selected until the user's finger has moved to the first active region on the screen (similar to a combination of `mouseEnter` and `mouseWithin` events in a mouse system). There was no statistically significant difference between the first-contact and the take-off strategies in this experiment done with Hyperties, even though fairly large and significant differences had been found in an earlier experiment [Potter et al. 1988] on selection in a traditional text environment. In the earlier, non-hypertext experiment, subjects had to select targets that were two characters in width and were separated by a two character space. For such a task, the first-contact strategy gave rise to a lot more errors but was somewhat faster than the lift-off strategy where users could see what they were selecting. In Hyperties, however, the anchors are typically whole words which are far apart on the screen so users have a much smaller risk of touching something by mistake and they don't need to rely as much on the feedback. The different outcome of these two experiments shows the importance of conducting usability tests of as high a validity as possible with regard to the actual final use of whatever is being tested. For selecting hypertext anchors, the first-contact and take-off strategies performed about the same, so the take-off strategy might be chosen by a designer because it is the simplest to explain to users. But for a text editing application, one should choose the first-contact strategy.

Can Text-Only Computers Be Used for Hypertext?

Many people may wonder whether hypertext will run only on modern personal computers such the Macintosh or IBM PS/2 or on expensive graphic workstations. Hyperties is one hypertext system that proves it is possible to have hypertext even on the old "plain vanilla" IBM PC personal computers without graphics capabilities.

Also, many hypertext products, such as Guide, will work on a "plain strawberry" IBM PC[1] with a reasonable-resolution graphics board such as EGA and 640 kilobytes of RAM memory.

The only real requirement for hypertext is to have some possibility for the user to point to an item on the screen and activate it.[2] This activation is most frequently done with a mouse, but if one does not have a true pointing device available, the same action can be performed by using the arrow keys to position the cursor on the desired word and then hitting ENTER.

It is thus possible to have hypertext even on dumb terminals connected to mainframe computers. Of course, the response time requirements inherent in hypertext make hypertext infeasible on timeshared computers unless they have sufficient capacity for subsecond response times.

In any case, only fairly primitive hypertext interfaces will work on a text-only screen. The more advanced methods for improved navigation orientation, discussed in the next chapter, require some kind of graphic support, and many applications of hypertext also work much better if there is a windowing system available. It must be said that large-scale hypertext use is naturally matched to the capabilities of the modern, graphic personal computers and workstations.

Many people will nonetheless have to use old text-based terminals for years to come, and they can still get some of the advantages of hypertext, for instance in their online help systems.

One should also not completely discard the use of mainframe computers as a part of a hypertext architecture. Mainframes are good for handling the large databases one would need for really big

---

[1] A new expression coined to extend the ice cream metaphor.

[2] As a matter of fact, some limited types of hypertext can even be supported with line-oriented interfaces [Wahlen and Patrick 1989], which rely completely on commands typed by the user.

hypertexts, and they could also serve as host computers for distributed hypertexts accessed cooperatively by many users. This type of host computer should serve only as a backend repository, however, whereas the user interface should run on local personal computers with graphic capabilities.

This type of "cooperative processing" is not very common yet since most people who combine host mainframes and front end personal computers have the entire application running on the mainframe and use their personal computer only as terminal emulators. There are several products available for cooperative processing, however, and simple applications can actually be implemented without too much bother. For example, the network planning section of the Swedish telephone company Televerket did their own small HyperCard program to combine data from different databases stored on mainframes from several vendors. The user interacts with a single consistent HyperCard user interface that knows how to connect to the various hosts and how to access data in the different databases. This example is not really hypertext even though it uses HyperCard to combine data from a number of sources. True cooperative processing hypertext systems are part of the Xanadu architecture, however.

CD-ROM as a Storage Device

A special hardware problem is the storage space needed for the multimedia in hypermedia. For example, a single color television image takes up 105 kilobytes of storage, meaning that a minute of live video would take almost 200 megabytes. This obviously makes it impossible to deliver any form of hypermedia material with lots of video on traditional computer disks.

We have to turn to optical storage devices such as CD-ROM[3] to get room for these huge amounts of data. A CD-ROM disk[4] is physically the same as an audio CD, but instead of storing music it stores computer data. The similarity to audio CDs gives access to a great

---

[3] Compact Disk-Read Only Memory.

[4] "C" or "K"? There is no agreement about whether to spell it disc or disk. I have chosen to follow the spelling used by the *IEEE Spectrum* magazine and use "k." A less serious argument is that my own first name is spelled with a "k" but often misspelled with a "c" so I tend to like people who spell words with "k"s.

economy of scale for CD-ROMs since they can be pressed on the same factories that supply the huge world market for audio CDs. Thus a CD-ROM can be produced for about $2 plus a one-time fee of $1,500 for the master disk used in pressing the disks.

The CD-ROM players have certain similarities to home CD players but are still much more expensive since they do have to contain special electronics and be faster at nonsequential access to the tracks on the disk. After all, when listening to Mozart you almost never jump around on the disk so an audio player can be optimized to read the tracks one after another. But as mentioned in Chapter 1, the entire idea behind hypertext is to read the data nonsequentially.

The reason CD-ROMs are called *ROMs* is that they are a read-only storage device. This means that the individual user cannot change the contents of the disk. Actually, some writeable optical disks exist and are used, for instance in Steve Job's NeXT machine. But for many hypertext applications it would be OK to have the basic data stored on a read-only medium. Users could still be allowed to add links and annotations which could be stored on the user's traditional magnetic computer disk since it is most likely that user additions would be very small compared with the basic data and would therefore fit on a smaller disk. The hypertext system would then merge the data from the two disks whenever it needed to display it to the user, so the user would never know the difference.

A CD-ROM disk can store between 550 and 650 megabytes of data, which is equivalent to between 500 and 1000 standard textbooks or novels as long as we are talking text-only books. But as just mentioned, we also want to include other media with much greater storage requirements.

Actually, even a CD-ROM is not really large enough to hold the amounts of multimedia data we want for our hypermedia applications if the data are just stored in a plain uncompressed format. But compression can often yield room for significantly more data. For example it has been possible to store the entire Canadian telephone directory in a single CD-ROM even though it takes up 2 giga[5] characters in its plain text form and therefore should require four CD-ROMs instead of one. But because so many people have the same names it was possible to compress the data by a factor of four. For

---

[5] Giga = thousand mega = thousand million = a (U.S.) billion.

example, instead of storing five characters for every person named "Smith" one could just store a one-byte code indicating that the person has "name # 1" or something like that.

For multimedia data it is possible to achieve even greater compression factors. For color images, one can take advantage of the fact that they often contain large surfaces with a single color or with only small variations in color shades, and that therefore a smaller amount of information is needed to store each pixel.[6] For moving images (film) it is possible to achieve yet another degree of compression since two sequential movie frames are almost always close to identical. The actor may have moved a little, but the background stays the same.

As a result of various ingenious compression schemes it has proven possible to store a full hour of video on a CD that originally could store only an hour of less-demanding sound. There is an international standard for the physical CD-ROM format since it is the same as the audio CD format. There is also an international standard called "High Sierra" format, or ISO 9660, for the storage of plain data on CD-ROMs, but there are unfortunately two standards for the compressed data.

One standard is called CD-I (Compact Disk-Interactive) and is supported by Philips and Sony, whereas the other standard is called DVI (Digital Video Interactive) and is supported by Intel and IBM. Both standards are similar in allowing slightly more than one hour of video on a CD-ROM, but they are otherwise quite different.

CD-I is designed as a stand-alone system that is intended to be sold as a consumer electronics appliance for the home. A CD-I machine is self-contained with its own computer hidden inside. Users do not see the computer, however, but only the nice video images on their television screens, so CD-I may appeal to the "compuphobic" part of the population. CD-I does come in a computer-oriented format also, called CD-XA (Extended Architecture).

DVI is only a plug-in board for a computer that is supposed to do the rest of the processing as long as DVI provides the pictures. Thus DVI from the start is intended for highly interactive applications that

---

[6] Pixel = picture element (the dots making up a digitized image). Sometimes referred to as a pel.

take advantage of digital image processing, such as synthesizing an image as a combination of several smaller images stored on the disk.

It is currently impossible to tell which of the two standards will "win." One likely scenario, given the powerful companies supporting each standard, is that they will both survive, perhaps with CD-I being used mostly for home applications and DVI being used mostly for professional applications since it is more flexible.[7]

---

[7] Remember that Sony has been buying major U.S. film and record companies like Columbia Pictures and CBS Records together with their stockpiles of copyrighted material. These purchases could well be a major factor in determining the future of the computer market. Sony is definitely interested in the hypertext market as witnessed by their introduction of the dynabook-sized Discman in Japan in May 1990. The Discman reads three-inch CD-ROMs, each containing text corresponding to about 100,000 printed pages. Sony is cooperating with 28 Japanese publishers who have formed the Committee for the Electronic Book and estimate that the Japanese market for electronic books will correspond to 2.6 billion dollars in 1992.

8. Navigating Large Information Spaces

When users move around a large information space as much as they do in hypertext, there is a real risk that they may become disoriented or have trouble finding the information they need. To investigate this phenomenon, we conducted a field study where users were allowed to read a Guide document at their own pace [Nielsen and Lyngbæk 1990].

Even in this small document, which could be read in one hour, users experienced the "lost in hyperspace" phenomenon as exemplified by the following user comment: "I soon realized that if I did not read something when I stumbled across it, then I would not be able to find it later." Of the respondents, 56% agreed fully or partly with the statement, "When reading the report, I was often confused about 'where I was.'"

Users also had problems using the inverse operations of the Guide hypertext buttons to return to their previous system states, as can be seen from the 44% agreement with the statement, "When reading the report, I was often confused about 'how to get back to where I came from.'" One reason for the confusion felt by many users is probably that Guide uses different backtrack mechanisms depending on which type of "button" (link mechanism) was used originally. Several users complained that Guide does not reestablish a completely identical screen layout when returning to a previous state after a backtrack operation. This change makes it more difficult to recognize the location one has returned to and thus complicates the understanding of the navigational dimensions of the hyperspace.

There are several possible solutions to the navigation problem. The most simple from the user's perspective may be to remove the requirement for navigation by providing guided tours [Trigg 1988] through the hypertext somewhat like the original "trails" suggested by Vannevar Bush in 1945. A guided tour may be thought of as a

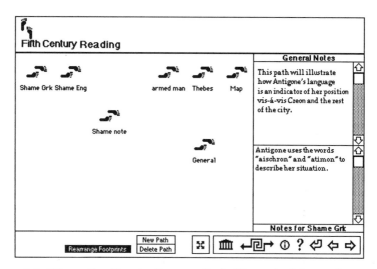

Figure 8.1. *The path editor in Perseus. Each "footprint" is a reference to a node in the hypertext. © 1989 by the President and Fellows of Harvard University and the Annenberg/CPB Project, reprinted with permission.*

"superlink" that connects a string of nodes instead of just two nodes. As long as users stay on the guided tour, they can just issue a "next node" command to see more relevant information. All nodes in the Perseus system (see Figures 4.10 and 4.11) have a "path" icon for use in moving back or forth along the selected guided tour. The system also provides the path editor shown in Figure 8.1 listing the names of all the nodes in a path and allowing users to add new nodes or remove or rearrange the existing nodes.

Guided tours can be used to introduce new readers to the general concepts of a hypertext, and one can also provide several different guided tours for various special-interest readers. The advantage of hypertext guided tours compared to tourist guided tours is that the hypertext reader can leave the guided tour at any spot and continue browsing along any other links that seem interesting. When the reader wants to get back on the tour, it suffices to issue a single command to be taken back to the point where the tour was suspended. The "guide" will be waiting as long as it takes.

Even though guided tours are nice, they really bring us back full circle to the sequential linear form of information. Even though guided tours provide the option of side trips, they cannot serve as the only navigation facility since the true purpose of hypertext is to provide an open exploratory information space for the user. Probably the most

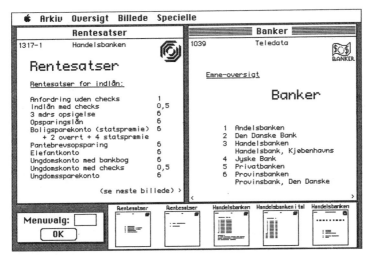

Figure 8.2. *A "visual cache" of miniatures of the five most recently visited nodes. From a prototype window-oriented videotex system designed at the Technical University of Denmark (implementation by Flemming Jensen).*

important navigation facility is the backtrack, which takes the user back to the previous node. Almost all hypertext systems provide some form for backtrack but not always very consistently, and we found in the Guide study mentioned above that inconsistency in backtracking could give users trouble. The great advantage of backtrack is that it serves as a lifeline for the user who can do anything in the hypertext and still be certain to be able to get back to familiar territory by using the backtrack. Since backtrack is essential for building the user's confidence it needs to fulfill two requirements: It should always be available, and it should always be activated in the same way. Furthermore, it should in principle be possible for the user to backtrack enough steps to be returned all the way to the very first introduction node.

Some hypertext systems provide more general history mechanisms than the simple backtrack. For example, some systems have history lists like Figure 2.10 to allow users direct access to any previously visited node. Since users are most likely to want to return to nodes they have visited relatively recently, it is also possible to use a "visual cache" like Figure 8.2 where a small number of nodes are kept visible on the primary screen. The design in Figure 8.2 represents the nodes by miniatures [Nielsen 1990f] of their graphic layout, but it is also possible to use icons or just the names of the nodes.

Hypergate and some other systems allow users to define bookmarks at nodes they might want to return to later. The difference between bookmarks and history lists is that a node gets put on the bookmark list only if the user believes that there might be a later need to return to it. This condition means that the bookmark list is smaller and more manageable, but it also means that it will not include everything of relevance. It frequently happens that you do not classify something as relevant until a later time, when its connection with something else suddenly becomes apparent. Then it is nice to be able to find it on the history list, which the system has automatically been keeping for you.

When the user defines a bookmark, the system may put the node's name on the bookmark list, or it may prompt the user for a small text to remember the node by. Bookmarks are more useful in hypertexts than in regular books because it is possible to use more of them. It is easy for a user to scan a menu of twenty node names that have been marked, whereas the same number of physical bookmarks in a book would be a complete mess to handle.

A special kind of bookmark would allow a user to resume the session with a hypertext system after an interruption and keep the state of the hypertext unchanged. A "smart bookmark" might even show some additional context to reorient the reader in the information space.

The Symbolics Document Examiner offers a special feature where users can build a list of references to nodes that they might want to remember to look at later. These references might be picked up from links in previously visited nodes and thus alleviate the problem of only being able to navigate to one new node at a time in most hypertext systems. This feature is called a bookmark list but might more appropriately be called a "shopping list."

Overview Diagrams

Since hypertext is so heavily based on navigation, it seems reasonable to use a tourist metaphor and try to provide some of the same assistance to hypertext users as one gives to tourists. One option is the guided tour as mentioned above, but as hypertext users are mostly supposed to find their own way around the information space, we should also give them maps. Since the information space will normally be too large for every node and link to be shown on a single map, many hypertext systems provide overview diagrams to show

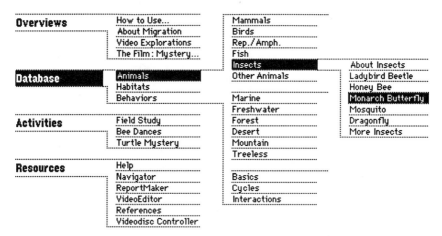

Figure 8.3. *A fisheye view-like browser from* Interactive NOVA. © *1989 by Apple Computer, Inc., WGBH Educational Foundation, and Peace River Films, Inc., reprinted with permission.*

various levels of detail. The system described in Chapter 2 uses both a global and a local overview diagram and displays both of them on the screen at the same time. An alternative would be to use a zoom facility to allow users to see more or less detail. There have also been a few attempts to design three dimensional overview diagrams [Fairchild et al. 1988].

A third alternative is to use a fisheye view [Furnas 1986] like the one in Figure 8.3 and to show the entire information space on a single overview diagram but in varying levels of detail. A fisheye view shows great detail for those parts of the information that are close to the user's current location of interest and gradually diminishing amounts of detail for those parts that are progressively farther away. The use of fisheye views therefore requires two properties of the information space: It should be possible to estimate the distance between a given location and the user's current focus of interest, and it should be possible to display the information at several levels of detail. Both conditions are met for hierarchical structures like that shown in Figure 8.3, but they may be harder to meet for less highly structured hypertexts.

In addition to showing users the layout of the information space, overview diagrams can also help users understand their current location and their own movements. To achieve this understanding, the

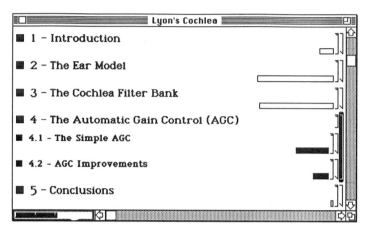

Figure 8.4. *An example of a "notebook" written in Mathematica. This is Apple Computer Technical Report # 13, "Lyon's Cochlear Model" (used for automatic speech recognition) by Malcolm Slaney, Apple Computer 1988, which was issued both in a printed format and on a Macintosh disk.[1] The latter format allows readers to try out the various mathematical formulae themselves. © 1988 by Apple Computer, Inc., reprinted with permission.*

overview diagram should display the user's "footprints" on the map to indicate both the current location and the previous ones.

To continue the tourist metaphor for hypertext, another facility that often helps users navigate is the use of landmarks in the form of especially prominent nodes. Tourists who visit Paris quickly learn where the Eiffel Tower is and how to use it and a few other landmarks for orientation. Almost all hypertext systems define a specific node in a document as the introductory node and allow fast access to it, but one can also define additional local landmarks for special regions of the information space and make them stand out on the overview diagrams. Landmarks are usually defined by the author of a hypertext system as part of the process of providing a usable structure for the readers. It might be possible for the hypertext system to define landmarks automatically by the use of connectivity measures (see the example in Table 10.1), but it is probably better to have the author choose the landmarks from a list of candidate nodes calculated on the basis of connectivity.

---

[1] The report is available from the Apple Corporate Library, 20525 Mariani Avenue, Cupertino, CA 95014, USA.

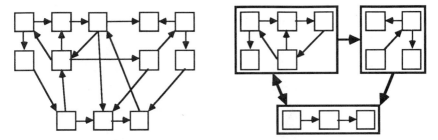

Figure 8.5. *Link inheritance during a clustering operation.*

Figure 8.4 shows an overview facility from the Mathematica "notebook" reader. The horizontal bars indicate the relative size of of the nodes and thereby give the user a prospective view of the information. Users will typically deal differently with small texts than with large texts, and the system ought to let users know in advance what they are facing.

The notebook reader in Figure 8.4 also shows the hierarchy of the information explicitly to the user by the vertical brackets. When the user clicks in one of these brackets, the system will highlight all the nodes belonging to the corresponding level in the hierarchy.

Contextual information can also be conveyed by more subtle contextual cues like the use of different background patterns in different parts of the information space. Even though such methods will not eliminate the disorientation problem, they are still needed to solve the *homogeneity* problem in hypertext. Traditional text is extremely heterogeneous as can be seen by comparing a mystery novel with a corporate annual report. You do not need actually to read the text to distinguish between the two. But the same two texts would have looked exactly the same if they had been presented online on a traditional computer terminal with green letters.

Printed books look different depending on their quality and age. They even automatically change to reflect how often they are used by being more or less worn. Modern graphic computer screens allow us to utilize similar principles to provide additional information to the user, but we still have to discover the best ways of doing so.

The main hypertext control structure is the `goto` statement in the form of a jump. In an analogy with software engineering, it might be possible to use alternative methods that are more similar to structured programming such as the nested hierarchies of Guide.

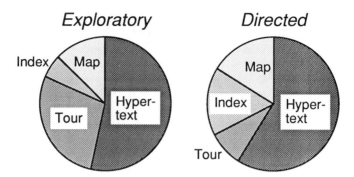

Figure 8.6. *Distribution of the methods used to transfer to new screens in hypertext on the history of York when users were asked to explore the information space and when they performed a directed search to answer specific questions. Data from Hammond and Allinson [1989].*

Another example of structured hypertext mechanisms is the use of link inheritance [Feiner 1988] to allow simplified views of an information space without having to show all the links. As shown in Figure 8.5, link inheritance replaces the individual links between nodes in an overview diagram with lines connecting clusters of nodes, thus simplifying the diagram considerably.

Hammond and Allinson [1989] have studied users of a hypertext history of the city of York. Some subjects used the system for an *exploratory task* wherein they first read the hypertext on their own and were later given a test to see how much they had learnt. Other subjects were given a *directed task* wherein they were given a set of questions that they were to answer using the hypertext system. Several different navigational methods were provided in addition to the plain hypertext links between associated parts of the text. One test compared the use of an overview map to the same system without the map and found that users performed slightly better (but insignificantly so) in both the exploratory and directed tasks when they had the use of the map. The same was true for an index mechanism. There were large, significant differences in both task conditions, however, in the ratio of new, different hypertext nodes visited compared to previously visited hypertext nodes being revisited. Both the map and the index led to users' seeing a significantly larger proportion of new nodes.

Furthermore, users in the exploratory task also visited more new nodes than users in the directed task. This difference is understandable since the exploratory users could not know what questions they would

Figure 8.7. *A central screen from* Inigo Gets Out. *This screen has a first-person perspective: To get the cat to climb the tree, you click the tree. © 1987 by Amanda Goodenough, reprinted with permission.*

be asked and therefore would feel encouraged to cover as much of the information base as possible in the time given.

Hammond and Allinson also tested a system wherein users had an overview map, an index, and a guided tour facility available. As shown in Figure 8.6, it turned out that users' use of these facilities varied significantly depending on their task, with the guided tour being used 28% of the time for the exploratory task but only 8% of the time for the directed task, the index being used 6% of the time for the exploratory task compared to 17% for the directed task, and the map being used about the same (12% vs. 16%).

Navigational Dimensions and Metaphors

Navigational dimensions and metaphors can help users better understand the structure of the information space and their own movements.

For example, the interactive fiction *Inigo Gets Out* mostly uses a navigational metaphor related to Laurel's [1989] definition of *personness* in interactive systems. Most of the story has a *first-person* feel wherein the user identifies with the cat and clicks at those points in the environment where the cat wants to go. See the screen in Figure 8.7

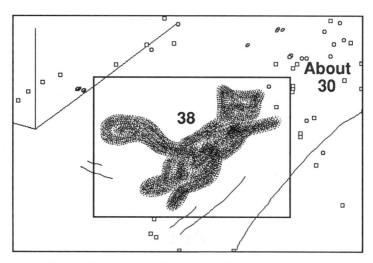

Figure 8.8. *Screen from* Inigo Gets Out. *This screen has a second-person perspective: To get the cat to run to the right, you click on the cat itself. The actual image from* Inigo Gets Out *has been overlaid with data from a field study of the use of the system in a Copenhagen kindergarten (the heavy border showing the button on the cat, the small symbols denoting mouse clicks outside the button, and the numbers counting clicks in various regions of the screen). Click markers inside the button denote cases where the user moved the mouse in between pressing down the mouse button and releasing it.* © 1987 by *Amanda Goodenough, reprinted with permission.*

where the user would click on the tree if that is where the cat "wants" to go at that point in the interactive fiction.

In a few locations, however, the story changes to a *second-person* feel where the user orders the cat around by clicking on *it* rather than on the environment. For example, in Figure 8.8 (one of the last screens of the story), the cat is shown running along the path to the house where it lives. Because of the general first-person feel of the story, many users click at the end of the path, thus expressing the sentiment "Now let's run in this direction." The system, however, requires the user to click on the cat itself, which leads to a sentiment more like "OK you cat, move along now."

We conducted a field study of children in a Copenhagen kindergarten using *Inigo Gets Out* [Nielsen and Lyngbæk 1990] and mostly found that the children had great fun reading the story and could navigate easily. But from logging user interactions in our field study we know that users in total made 30 clicks on the screen in

Figure 8.8 from the (erroneous) first-person perspective and 38 clicks from the second-person perspective. Any first-person click on this screen must have been made before a second-person click, since users would not be moved to the next screen until they realized the need for a second-person click. These data do not prove that first-person stories in general are more intuitive than second-person stories, but they do indicate the need for consistent navigational metaphors in hypertexts.

The hypertext system described in Chapter 2 is based on two navigational dimensions. One dimension is used to move back and forth among the text pages within a given node, and another dimension is used for hypertext jumps. To reinforce users' understanding of these two dimensions, two different animation techniques are used when shifting from one screen to another.

Movement between pages within a node is seen as a linear left–right dimension, corresponding to the orientation of the scroll bars at the bottom of the screen and to the way printed books are read in Western society. A change to a new page along this dimension is visualized by an animated right or left wipe, using built-in visual effects from HyperCard that look quite like the turning of a page.

Hypertext jumps are seen as being orthogonal to the left–right page turning and are visualized as an in–out dimension using an animated iris that *opens* for anchored jumps and *closes* for return jumps. The opening iris gives users the impression of diving deeper into the hyperspace when they take a hypertext jump, and the closing iris for return jumps gives the inverse feeling of pulling back again.

Another example of orthogonal navigational dimensions is the "season knob" in the *Aspen Movie Map* described in Chapter 3. It could be operated independently of the navigation through the streets, and navigation in time and geographical navigation were thus done along orthogonal dimensions.

Information Retrieval

A search for information in a hypertext might be performed purely by navigation, but it should also be possible for the user to have the computer find things through various search mechanisms.

Navigation is best for for information spaces that are small enough to be covered exhaustively and familiar enough to the users to let them find their way around. Many information spaces in real life are

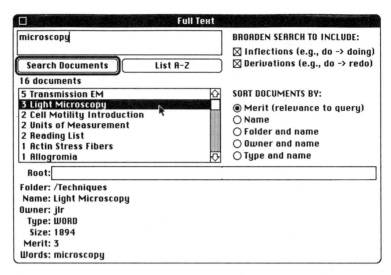

Figure 8.9. *Intermedia's full-text interface allows users to search the entire Intermedia database to find every occurrence of the specified text in all documents, regardless of type. The list of retrieved documents can be sorted according to five different criteria. Clicking on the document name in the list will allow the user to view information about the document. Double-clicking on the document name will open the document. © 1989 by Brown University, reprinted with permission.*

unfortunately large and unfamiliar and require the use of *queries* to find information.

The simplest query principle is the full text search which finds the occurrences of words specified by the user. Some hypertext systems simply take the user to the first occurrence of the search term, but it is much better to display a menu of the hits first as shown in the example from Intermedia in Figure 8.9. The problem with jumping directly to the first term occurrence is that the user has no way of knowing how many other hits are in the hypertext. The general usability principle of letting the user know what is going on leads to a requirement for an overview, even in the case of query results.

One can also integrate the search results with the overview diagram by highlighting those nodes that contain "hits."[2] SuperBook

---

[2] "Hits" indicate the number of the user's search terms that can be found in the node. It is possible to use more advanced query facilities and also add to the hit score if words are found which are synonyms or otherwise related to the search terms.

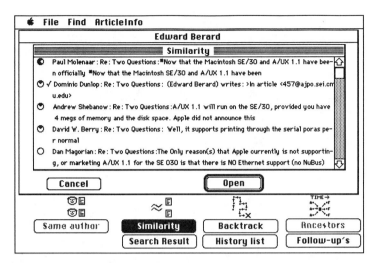

Figure 8.10. *A screen from the HyperNews system showing icons rating the links to other articles.*

[Egan et al. 1989] annotates the names of nodes with the number of hits to allow users to see not just *where* there is something of interest but also *how much* there is. It would be possible to use this type of search result to construct fisheye views since the number of hits in a given region of the information space would indicate how interesting that region must be to the user.

One can also use more sophisticated methods from the field of information retrieval. This brief section cannot do justice to that field, which is an active research area in its own right, so the interested reader should read a good textbook like Salton's *Automatic Text Processing* [1989] or at least a full survey article like [Bärtschi 1985].

As an example, Figure 8.10 shows a hypertext system [Andersen et al. 1989] for reading the Unix network news, which is a world-wide bulletin board system with a huge number of messages about various computer-related topics. Since there are far too many nodes in the system to rely on manually constructed links, we use a full text similarity rating calculated by counting the overlap in vocabulary between any two nodes. A list of the articles that are rated as the most similar to the current article is displayed when the user clicks on the "similarity" button.

In a case where we have a hypertext available in which the links have already been constructed, we should be able to utilize the information inherent in the linking structure to perform

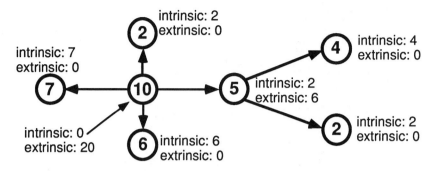

Figure 8.11. *An example of a calculation of query scores as a combination of* intrinsic *scores (how well the individual node itself matches the user's query) and* extrinsic *scores (how well the nodes it is linked to match the query). Here we have used a rule that gives a node a search score equal to its intrinsic score plus half its extrinsic score (the sum of the scores of the nodes it is linked to).*

more semantically meaningful searches than just plain full text searches. This step is possible because a hypertext can be considered as a "belief network" to the extent that if two nodes are linked, then we "believe" that their contents are related in some way.

Thus if a node matches a search, then we should also assign a higher score for the other nodes it is linked to since our "belief" that the connected nodes are related justifies the propagation of scores among them. One way of calculating this score is by assigning the final search result for a node as the sum of the number of hits in the node itself (called the *intrinsic* score) and some weighted average of the scores for the nodes it is linked to (called the *extrinsic* score). As a simple example, we could assign the final query score as the intrinsic score plus half the extrinsic score.

In the example in Figure 8.11, we see that the central node ends up getting the highest query score even though it does not contain any of the search terms (as can be seen from the fact that it has an intrinsic score of zero). This is because the central node sits in the middle of a lot of information related to the user's query and is therefore probably also highly relevant.

In addition to just finding information, query mechanisms can also be used to filter the hypertext so that only relevant links are made active and only relevant nodes are shown in overview diagrams. Even though the "raw" hypertext may be large and confusing, the filtered hypertext can still be easy to navigate. Such a combination of query methods to select a subset of the hypertext and traditional navigation to look at the information might be the best of both worlds if done right.

Finally, it could also be possible to filter a hypertext based on relevance feedback from other users in a kind of "voting filter." Users with little patience might choose only to see hypertext elements judged relevant by many previous users while more adventurous users might want the raw hypertext with everything in it.

9.   Hypertext Usability

Usability is traditionally associated with five usability parameters:

1) *Easy to learn:* The user can quickly get some work done with the system.

2) *Efficient to use:* Once the user has learnt the system, a high level of productivity is possible.

3) *Easy to remember:* The casual user is able to return to using the system after some period of not having used it, without having to learn everything all over.

4) *Few errors:* Users do not make many errors during the use of the system, or if they do make errors they can easily recover from them. Also, no catastrophic errors must occur.

5) *Pleasant to use:* Users are subjectively satisfied by using the system; they like it.

Since most hypertext systems are not used for such critical applications as process control, medical applications, or financial asset management, the subcriterion of preventing catastrophic errors is of less importance. To the extent that hypertext is used for authoring, we would still like users to be prevented from easily wiping out their entire work, however. Except from this qualifying comment, it seems that usability of hypertext systems really fits the general definition of computer system usability quite well, so it will also be used in this chapter.

Several methods exist for evaluating how well a given user interface scores on each of these primary usability parameters and for refining them to even more precisely measurable secondary parameters. See e.g. Gould [1988], Whiteside et al. [1988], and Landauer [1988] for lists of such methods and for issues to study in a general usability evaluation process and see Nielsen [1990d] and Perlman et al. [1990] for a discussion of hypertext usability evaluation.

It turns out that most discussions of hypertext usability are not founded in measurements of the usability parameters but are more in the nature of conjectures based on personal experience. Some empirical evaluations of hypertext systems do exist, however, and are reviewed here. First I try to refine the definition of the usability parameters for the purpose of evaluating hypertext; I then survey research that has resulted in benchmark measures comparing the performance of different systems, and the chapter ends with a discussion of non-benchmark studies.

Usability Parameters for Hypertext

The overall acceptability of a computer system is a combination of its *social acceptability* and its practical acceptability. As an example of social acceptability of hypertext systems, consider the French LYRE system [Bruillard and Weidenfeld 1990] for teaching poetry. LYRE allows the students to see the poem from various "viewpoints," each highlighting certain parts of the poem as hypertext anchors to relevant annotations and allowing the student to add new annotations. LYRE does not, however, allow the student to add *new* viewpoints since that capability is reserved for the teacher. The premise is that students should work within the framework set up by the teacher and not construct completely new ways to analyze the poem. This premise is obviously socially acceptable in the southern European tradition in France, and indeed an alternative design might well have been deemed socially *un*acceptable in that country because it would have undermined the teacher's authority. On the other hand, many people in Denmark where Scandinavian attitudes are more prevalent would view the current design of LYRE as socially unacceptable because it limits the students' potential for independent discovery.

Given that a system is socially acceptable, we can further analyze its practical acceptability within various categories, including traditional categories such as cost, support, reliability, compatibility with existing systems, etc., as well as the category of *usefulness*, which is of special interest to us in this chapter. Usefulness is the issue of whether the system can be used to achieve some desired goal. It can again be broken down into the two categories of *utility* and *usability*, where utility is the question of whether the functionality of the system in principle can do what is needed and usability is the question of how well users can use that functionality. Note that the concept of "utility" does not necessarily have to be restricted to the domain of hard work. An educational hypertext has high utility if students learn from using

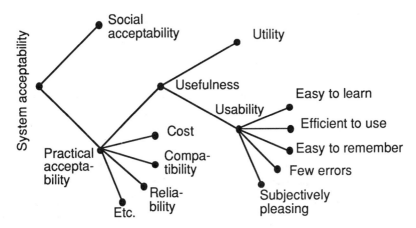

Figure 9.1. *The various parameters associated with system acceptability.*

it, and an entertainment product has high utility if it is fun to use. Figure 9.1 shows the simple model of system acceptability outlined here.

For a discussion of the usability of specifically hypertext systems, we can refine the primary usability parameters somewhat. The first point is that the usability of a hypertext system is determined by a combination of the usability of the underlying hypertext system *engine* (i.e. the basic presentation and navigation support available) and the usability of the *contents* and *structure* of the hypertext information base, and by how well these two elements fit together. From the user's perspective, all of these elements are of course seen as one single interface, and the user will not care whose "fault" it is if something is not usable. But from an analytical perspective, this distinction between the underlying system and the information base is probably an advantage. Furthermore, the relevant secondary parameters will be different for readers than for authors in many cases. Normally, the "easy to learn" parameter will be of less importance for a hypertext author who will spend a lot of time with the system.

1) Easy to learn: The hypertext engine itself is easy to learn. Users are quickly able to understand the most basic commands and navigation options and use them to locate wanted information.

When users enter an information base for the first time, they are immediately able to understand the first screen and to browse from it. Users are quickly able to learn the basic structure of the hypertext network and where or how to look for specific information.

Users of educational or entertainment hypertexts can learn something or enjoy the session without having to familiarize themselves with the entire hypertext structure.

The contents of the hypertext information base is easy to understand: Each node contains text (or other information) that is easy to read.

For authors: Authors who are editing an information base constructed by somebody else can easily understand the basic structure of this hypertext and are able to modify it without knowing the entire contents of the information base.

2) Efficient to use: Given that users want to find a certain piece of information, they either get to it quickly or soon discover that it is not in the information base. When users arrive at a node, they are quickly able to orient themselves and understand the meaning of the node in relation to their point of departure.

For educational hypertext: Users learn the facts or concepts that are most relevant for their purpose without having to learn or go through non-relevant material or material they already know more than necessary.

For authors: Authors can quickly construct a hypertext structure to reflect their understanding of the domain. It is easy to modify and maintain this structure.

3) Easy to remember: After a period of not having used the hypertext engine, users have no problems in remembering how to use and navigate in the hypertext.

After a period of not having used an information base, users can remember its general structure and are still able to find their way around the hypertext network and to recognize landmark nodes. Users can remember any special conventions or notations for special anchors, links, and nodes.

Users can transfer their knowledge of the use and navigation of one information base to the use of another information base with the same engine.

For authors: When a hypertext structure needs revision after some time, it is easy for the author to return to the information base and update it. The author can remember or is reminded about the basic structure of the information and does not need to remember details in order to update it.

4) Few errors: Users will rarely follow a link only to discover that they really did not want to go to wherever the link leads. In case users have erroneously followed a link, it is easy for them to return to their previous location. Users can in general easily return to locations where they have been, in case they decide that some lengthy digression should be abandoned.

For authors: The hypertext has very few links that erroneously lead nowhere or somewhere else than where they are supposed to go. The information contained in the nodes is correct.

5) Pleasant to use: Users prefer using the hypertext system to existing alternative solutions such as paper or other, non-hypertext computer systems. Users are rarely frustrated with using the hypertext engine or disappointed about the result of following links. Users feel that they are in control with respect to the hypertext and that they can move about freely rather than feeling constrained by the system.

For non-work related hypertext such as interactive fiction, users find using the hypertext an entertaining and/or moving and/or enriching experience.

A Semantic Differentiation Scale for Usability

Guillemette [1989] asked users to evaluate traditional (non-hypertext) documentation and found that their replies could be characterized by the following seven factors, which explained 65% of the variance:

- *Credibility* (correct–incorrect, reliable–unreliable, believable–unbelievable)
- *Demonstrative* (precise–vague, conclusive–inconclusive, strong–weak, complete–incomplete)
- *Fitness* (relevant–extraneous, meaningful–meaningless, appropriate–inappropriate)
- *Personal affect* (varied–monotonous, interesting–boring, active–passive)
- *Systematic arrangement* (organized–unorganized, orderly–chaotic, structured–unstructured)
- *Task relevance* (useful–useless, informative–uninformative, valuable–worthless)
- *Understandability* (clear–confusing, understandable–mysterious, readable–unreadable)

The terms in parentheses after each factor are the semantic differentiation scales associated with each factor. These seven factors are of course somewhat related to the five usability parameters but can also be viewed as a new set of dimensions according to which one could evaluate hypertext. They have the advantage of matching the way users view documentation but the disadvantage of overlooking that hypertext can be used for many other applications than online documentation. It is not clear whether the factors will cover other application areas too.

Survey of Benchmark Research

A fair amount of research has resulted in benchmark numbers comparing the usability of various approaches to accessing text online. Rather few studies exist that have looked at the hypertext problem as such, but there are some studies of non-hypertext systems that are relevant for the usability of hypertext and which are also reported here.

Impact of User Interface System Software

Online information systems can be implemented using several different kinds of common user interface system software. One of the most common at the moment is the use of multi-window systems, and Tombaugh et al. [1987] have conducted a test of the impact of such systems on users' abilities to once again find information they have previously read. The test was conducted both with novice subjects who had not used window systems before and with subjects who already had skills in the use of the windows themselves. For both novice and experienced users, the plain reading of the text was slightly slower when it was presented split up into several windows than when it was presented in one scrolling window (17 min. vs. 15 min. for novices and 17 min. vs. 16 min. for experienced users). But when it came to retrieving parts of the previously read text in order to answer questions about it, novices continued to do slightly worse in the multi-window interface (85 sec. vs. 72 sec. per question) whereas the experienced users performed better with the multi-window system than with the single scrolling window (50 sec. vs. 65 sec.). The slower reading time for the multi-window condition is probably because it is slower to shift between windows than simply to keep the mouse on the scroll bar and scroll the text in a single window. For the novice users, the multi-window situation was also slower for re-reading the text to answer questions because of unfamiliarity with the skills for window manipulation. But for the experienced users, having multiple overlapping windows allowed faster access to more text, and the window title bars probably helped in locating previously seen information in the deck-of-cards window layout used in this experiment.

Considering the two very different conclusions about whether multiple windows help people relocate information, this study also demonstrates the importance of using a group of test subjects who are representative of the intended users of the system. In this case, one can probably assume that most users will be familiar with multi-window interfaces if they have a personal computer or workstation using such an interface. But for systems to be used by the general population, one should probably pay more attention to the results from the novice subjects in this study.

The impact of system response time on users' browsing behavior was studied by Patterson and Egido [1987], who found that users (not so surprisingly) solved problems faster when the system response time was fast but also that they looked at more nodes before making decisions to change the active set of objects they were browsing in the image database (1.6 vs. 1.0 nodes on average). Patterson and Egido do not know whether the users made *better* decisions because they looked at more nodes, but they do conclude that response time affects the way information is collected to make a decision to the extent that users explore more when it can be done faster.

Hypertext vs. Scrolling Text Files

Hypertext should be compared with traditional means of accessing text on a computer. This method is mainly scrolling text files in ordinary word processors, and Monk et al. [1988] performed such an experiment with the comprehension of the text of a Pascal program. They found that the subjects performed faster with the traditional scrolling files than with a hypertext system (13.2 min. vs. 18.3 min. to answer 15 questions about the program). The hypertext system they originally used did not include an overview diagram of the structure of the information base, so they conducted a simple follow-up experiment by drawing such a diagram by hand and pasting it to the computer used in the experiment. This addition improved the performance with the hypertext system to 13.0 min. so that it was slightly better than the scrolling text file. Of course there are two problems with this experiment. One is that by using an added paper diagram to simulate hypertext overview diagrams, they actually also simulated using a larger screen, which is normally seen as an advantage in itself. Secondly, the improved performance may not have been due to any advantage of overview diagrams in hypertext in general, but could instead be based on the specific advantage an overview of a program structure gives in comprehending that program. So the overview may help with this specific task but not with others.

A different kind of comparison was made by Gordon et al. [1988]. They used a hypertext system that is not named in the paper but seems to be a home-made design somewhat similar to Hyperties but with fewer browsing facilities. They tested four existing magazine articles, two on general interest topics ("Falling in Love" and "Reverse Sterilization") and two on technical topics ("Attentional Factors in Jet Aircraft Crashes" and "Speech Synthesis and Recognition"). Subjects read the articles on a computer screen using either a hypertext format or the original linear format and were then asked to recall as many concepts as possible from the article. Readers of general interest articles performed significantly worse on the hypertext system than on the linear file system (17% vs. 31% of concepts recalled) while readers of the technical articles performed about the same (22% vs. 21% recall). The authors speculate that one reason for this difference could be that readers of technical material would apply more effort to learning the material while readers of general interest material would tend to be distracted by the hypertext system. Another reason for the poor performance of the general interest hypertext might have been that the text had been written for the linear format and was probably not well suited to being split up into smaller nodes of information while the technical texts might have been more structured, even if they too were originally written for the linear format. Furthermore, the subjects in the experiment had not received any training in the use of the hypertext system, which in itself would be enough to make them more negative towards it.

Hypertext vs. Other Traditional Computer Systems

Information could be made available through a set of traditional menus instead of by hypertext. Shneiderman [1987] studied access to a small data set through either Hyperties or a traditional menu selection system and found that subjects answered significantly more questions when using Hyperties than when using the menu system (15.2 vs. 12.2 questions answered in 15 min.). The subjects' subjective preferences were also significantly in favor of the hypertext system (5.9 vs. 4.2 on a 1–7 scale).

Since hypertext is very similar to the database concept, comparisons between hypertext and traditional, command-based database access are also of interest. Canter et al. [1985] compared the strategies with which users moved around in the data in a hypertext-like system and in a command-based database. They found that users visited about the same number of different nodes of data but that the hypertext users revisited these nodes more, leading to a lower proportion of different nodes visited to total number of nodes visited for the hypertext users (33% vs. 68% of all visits were to previously unvisited nodes). Hypertext users had significantly more rings (returning to a previously visited location) and spikes (returning by exactly retracing a backtrack path through the locations visited) in their navigation than did the command-based users (61 vs. 28 and 17 vs. 5). So Canter et al. conclude that users move through the same data in different ways when they gain hypertext-like access capabilities.

Some applications of hypertext are very similar to expert systems, and Peper et al. [1989] compared an internal IBM hypertext system to a commercial expert system shell for the representation of information needed to diagnose problems in a world-wide computer network. The same information was represented in both forms and tested with a set of sample problems to be solved by twelve users who were either involved in network problem determination or had had such responsibilities earlier in their careers. These test users solved 81% of the problems correctly when using the hypertext system compared to only 67% when using the expert system. Using the expert system was faster, however, with 4 min. per problem compared to 5 min. when using the hypertext system. When asked what systems they would prefer to use on the job, 50% of the subjects chose the hypertext system, and 25% chose the expert system. From the authoring perspective, Peper et al. claim that it is "a very simple task" to update the information in the hypertext system while it is "difficult" to maintain the knowledge base in the expert system. Unfortunately they give no futher results from this aspect of comparing hypertext with expert systems except to note that the operators themselves were able to update the hypertext on the spot with annotations.

Hypertext vs. Paper

Perhaps the most important comparison is that between complete hypertext implementations of a set of information and a paper implementation of the same information in the form of a book or an article. Shneiderman [1987] compared two versions of a set of historical articles taking up 138 pages in the printed version. The electronic version was implemented in Hyperties. When subjects answered questions for which the answer could be found at the start of an article, they did worse in Hyperties than on paper (42 sec. vs. 22 sec.), whereas they were only insignificantly slower when the answer was in the body of an article (58 sec. vs. 51 sec.) and took the same time when the answer had to be found by combining facts from two articles (107 sec. in both conditions). These data seem to indicate that hypertext is of some help in situations where the user has to jump around in the information, and that hypertext slows the user down in situations where the information can be found by a glance on a page.

Users' Subjective Judgements

I asked a group of computer science students to judge whether they would prefer having their manuals, their textbooks, and fiction available in an online form instead of in a printed form [Nielsen 1986]. The question was asked both for online systems including the possibility for user annotations (a form of hypertext) and for plain online text without an annotation feature. Users were asked to rate their agreement with the statement that the online system would be an advantage on a scale from 0 to 4 (disagree much, disagree a little, neutral, agree a little, agree much). We should note that the validity is fairly low when one asks people to rate the usefulness of systems with which they do not yet have any experience since people often change their minds once they have tried something. But users' preconceived opinions about hypertext are still of interest since they will determine the speed with which the new technology can penetrate the market. The group studied here (computer science students) is not typical of the general population, which will probably tend to be more negative towards technological innovations.

For the questions assuming a facility for user annotations, results showed that the students viewed online manuals as a big advantage and online textbooks as a small disadvantage, whereas online fiction was viewed as a very big disadvantage. Comparing the responses for questions about systems with and without an annotation facility shows that users found annotations to be a small advantage for online manuals and a big advantage for online textbooks, but not to be any advantage for online fiction.

In another study, Marchionini [1989] had sixteen high school students use the *Grolier's Academic American Encyclopedia* in both print form and electronic form. The subjects were then asked to compare the print and electronic encyclopedias. Half said that the electronic version was faster, three said that it contained more information than the printed version, and one said that it was more up to date. This result was in spite of the facts that the two versions of the encyclopedia actually contained the *same* text and that the subjects were measurably slower with the electronic version. This indicates some of the problems with subjective evaluations and the seductive qualities of novel technology.

Finding Information

Egan et al. [1989a; 1989b] have conducted tests of the use of a statistics book in a hypertext version in the SuperBook system and in its traditional printed version. The book was originally written with printed publication in mind, so it might be possible to design a version specifically for hypertext that would do better than the one tested here. Users were asked to find the answers to certain questions about statistics, which could be answered from the book, and they were timed. When key words from the question were words occurring in the headings of the book, users performed best in the printed book (3.5 min. vs. 4.4 min.). This result is probably because queries using words from a book's headings match the author's structuring of the book pretty well. The typographical nature of the printed book also supports access to the text in that structure in the form of quick scanning of the table of contents and running headings when flipping through the pages of the book. When the relevant page has been found, it is easy to locate the subheading that starts the section the user is to read.

The situation was the opposite, however, when the questions used words that did occur in the running text of the book but not in its headings. Then the online version was faster (4.3 min. vs. 7.5 min.), probably because it included a full text index.

Egan et al. also measured whether the users gave correct responses to the questions and found that the hypertext version was better than the printed book. The users were then asked to write an essay based on the book, and those essays were graded by an impartial judge who was not informed about what version of the book each writer of an essay had used. These ratings were significantly higher for the hypertext version (5.8 vs. 3.6 on a 7-point scale). To investigate why users performed better even when it came to the contents of the book, Egan et al. conducted another experiment [1989a]. They identified a number of key facts about statistics that ought to be represented in an essay of the type the subjects had been asked to write. The essays were then scored for any mentioning of these facts, and it turned out that there were more facts in the essays written by hypertext users (8.8 vs. 6.0 out of 15). Upon closer analysis, it turned out that most of the difference in number of facts could be seen by looking at just three facts that were discussed in the same single paragraph of the statistics book. The hypertext users included almost all of these so-called "discriminating facts" in their essays whereas the paper book users included rather few (2.7 vs. 1.2 out of 3).

Egan et al. then videotaped users while they read the book and wrote the essays to find out why users of the paper book did not find the discriminating facts. All the users in both conditions actually looked at the page containing the critical section of text with the discriminating facts. The problem with the printed version was that it did not specifically highlight the critical section any differently from the rest of the page and this section appeared approximately two-thirds of the way down the page. The hypertext system, in contrast, highlighted the user's search terms, thus pointing out that the critical section contained something of special relevance.

The results reported here were derived from studies of a revised version of SuperBook. Egan et al. [1989c] have also reported results from conducting the same studies with the original version of SuperBook. The redesign was done on the basis of observations from usability studies of the first version, and the results show that the revised version was indeed the best, since the mean search time for answering all types of questions was 5.4 min. with the revised version and 7.6 min. with the original. The proportion of correct responses to the questions also rose (75% vs. 69%).

Use of Hypertext in Education

Catano [1979] used one of the first hypertext systems, FRESS, to teach poetry. Results were measured by giving students a poem for analysis in essays that were graded by an external evaluator. This test was done both before and after the class, and for students in both a class using the hypertext system and a class taught by the same teacher using printed materials. The ability of students to analyze poems increased slightly more for the students taking the hypertext class (1.2 vs. 1.0 points). When the experiment was repeated the following year, the hypertext class improved less than the regular class, however (1.4 vs. 2.5 points), so this study is not conclusive. In any case, this study of a pioneering system may not be indicative for the currect generation of modern hypertext systems. The study is interesting, however, because it actually tried to measure what students learned from using a hypertext system while comparing them with a control group taught by the same teacher using traditional materials.

Field Studies

The main difference between field studies and laboratory studies is that field users use the system for a real-world reason (not because an experimenter has set up the system for them to try) to solve self-defined tasks (rather than tasks defined by the experimenter). Since one of the main ideas behind hypertext is to empower users to navigate an information space according to their own individual wishes and at their own speed, it is important to look at people using hypertexts in their own natural environments.

Nielsen and Lyngbæk [1990] had users read a hypertext document in Guide on their own time and report back on the usability of the three forms of hypertext used in Guide. On the question whether the hypertext facility was easy to understand, the Guide note button (used for pop-up) and replacement button (used for in-line hierarchical expansion) scored significantly higher than the reference button (used for `goto`): 1.5 vs. 1.5 vs. 2.2 on a 1–5 scale with 1 being best. On the question whether the hypertext facility improved the document, the note button scored significantly better than the replacement and reference buttons (2.0 vs. 2.5 vs. 2.8). So these users view the reference goto button as the poorest form for hypertext support and the note pop-up button as the best.

Conklin and Begeman [1988] had 32 people use the gIBIS hypertext tool for one year to build argumentation structures about various design decisions. gIBIS uses typed links between nodes, and for links to nodes commenting on a previous position there was a strong trend to having more of the type "supports" than of the type "objects to" (450 vs. 190), so users like to be positive towards their colleagues.

Many aspects of system use can be observed only in the field. Baird et al. [1988] observed the use of the *Glasgow Online* hypertext, which was made available to the general public at the Glasgow Garden Festival where about 500 people looked at it, corresponding to 11% of the total number of visitors to the university pavilion where it was displayed. Of these 500 people, about 70 were young people of 20 years of age or less, while about 430 were older than 20 years. Yet, of the about 50 people who went from the passive status of looking at the system to the active status of actually using it, about 32 came from the small, younger group and only 17 came from the much larger, older group.

The ultimate field studies look at the impact of the hypertext on the users' performance in the real world task, which is their reason for having the hypertext system in the first place. Unfortunately, very few such studies exist, possibly because hypertext systems have not been used all that much for real tasks yet. Nielsen and Lyngbæk [1990] studied children in a kindergarten who played with the interactive fiction *Inigo Gets Out* (see Figures 8.7 and 8.8) and found that they enjoyed doing so. For this system, enjoyment is its reason for existing, so it must be said to have been successful. Unfortunately, we could not *measure* the children's enjoyment on a quantitative scale.

Peter Brown [Brown 1989b] has reported on the use of Guide at the British computer company ICL for the task of diagnosing the fault when a customer calls ICL for service. This task is called "laundering" and is used to determine whether or not a visit by a repair technician is needed and what spare parts the technician should bring to the customer site. Making the right diagnosis therefore has real financial implications since it is expensive to send technicians bringing the wrong spare parts or to discover some trivial problem that the customers could have corrected themselves. It turned out that the proportion of customer calls handled correctly was 68% when the launderers used a paper representation of the information and 88% when they used hypertext (rising to 92% after six weeks of use).

Individual Differences

The users' level of expertise will have a large impact on how they use the system. Tombaugh et al. [1987] had users answer questions about texts that were displayed in several windows on a screen. Users who had been given just 30 minutes of practice in manipulating the very simple window system performed much better even at the end of a 90 minute experiment than users who had started the experiment as complete novices with regard to windows (50 sec. vs. 85 sec. to answer each question about the text).

In a study of an online engineering manual, Joseph et al. [1989] found that users changed their relative frequency of use of the various access mechanisms as they became more experienced. On the first day of using the online manual, users would use the table of contents quite a lot (20% of their information access was through the table of contents). This volume was probably because of their expectations based on having used similar engineering manuals in paper form. But the online table of contents was not very usable in this system because it displayed only chapter names and not the section listings that are found in the printed manual's table of contents. Going by the names of the chapters alone, information about arch bridges could have been in at least three of the chapters listed, and users selecting chapters from a table of contents actually made the wrong choices 80% of the time. Because of this poor experience, users changed to using the table of contents for only 5% of their information access on the third day of using the system.

Some people are more active in discussions than others, whether due to motivation, knowledge of the field, energy, extroverted nature, or whatever. In a study of the use of the gIBIS hypertext system for shared group-wide discussion of design issues, Conklin and Begeman [1988] found a huge individual variability in the number of hypertext nodes created by various users. Discussion group B had only two participants, and one created 190 nodes while the other created only 30. Discussion group A had four participants, and the most active created 221 nodes whereas the second most active participant created only 22. In the other discussion groups studied, the variability was less extreme but still very large.

Campagnoni and Ehrlich [1989] tested the Help Viewer online help system for the Sun386i. The subjects were given a standard test of spatial visualization ability, which showed that users with higher visualization scores needed less time to locate the answers to the questions, mostly because they had less need to return to the top level table of contents. This result indicates that users with good visualization abilities were better able to construct a conceptual model of the structure of the information space. There was a good regression fit between visualization scores and performance in the use of the hypertext system (correlation 0.75), indicating that people with high visualization scores could answer a given set of questions in 700 seconds while people with poor visualization scores needed 1,350 seconds.

Just being fatigued can change a user's work. As mentioned above, Wilkinson and Robinshaw [1987] had subjects proofread a traditional text file from computer screens continuously over periods of one hour and found that performance was significantly better during the first ten minutes than during the last ten minutes (error rate 25% vs. 39%).

Conclusions about Benchmark Studies

One of the very interesting questions one could ask about these studies is whether hypertext is in fact any good. The answer is simply, "It depends," since it seems that some studies indicate advantages to hypertext while others indicate disadvantages. It depends on the hardware and system software used, it depends on the design of the hypertext system, and it depends very much on the user's task and individual characteristics.

It is also interesting to consider the most extreme ratios between the conditions studied. The unqualified winner is the factor of more than 11 for proportion of young people compared to the proportion of older people who went from looking at Glasgow Online to actually using it. This difference between the two age groups of more than an order of magnitude makes all the 20% to 50% differences so carefully measured in other studies pale in comparison. This indication of the importance of age in the acceptance of new technology is a lesson we should take seriously, especially when considering that most of the studies reported here have been conducted with young college students as subjects.

Non-Benchmark Studies

Several studies of hypertext usability have avoided coming up with measurable comparisons of two or more conditions. This avoidance has typically been either because only a single system has been tested or because qualitative approaches have been judged more relevant for the purpose of the study.

Users' Conceptual Models of Domain Knowledge

Teshiba and Chignell [1988] measured the fit between the structure of students' conceptual model of the U.S. Constitution and related issues and an ideal model of this domain generated by experts. The models were found by having the students sort cards with various terms by perceived similarity into piles that they grouped hierarchically. The hierarchies generated by the students were then compared with the ideal hierarchy by Hubert's [1978; 1979] gamma measure of proximity between two hierarchies, and the authors found that this proximity measure increases slightly (but not significantly) over time with the use of the hypertext. These results are actually useless for an assessment of the usability of the authors' hypertext system since we do not know whether a larger increase would have resulted from having the students spend the same time on studying constitutional issues in a more traditional way. But the paper is interesting because it shows a way to measure the conceptual model-building effect of using hypertexts.

Logging User Interactions

Computer systems can be instrumented to monitor automatically users' interaction behavior. The advantages of this approach are that no human experimenter is needed to collect the data, that the data is collected unobtrusively without influencing the user's working style (but with the associated problems relating to privacy), and that because of these two characteristics data can be collected in the field and over long periods of time.

Some studies exist of logging data from hypertext. Egan et al. [1989a] logged readers' use of the SuperBook system in their study discussed above of why more facts were found by SuperBook readers than by readers of a printed book. In a typical use of logging data, Egan et al. [1989c] used knowledge of which operations users performed frequently to improve the average response times of SuperBook by tuning a redesigned version. Yoder et al. [1984] logged the use of the ZOG system on board the aircraft carrier USS *Carl Vinson* to determine which tasks the users performed with the system and what errors they made. Since ZOG (now known as KMS) is strictly frame-based, it was easy to record the time spent by users at each node in the hypertext as a set of discrete data. This approach is somewhat harder in hypertext systems based on the scrolling file paradigm.

Shneiderman et al. [1989] logged the navigation behavior of users of Hyperties at three museums. One information base was used at two of the museums and another information base was used at the third. A computer with an information base on the photographer David Seymour was exhibited at both the International Center for Photography and the B'nai B'rith Klutznick Museum, and a total of 734 user sessions were logged. It was possible for users to start from the welcome screen by reading either an introductory article or by going to the index. At both museums, about 80% of the users started by reading the introductory article, and of these users about 50% then went directly on to the index from the introductory article rather than following the hypertext links leading out from the introduction. For the approximately 20% of the users who went to the index first, the most popular article to select from the index was an article about Israel for the visitors to the B'nai B'rith Klutznick Museum and an article about the photographer for visitors to the International Center for Photography, thus showing that different groups of users may access an information base in different ways.

Shneiderman et al.'s third study logged 4,461 user sessions with an information base about archaeology at the Smithsonian Institution. The list of articles (Hyperties nodes) sorted by frequency of access was topped by most of the articles mentioned in the introductory article, indicating that a listing in such a central location is a good way to attract user attention. The list of articles accessed by selection from the index indicated a strong preference for articles having names in the beginning of the alphabet: Of the 20 top articles, 18 had names beginning with A, B, or C, probably revealing that the index mechanism was not very usable since it was long and arranged alphabetically instead of by topic. Shneiderman et al. also comment that the very names of articles (which are used as anchors in Hyperties) seemed to impact their popularity among users who were most attracted to articles with names indicating that they contained specific information. Finally, Shneiderman et al. comment that they actually got the most useful information for their own design of the hypertext interface from more informal observations of the users and not from the logging data.

Nielsen and Lyngbæk [1990] studied the use of nonverbal interactive fiction by children in a kindergarten. A Macintosh running the hyperstory *Inigo Gets Out* was made available for the children for a day where the computer logged all the mouse clicks made by the children while navigating the artificial world of the story. For the analysis of this data, we had the computer draw diagrams of the screens that graphically showed where the users had clicked. An example is shown in Figure 8.8. This data representation provided much more insight into the usability of the hyperstory than a more statistically oriented analysis of the data, but this advantage is of course partly based on the graphic nature of the user interface being studied.

Observing Users

Several studies have been conducted using various variations of observation or thinking aloud methods. Hardman [1989b] studied the usability of *Glasgow Online* using the thinking-aloud methodology and found several problems in its user interface. Most of these problems were actually more related to traditional issues in human-computer interaction, such as readable screen design. But some of Hardman's observations are directly related to the hypertext nature of *Glasgow Online*. She found that users had problems using the "next" operation because it was based on a confused linking paradigm. She also found that many users did not use the backtrack facility but instead started all over from the welcome screen and retraced their path through the information base. This preference was probably because backtrack is inconsistently implemented in *Glasgow Online*.

Iterative Interface Refinement

Current practice in usability engineering [Whiteside et al. 1988; Nielsen 1989c] is to refine user interfaces iteratively since one cannot design them exactly right the first time around.

One example of a usability study that can be used for such a purpose is Hardman's [1989a] evaluation of the understandability of the icons used in *Glasgow Online* to denote various services at hotels in a manner similar to many guidebooks. When test subjects went through the hypertext in the study discussed above, Hardman stopped them when they first reached a screen showing information about a particular hotel (where the hotel service icons were found) and asked them to tell her how they would interpret each of the icons. For each subject she then made a list of the icons guessed correctly as well as the icons the subject could not guess or guessed wrongly. For example, one user thought that an icon showing a globe of the earth meant that the hotel offered facilities for exchanging foreign currency whereas it actually was intended to mean that the hotel had conference facilities (presumably the idea was to induce an association with international meetings). Several other users believed that an icon showing a pineapple meant that the hotel had fresh fruit in the rooms or that it served fresh fruit, whereas the intention was to indicate that the hotel catered to special diets (such as vegetarians).

This information about wrong guesses can be very useful when it comes to redesigning icons to reduce the probability for mistakes. One would especially want to redesign icons where some users make disastrously wrong guesses. Hardman also accumulated the number of correct and wrong guesses for each icon to a list indicating their overall understandability. One would also want to redesign those icons where many subjects made wrong guesses, even if none of the guesses were disastrous.

Many of the other studies discussed in this chapter have also been conducted with the purpose of allowing the experimenters to refine the next version of their system.

The Larger Picture

Among the benchmark studies we see that individual differences have the largest impact on the performance when using hypertext systems. Another major factor is the different tasks users have when they use hypertext systems. These two issues are absolutely the most important when is comes to measuring hypertext usability.

One should take care not to identify usability evaluation with quantitative benchmark studies only, since we have seen that many of the most interesting insights leading to improved hypertext user interfaces have come from more qualitative observational studies.

10. Writing Hypertexts

Unfortunately, even though you can easily get some ideas about hypertext authoring from your experience as a hypertext reader, we face the general problem that people have not learnt how to structure information in hypertext networks the same way they have learnt to write linear reports through writing endless numbers of essays in school. Early experience with the use of NoteCards [Trigg and Irish 1987] indicated the need to give users a "strategy manual" about the design of hypertext networks and the useful conventions they might respect. Just giving users the four types of NoteCards objects and letting them loose was not enough.

Some advice for authors of hypertexts comes from our understanding of the reading situation. For example it is a good idea to keep each node focused on a single topic to make it easier to understand and recognize in overview diagrams, history lists, etc. Having a single topic for each node also makes it easier for the author to know what links to construct.

Because we know that reading speed is slower from screens than from paper, we need to make hypertext nodes shorter than paper articles. The very nature of hypertext helps the author achieve this goal because subsidiary topics, definitions, etc. need not be elaborated in the primary text. One should construct additional nodes to hold this information.

One general strategy is to be critical of the links and to avoid adding every possible link between remotely related concepts. A "clean structure" is easier for users to navigate and many hypertext systems allow the readers to add extra links if they really want them. Remember that it is an author's job to set priorities for the readers (even in hypertext).

I would expect that our knowledge of what constitutes good hypertexts will build as we see more examples of what works or does not work. Eventually students might learn hypertext authoring in schools just as they currently learn essay writing, and the problem will go away. For the short term, the best recommendation probably is to pay close attention to the authoring principles implicit in other writers' hypertext and try to emulate the principles you like.

Usability for Authors

It is important to keep in mind that the users who require usable systems are not just the end-users but also the authors who develop the hypertext structures read by these end-users. For some tasks, such as brainstorm support, the readers and the writers are the same people, and certain hypertext systems provide exactly the same user interface for readers and writers. But in many cases, extra facilities are available for information authors, and it is important to ensure the usability of these facilities. Unfortunately, the authoring of hypertext has been even less studied than the reading of hypertext.

One example of an authoring facility is the list of dangling references in Hyperties [Shneiderman 1989] showing links not yet completed by the author. Based on personal experience with developing a hypertext structure in a system *without* such a facility [Nielsen 1989a; 1990b], I am convinced of the need for a dangling reference facility in an authoring system. But this kind of personal experience does not indicate the best way of implementing such a facility or of integrating it with the rest of the system. And to evaluate the usefulness of more advanced or complex types of authoring support, purely personal opinions may not suffice.

Other evidence from informal studies indicates a severe problem with premature structuring [Halasz 1988] because many hypertext systems force the author to structure the information at too early a stage. A simple example is the need to enter a name for a new node before one even knows what it will really be about [Walker 1988]. This latter problem can be alleviated by a "rename" command that also automatically updates all links. The very distribution of the information over nodes may be harder to change even though it is also likely that authors will change their way of thinking about the domain as they write.

In a study of authors revising their works, Haas [1989] asked the test subjects to think aloud, and counted the proportion of their utterances that referred to the editing medium itself rather than to the text being edited. This proportion was only 3% when they used paper but 8% on a mouse-based workstation and a whopping 21% on a keyboard-based personal computer, thus indicating that the use of pen and paper was significantly more transparent even though the test users all had at least four years of computer experience. This study points out the importance of having as transparent authoring tools as possible so that authors are allowed to focus on the task of communicating their domain knowledge to the readers.

Unfortunately hardly any studies exist of the usability of authoring interfaces, possibly because they are harder to study. For a reading interface, specific tasks can be set and one can measure how fast readers solve these tasks. It is also fairly easy to assess how much the readers have learnt by asking them questions about the content of the information. But for writers, we need to assess the quality of the information they create and this judgement is very hard to make as long as we do not have a firm understanding of what makes a good hypertext structure in the first place. A fully valid test would probably need to measure the usability of authoring facilities by having several authors create information bases that would then be measured in use by groups of end-users. This approach leads to exorbitant requirements for end-user test subjects and is probably infeasible in almost all cases.

An alternative is to follow the Hansen and Haas [1988] test of letter writing with various screen sizes (discussed in Chapter 9) and have judges evaluate the quality of the result of the authors' work. This is easier to do as long as the result is linear texts, which we are used to judging, but work on heuristic evaluation techniques for hypertexts could lead to the possibility for also judging non-linear texts such as was done informally by Nielsen [1990a] who evaluated the usability of three systems by using various usability heuristics such as the need for consistent backtracking, history facilities, and support for navigational dimensions.

A field study [Kerr 1989] of the working style of designers doing everyday production of videotex frames showed that, over time, designers tend to be bored since most routine frame creation work is not very interesting. The study revealed a conflict over the place of individual creativity in videotex work where the designers chafe at restrictions imposed by managers because using the hardware and software in unusual and exploratory ways is a principal motivation in designers' daily work.

In contrast, Shneiderman [1989] in his discussion of the lessons learnt from building more then thirty hypertext structures for Hyperties emphasized the key lesson that each project was different and had to have its information structured according to a principle that was suited for its specific domain. Shneiderman's experience also showed, however, that it is necessary to have a single managing editor to coordinate a project and to copy edit the final result. So there is certainly the potential for tension among the people whose work it will be to create future, large information bases. Just as software developers may feel frustrated by user interface standards restricting their design options, information base developers may be frustrated by having to place consistency over their individual creativity. One hopes that the unique individual needs of each project will provide enough variation to keep this problem to a minimum, but only further experience can tell.

Separate Interfaces for Writers

The fundamental question in relation to hypertext authoring is whether there should be a separate interface to the hypertext for the writers or whether all users should share the same interface.

Several hypertext systems are based on the principle that "readers" also need to write. KMS has no specific reading or writing modes but allows users to add text or links to any frame at any time. This approach eliminates the need for users to remember what mode they are in or to understand the difference between the commands and data representations available in the two modes.

Other systems do allow both reading and writing but in slightly different modes. For example, HyperCard includes a "user level" mechanism that can be set to several different values, allowing more or less radical changes to the documen. One of these user levels is a browse-only mode without any authoring capabilities. Even when the user level is set allow authoring, the author needs to enter special modes to add new buttons or fields to a card. The advantage of this approach is to reduce complexity in each of the modes because they can be optimized for a single task. Users maintain the possibility of changing the document, but they do not risk doing so inadvertently.

Finally, a few hypertext systems including the Symbolics Document Examiner and Hyperties provide separate authoring environments, typically because they want to provide extremely simple interfaces for their readers.

Concordia

The Symbolics writing environment is called Concordia [Walker 1988] and is based on the premise that writers have different needs from readers. Also writers have more motivation for learning the hypertext tool itself, so they can be provided with a more full-featured but perhaps more complex user interface.

Concordia is a structure-oriented editor and gives writers templates for their nodes with special slots for standard information like keywords and section headings. It also manages meta-information for each node in addition to the text seen by the readers. This meta-information includes auditing data (determining whether the text has been checked) as well as the writers' own notes for future versions. Even though the Symbolics Document Examiner has only one-directional links for the readers, Concordia provides bidirectional links for the writers in the form of a list of incoming links for the current node. This facility was included because writers needed to know what other nodes in the hypertext referred to the one they were working on in order to provide a decent "rhetoric of arrival" by making their text understandable in the context of the reader's potential navigation paths.

Concordia uses a generic markup language to separate form from content in the text. A special "book design" database defines the appearance on the screen of the various text elements and enables global formatting changes for the purpose of, say, going from a color screen to a monochrome screen. The structure oriented editor takes care of inserting appropriate markup tags, but the writers also have a facility available to change the display to show the text in the final formatting readers would see under a given book design database.

Authoring Toolkits

A toolkit for hypertext authors should obviously first of all contain the basic tools needed by any writer, such as integrated spelling check and drawing packages for making good illustrations that can easily be modified. Unfortunately almost all current hypertext systems are monolithic programs and do not integrate well with the other facilities of the user's computational environment. This means, for example, that users need to construct illustrations in external graphics programs and import them to the hypertext where they are considered static images. If an illustration has to be changed, the user has to reexport it back to the graphics program it came from and edit it there.

The lack of integration between stand-alone hypertext programs and the rest of the user's computational environment was one of the major user complaints in several surveys conducted by Leggett et al. [1990]. This sad state of affairs does not necessarily have to continue, however. There is some work being done on providing link services [Pearl 1989] to integrate all applications on a given computer, and that work could well prove to be a great help for the hypertext authoring interface also.

The integration of traditional writing aids into hypertext authoring systems may be difficult in practice, but at least we know what to aim for. With respect to specialized tools for writing specifically hypertext, we are less well off because we do not yet know what to aim for.

There is an obvious need for tools to import text from other programs, whether they are other hypertext systems or more traditional text systems. Hypertext interchange is discussed further in Chapter 6, and the conversion from plain text to hypertext is discussed in Chapter 11.

Recommendations for hypertext authors would probably include the traditional advice: to begin with making a synopsis to structure the information in a top-down fashion. In real life, however, many authors seem to prefer a bottom-up approach of writing hypertext nodes as they think of them. This attitude has been found to be the case in a study of HyperCard authors [Nicol 1988] who mostly worked in a "button-up" manner of constructing their hypertext one button (link) at a time.

Because of this phenomenon there is a need for authoring tools to help writers structure their hypertext after the fact. As mentioned above, Hyperties has a nice facility for keeping track of dangling links. Other tools to help the author understand the emerging network would include the overview diagrams that many systems already produce for readers (see Chapter 8), but for authors the diagrams could also be used for dynamic restructuring of the information space.

The system could also give the author helpful statistics calculated from the structure of the hypertext network. Clustering methods can be used to show the underlying structure in the network, and connectivity

Connectivity scores calculated giving high weight to incoming links and low weight to outgoing links (i.e. nodes that are referred to a lot)	*Connectivity scores calculated giving low weight to incoming links and high weight to outgoing links (i.e. nodes from which you can go to a lot of places)*
74 Bibliography: References 73 Browsing 59 Hyperties 54 HyperCard 53 Windows 52 Links 51 Authoring Overview 50 Graphics 50 Shneiderman 50 Guide	77 Introduction 58 Systems Overview 49 Guide 49 Authoring Overview 48 Bibliography: References 48 Getting started 48 Hyperties 48 Links 43 Dictionaries 41 Hyper hype?

Table 10.1. *Connectivity of nodes in* Hypertext Hands-On! *by Ben Shneiderman and Greg Kearsley. Only the top ten nodes are listed for each way to calculate connectivity. Numbers calculated using the HyperBook system implemented at the Technical University of Denmark by Michael H. Andersen and Henrik Rasmussen.*

measures can indicate potential landmarks by listing those nodes that are central in the hypertext.

Table 10.1 shows two calculations of connectivity for the nodes in *Hypertext Hands-On!* by Ben Shneiderman and Greg Kearsley. These calculations were performed using the transitive closure of the links with steadily decreasing weights for nodes that were more than one jump away. This means that the connectivity score for a given node is calculated by counting all those other nodes in the network that are connected to it by paths of one or more links, taking the length of this path into account. The left column was calculated by giving the highest weight to incoming links while the right column shows the result of putting the emphasis on the outgoing links.

Five nodes (Bibliography, Hyperties, Links, Authoring overview, and Guide) actually occur on both lists, indicating that they have a truly central location in the information space of this hypertext. For the calculations in Table 10.1 we have given all links and nodes equal weight but it would be possible for the author to assign different importance ratings to the links and nodes in a hypertext and have those values reflected in the connectivity scores. A node would get a higher score if the links connecting it with other nodes were deemed to be especially important or if those other nodes had a high importance rating.

Cooperative Authoring

Much work with modern computer systems is collaborative in nature and involves groups of people working together. This is certainly true of most large writing projects such as the writing of the text for the Symbolics Document Examiner online manual. Fortunately hypertext is quite well suited for supporting collaboration since its linking structure allows the coordination of nodes written by multiple authors. Hypertext annotation facilities and the possibilities for linking through distributed networks also offer support for group work. Actually some hypertext systems like gIBIS (see Figure 4.2) have group support as their main purpose.

Several problems arise when more than one user works on a shared hypertext. The disorientation problem discussed in Chapter 8 could well become much worse when the information space changes behind the back of the individual user because of the activities of other writers. In one case of collaborative use of NoteCards [Trigg et al. 1986], the solution to this problem was to establish a special area of the hypertext for communication among the authors and to use different typefaces for the text written by each author.

In general, the hypertext system might keep the identity of the authors as attributes of nodes and links and use that information to determine authorizations to change or delete the information. It could also be possible for a user to ask the system to filter the hypertext with respect to the author IDs to see only nodes and links added by particular categories of users and to make the information "owned" by that user especially prominent in overview diagrams.

In some cases the users can be divided into two or more categories with different access privileges. A typical example is the use of Intermedia for teaching where the professor would be authorized to add or change the "canonic" hypertext structure whereas the students would be authorized only to add links and annotations.

Version control [Delisle and Schwartz 1986] is a final problem that becomes even more serious in multi-author hypertexts even though it is also present in single-user systems. What should happen if node **A** links to node **B** and someone suddenly changes **B**? For example, the text in **B** might be split over two new nodes and the link from **A** could be redirected to the more appropriate of them. The choice of "more appropriate" is probably impossible to make automatically, so the best we can hope for is a hypertext system that informs the person making the change that there is a need to update the links.

The Authority of the Author

Hypertext basically destroys the authority of the author to determine how readers should be introduced to a topic. From the readers' perspective, this is one of the great advantages of hypertext since it means that they are free to explore the information as they see fit. Remember the SuperBook study described in Chapter 9 showing that readers could access the information in the hypertext just as easily when they approached it with questions that had not been included in the author's original structuring of the text.

It might also be good news from the author's perspective. Authoring takes on an entirely new dimension when your job is changed to one of providing opportunities for readers rather than ordering them around. These opportunities should not be endless, however. The author still has the responsibility to provide certain priorities for the readers and to point them in relevant directions.

The old saying "more is less" is also true of hypertext linking: If you add every conceivable link to your hypertext, readers will benefit less than if you add only those links that are truly important and relevant. Every extra link is an additional burden on the user who has to determine whether or not to follow it. And if there are too many links leading to uninteresting places (because "they might be relevant for some readers") then readers will quickly become disappointed and learn not to trust your judgement.

In writing fiction in hypertext [Howell 1990], the loss of the absolute authority of the author leads to the loss of a single narrative stream of action which again destroys most traditional ways of writing in Western civilization. Instead the role of the author becomes much more closely connected to the tradition from science fiction of "building worlds" that the reader can explore.

11.   Converting Existing Text to Hypertext

The ideal situation with respect to hypertext would be to write all the nodes from scratch since the text is to be presented in a new medium. Just as the best films are not made by putting a camera in the front row of a theater, the best hypertexts are not made from text that was originally written for the linear medium. But in the real world we have to respect that large amounts of extremely useful text already exist and can be converted to hypertext much more cheaply than the same information could be rewritten. This chapter first covers some of the issues in the conversion of existing text to hypertext and then gives more detail about two concrete conversion projects: a medical handbook and a large dictionary.

Conversion projects have to split the existing text into nodes and come up with links and their anchors. This process may be done automatically if the text is already suitably encoded or is regular enough to allow the writing of a simple pattern recognizing program. But in many cases it is necessary to do at least some of the conversion manually. Link structures can often be derived from existing sources like a printed index or table of contents, whereas node structures are often defined as the smallest named units of the text (typically sections).

The vendor of the Guide hypertext system, OWL has released a system called IDEX [Cooke and Williams 1989] for the conversion of text files to hypertext. IDEX works on text encoded in the SGML[1] [Barron 1989] standard formatting language and maps the SGML tags to hypertext nodes and links. SGML is based on describing the *meaning* of the text rather than its typographical appearance so it includes, for

---

[1] Standard Generalized Markup Language—an ISO international standard for text formatting.

instance, tags telling the formatter, "This is a chapter heading" or "This is a section heading."

IDEX can utilize this information automatically to fold the text file into hierarchical replacement structures according to its chapter–section–subsection format and to put footnotes, literature references, etc. in pop-up notes.

Sometimes a small software development effort can result in a customized system to generate hypertext structures automatically. As an example, the software mail order company the Savings Zone has distributed several versions of their price list in a hypertext format. The first few versions were produced by hand, but they quickly realized that they spent about 30–40 hours for each new version on updating information by hand. The problem was solved by writing a HyperCard program that could take a dump of the information in their product database and produce the hypertext version automatically. This conversion program was fairly easy to implement because of the fixed data format in the database dumps.

To the extent that the conversion from text to hypertext is not done completely automatically, the converter has the option of adding new links to the information structure. Kahn [1989b] distinguishes between "objective links" derived directly from the original text and "subjective links" that are added because the converter feels they are relevant. Objective links would include cross references in the text or a link from the name of a city to its location on a map. Subjective links, in contrast, are located in concepts seen by the converter as being associated.

Obviously many of the "objective" links are only objective as far as the converter is concerned. For the original author, the decision of which other works to reference and which internal cross-references to add to the rest of the author's own document was mostly subjective. As more text is written in hypertext from the start, subjective links will probably tend to outnumber objective links. There are still some objective links left, such as the link from a person's name to the biography of the person if such a biography is present on the system. Many of these links may tend to become implicit, however.

The addition of new links or hypertext structure to an existing text gives rise to a problem similar to that of "colorizing" old black-and-white films. There is a risk that the hypertext version of the information will be subtly altered by the new structure or new way of connecting things and that the original author's intentions are violated. One example was the conversion of an issue of the journal *Communications of the ACM* to the "Hypertext on Hypertext" product. The KMS version had to include new structure because its frame-oriented nature could not accommodate an entire journal article in a single node. This specific modification does not seem to have caused any problems, but one should be aware of the potential risks.

In many cases one probably needs a different information structure for hypertext than the structure of the existing document. If an automatic conversion is deemed necessary anyway, one should at least allow the readers more freedom than they would normally get to add their own links and to annotate or customize the information.

The reverse problem of converting a traditional text to hypertext is to linearize a hypertext structure for printing. There are several reasons for doing so, including the pragmatic one that a lot of material is still distributed on paper. Even in the remote future when computers may have replaced paper completely there will still be a need to give oral presentations to an audience. And presentations simply *have* to be linear in time.

It is fairly easy to linearize a hypertext having a strict hierarchical structure by performing a depth-first tree traversal, meaning that you start by printing the first chapter and all the sections it contains before moving on to the second chapter. Another easy way out is to follow any guided tours the author may have defined through the hypertext. But in the general case where the hypertext is a highly connected network without any special order, it is very difficult to produce a good linearization. Experience with the use of NoteCards to write traditional reports [Trigg and Irish 1987] showed that many writers had to perform a final round of editing on the linear document after it had been generated by a conversion of the NoteCards hypertext structure.

The Manual of Medical Therapeutics

The Washington University *Manual of Medical Therapeutics* is a 500-page book with guidelines for medical diagnosis and therapy that has been converted into hypertext in a variety of research prototypes [Frisse 1988] in NoteCards and HyperCard, and on the NeXT machine.

The printed book had a highly hierarchical structure as can be seen from the following example of a series of steadily more deeply nested section headings:

Chapter 6. Heart Failure
   V. Digitalis
      D. Digitalis Toxicity
         3. Treatment
            c. Ventricular Arrhythmias

This regular structure made it easy to construct a hypertext representation of the text automatically. Each subsection was made into a node that was given an identifier corresponding to the section number in the printed text. In the above example, the section number and node identifier is 6.V.D.3.c. Since this section number is basically incomprehensible for anybody who is not extremely experienced in using the *Manual*, each node was also given a title consisting of the first six words in its text. These names are certainly not optimal, but given the specialized nature of the medical terminology and the way the sections were written, they are nevertheless still quite readable for physicians. The names are shown as labels for hypertext links and as the search results after user queries.

Furthermore, the system can automatically construct hypertext links between a section and all its subsections and from a subsection to its parent node. Readers can use these hypertext links to browse the book, but they can also perform queries based on a combination of keyword search and hypertext navigation.

Assume that we have to find information about how to cure a patient having certain heartbeat irregularities. A physician knowing the correct terminology might give the computer a command like the following:

    find "treatment of digitalis-induced ventricular arrythmias"

Even though subsection 6.V.D.3.c of the *Manual* contains the answer (as can be seen from the above example of the section hierarchy), it would not be found because it does not contain all the keywords specified by the user. Several of the keywords only occur in the higher-level sections of which 6.V.D.3.c is a subsection. This way of writing the nodes made sense when the text existed in a printed form since the author could assume that the reader knew the context of a given piece of text in the chapter-section-subsection hierarchy.

Therefore the hypertext version of the text must provide a more context-dependent search facility if it is to reuse the text from the printed book. This is done by computing search results as a combination of the intrinsic and extrinsic query scores as explained in Chapter 8. In other words, the degree to which a given node is said to match a user query takes into account how well the match is for other nodes it is connected to by hypertext links. In the example, the node for section 6.V.D would match "digitalis," the node for section 6.V.D.3 would match "treatment," and the node for section 6.V.D.3.c would match "ventricular arrythmias." These three nodes would be listed in a menu of search results in an order determined by the exact search weights, and the user could browse through them using the hypertext links until all the necessary information was found.

Oxford English Dictionary

The *Oxford English Dictionary (OED)* is one of the largest texts to be converted to a hypertext format [Raymond and Tompa 1988]. The printed version was originally published in twelve volumes from 1884 to 1928, and a four volume supplement was published in the period 1972–1986. Because it is so old, the *OED* did not exist in machine-readable form but had to be rekeyed manually in a process taking eighteen months.

It might have been possible to scan in the text from the printed books by optical character recognition but that would have generated a fairly "stupid" representation of the text. By having humans type in the text it was possible to have the basic text supplemented by tags to indicate the nature of the various text elements. For example it was desirable to distinguish among the actual dictionary entries, their definitions, their etymologies, and the quotations from other literature.

The data is stored as one contiguous 570 megabyte stream of text, recorded using these descriptive SGML-style markup tags. Thus there are no nodes explicitly stored as separate units and there are no explicit links stored as pointers. The software used to access the text is based on indexes stored externally to the main data stream. Therefore one can view this software as converting a flat text file to hypertext every time it is used.

The original *OED* contained 252,259 entries (words that can be looked up), and the supplement contained 69,372 entries. To complicate matters further, there was some overlap between the original dictionary and the supplement since some words had acquired new meanings or quotations. Just merging the two sets of entries was thus in itself a service to users and the new edition furthermore includes an additional 5,000 new or revised entries. The complete second edition of the *OED* will be published on CD-ROM in the early 1990s to replace a current CD-ROM containing only the original *OED*. A third edition is expected sometime after the year 2000, but the hypertext medium should also make it possible to release continuously updated revisions every year or so.

One reason hypertext is a good access mechanism for the *OED* is that it contains 569,000 cross references within the dictionary itself. Many of these references link to variant forms of a word, to words with a similar meaning, or to entries about prefixes or suffixes. Since the *OED* contains definitions of almost every word in the English language, it also contains an astronomical number of implicit links since users may jump from every word in the complete text to that word's entry even if the editors have not included an explicit link.

The *OED* contains 2.4 million quotations to illustrate the way various authors have used words throughout the history of the English language. These quotations can really be seen as references to other literature, so a "universal hypertext" like Ted Nelson's Xanadu would replace them with links to the full text of the original sources allowing the user to see not just the sentence in which a word was used but also the broader context of that use.

Unfortunately it was not possible to design a single simple hypertext interface to the *OED*. The stumbling block was the great variability in the size of entries and the different uses to which the dictionary might be put. The distribution of the length of dictionary entries is extremely skewed. Only 5% of the entries in the *OED* are larger than 4,000 characters but they account for 48% of the total text. As an example, the entry for the verb "to set" is almost half a megabyte. At the same time, 20% of the entries are smaller than 50 characters. Obviously one cannot use the same principles for access to 50 character entries as for 500,000-character entries.

The larger entries can normally be structured according to the various meanings and sub-meanings of the word. These "senses" form a hierarchical structure that is suited for hypertext browsing since users often only care about a word in a few of its main meanings. The hypertext version of the *OED* automatically constructed this hypertext hierarchy from the encoding of the raw text with tags. The other types of information had tags that mostly followed a flat structure such as the year for various quotations. Therefore one form of hypertext support for browsing quotations could be a timeline.

Finally, the interface to the *OED* needed to allow alternative displays of entries according to the user's task since some users are very interested in the linguistic evolution of the words and ancient quotations whereas others only need the word definitions. This difference can again be supported quite well by hypertext. Instead of having a system that automatically formats the text in a single predefined way, the *OED* hypertext interface allows dynamic restructuring of the text according to the individual user's specification.

We should also note that the *OED* is one of the few examples where hypertext is actually more readable than paper. Most people who have the *OED* on paper do not have the full-sized twenty volumes but a three-volume edition in microscopic print.[2] The hypertext version can of course use as large a display font as the user wants and is therefore easier on the eyes. The variable font size is a real benefit for many handicapped readers.

---

[2] The microprint edition has two volumes corresponding to the original sixteen volume *OED* as well as a further single volume containing the supplement.

12. The Future of Hypertext

It is very hard to forecast the future of hypertext [Kain and Nielsen 1991]. Of course it is always difficult to forecast the future, but it is especially difficult in the case of hypertext because we do not have enough experience yet with real-life use of hypertext to know what the trends are going to be.

Short Term Future: Three to Five Years

In the short term of three to five years, I don't really expect significant changes in the way hypertext is done compared to the currently known systems. Of course new stuff will be invented all the time, but just getting the things we already have in the laboratory out into the world will be more than enough. I expect to see two major changes:
- the emergence of a mass market for hypertext
- the integration of hypertext and other computer facilities

A Mass Market for Hypertext

Currently there is no market in selling prepackaged hypertexts to the general public. Hypertext is only really being used for in-house production of specialized information. One major reason for this restriction is that the actual hypertext engines are not yet owned by a sufficiently large number of people to make a viable market.

The only exception to the lack of a hypertext market is HyperCard, which is owned by a few million people because it has been distributed for free with every Macintosh sold since 1987. And we have actually seen a few commercial hypertexts sold in HyperCard format such as the *Inigo*[1] series from AmandaStories and *The Manhole*[2] and *Cosmic Osmo* from Activision. These hypertexts have been interactive fiction

---

[1] See the screen shots from *Inigo Gets Out* in Figure 8.7 and 8.8.

[2] See the screen shots from *The Manhole* in Figure 4.15 and 4.16.

for children since they constitute a very broad market that does not require the same degree of complexity and specialization as fiction or textbooks for adults. Another current example of a commercial hypertext is the Bible—again a broad product with a wide readership.

Without actually knowing their sales figures, I would hazard the guess that these current hypertexts have not made all that much money compared to traditional book publishing.

The difference over the next few years will be that the number of HyperCard installations will automatically grow from a few million to many millions with the growth of the Macintosh market. Therefore we should expect to see "real" fiction and various forms of textbooks for sale in HyperCard format.

Furthermore, we should expect to see hypertext systems other than HyperCard obtain a large enough installed base to support a mass market. For example it might turn out that a sufficient number of universities buy Intermedia to allow independent authors to construct Intermedia information bases on new topics. A potential event could be that enough copies of some Intermedia information base were sold to also support third-party sales of *webs*[3] over that information base, but I view that possibility as extremely unlikely to happen in the short term future.

A true mass market would probably have to be based not just on the Macintosh but also on other popular machines such as the IBM PC. Even now, Activision has been preparing a version of *The Manhole* for MS-DOS IBM compatibles.

The really interesting result of a hypertext mass market would be a focus on the *contents* of the hypertext and how to structure it for optimal results. The current hypertext market seems to be mostly focused on sales of systems and features instead of actual content.

Integrating Hypertext with Other Computer Facilities

The reader will probably have noticed that I am quite enthusiastic about the possibilities of hypertext. Even so, it must be said that many

---

[3] An Intermedia web is a set of hypertext links among pieces of the text contained in the primary information base. Third-party web sales would therefore be unique to hypertext and would be an example of the "trail blazing" dreamt of by Vannevar Bush in 1945.

of the better applications of hypertext require additional features to plain hypertext.

As an example consider the problem of supplying the annual report from the Technical University of Denmark in an electronic format. Hypertext would obviously play an important role in such a project, and one could use hierarchical hypertext features such as those in Guide for nesting information about the various parts of the university, the various departments, and the various research groups within the departments. Cross-reference links would connect researchers who worked with colleagues in other departments.

But pure hypertext would not be enough for a usable annual report. Some readers would want to perform searches for specific people or topics, so there would be a need for some kind of full text search. Since many Danes share a small number of traditional family names, the search for a person's name would often generate a large number of hits, so there is also a need for some kind of sophisticated menu of hits that would show, for instance, the full name of each person as well as brief information about department and research interest. Furthermore, the system should provide phonetic classification of the search terms since people often don't know the exact spelling of names.

Additional facilities might also be useful, but the general conclusion in any case must certainly be that an integrated system to provide both hypertext and other appropriate facilities is needed.

We are currently seeing such a trend for hypertext systems to be integrated with other advanced types of computer facilities. For example, there are several systems that integrate hypertext with artificial intelligence (AI).

One such system is built by Scott M. Stevens [Stevens 1989] at the Software Engineering Institute at Carnegie Mellon University for teaching the software engineering technique called *code inspection*. Code inspection basically involves discussing various aspects of a program during a meeting where the participants each have specified roles such as reviewer, moderator, or designer of the program. It turns out that it is impossible to teach people this method without first having them participate in a number of meetings where they are assigned the various roles. This process can be quite expensive if the other meeting participants have to be experienced humans.

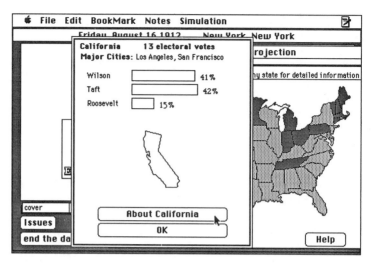

Figure 12.1. *Screen from* The Election of 1912 *showing the simulation part of the system. The user has called up a map showing the results of a (simulated) opinion poll and has asked for further information about one of the states.* © 1987 by Eastgate Systems, Inc., reprinted with permission.

It is possible, however, to simulate the other participants on a computer by the use of artificial intelligence. By doing so, the person learning the code inspection method can have as many training meetings as necessary, and the student can even go through the same meeting several times to take on the different roles. The major part of the meeting simulation system is therefore an AI method for finding out how the other meeting participants would react to whatever behavior the student exhibits. But the system also includes a lot of text in the form of the actual program being discussed, its design specifications, and various textbooks and reports on the code inspection method. These texts are linked using hypertext techniques.

Another example of the integration of hypertext with other techniques is the commercial product called *The Election of 1912* from Eastgate Systems running in their Hypergate system on the Macintosh. Whereas the code inspection meeting simulator was primarily an AI system with hypertext thrown in for support, *The Election of 1912* is primarily a hypertext system but also includes a simulation.

Most of the *1912* system is a hypertext about the political events in the United States in 1912 with special focus on the presidential election of that year. It is possible to read the hypertext in the normal way to learn about this historical period and its people. There is also a political

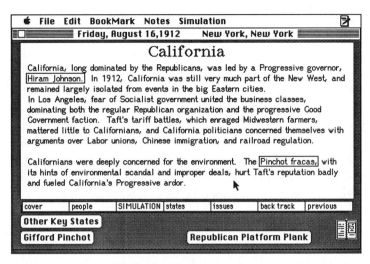

Figure 12.2. *Screen from* The Election of 1912 *hypertext showing the result of following the "About California" link from the simulation part of the system.* © *1987 by Eastgate Systems, Inc., reprinted with permission.*

simulation to increase student motivation for reading through the material.

Basically the simulation allows the user to participate in "running" for president in 1912 by "being" the campaign manager for Teddy Roosevelt. The user can plan the travel schedule for the candidate, what people he should meet with, and what issues he should speak out on in which cities. During the simulation, the user can call up a map showing the "result" of opinion polls for each state as shown in Figure 12.1.

The simulation is hooked into the hypertext system in such a way that the user can jump from the simulated information about a state to the actual historical information about a state (as shown in Figure 12.2) to understand why the voters in that state have reacted as they have to the candidate's speeches.

There are also hypertext links from the meetings with various possible supporters and famous people in the simulation to the hypertext's information about these people and from the issues in the simulation to the discussion about these issues in the real election.

Medium Term Future: Five to Ten Years

Towards the end of the nineties we should expect to see widespread publishing of hypertext material. It is also likely that the various forms of video, which are currently quite expensive, will be part of the regular personal computers people have in their homes and offices. So we should expect to see true hypermedia documents for widespread distribution.

Within this timeframe there is also some hope for a solution to the practical problems of data compatibility between systems. Currently it is impossible for a user of, say, an IBM PS/2 to read a hypertext that has been written on, say, a Unix Sun in KMS. In the world of traditional, linear text, the data compatibility problem has been more or less solved some time ago, with the possibility to transfer word processor and spreadsheet documents between IBMs and Macs being just one of the more spectacular success stories.

Current work on the "hypertext abstract machine" (HAM)[4] or similar ideas for interchange formats will almost certainly succeed to the extent that it will be possible to consider publishing the same hypertext on several different platforms. This change will increase the size of the market even more and will therefore add to the trend toward focusing on content. Of course there will still be many hypertexts that will need to take advantage of the special features available on some specific platform like the Macintosh, and these hypertexts will then not be universally available.

The availability of hypertext documents on several platforms is not just a commercial question of the size of the market for the seller. It is also a social issue for the readers of hypertext. Just imagine how you would feel as a reader of traditional printed books if there were some mechanism which restricted you to reading books printed in a specific typeface like Helvetica. But this is exactly the current situation with hypertext: If you own Hyperties, then you can read hypertext documents written in Hyperties but not those written in KMS, HyperCard, Guide, Intermedia, NoteCards, ...

An interchange format will partly resolve this problem. But the problem will be solved only *partly* because of the special nature of hypertext, which involves dynamic links to other documents. It is not even remotely likely that we will see Ted Nelson's original Xanadu vision of having all the world's literature online in a single unified system fulfilled in the medium term future. Therefore hypertext documents will get into trouble as soon as they start linking to outside

---

[4] See Chapter 6.

documents: Some readers will have them, and others will not. It is likely that most hypertexts in the medium term future will remain as isolated islands of information without a high degree of connectedness to other documents. This has been called the *docuislands* scenario.

Several of the current practical problems with hypertext documents should be expected to be solved in the medium term future. For example, there is currently no standard way to refer to a hypertext document the way there is with traditional books, which have a standard ISBN numbering system and recognized publishers with established connections to bookshops. If you want a book, you go to the bookshop and buy it. And if they don't have it, they can get it for you.

Hypertexts are published by a strange assortment of companies to the extent that they are published at all. Many a good hypertext is available only from the individual or university who produced it. And the sales channels for hypertexts are either nonexistent or a mixture of mail order and computer shops, most of which do not carry hypertext.

In a similar way, regular libraries almost never include hypertexts in their collections and wouldn't know how to deal with electronic documents anyway. There are a few online services that store a small number of electronic documents, but since there is no systematic way to determine where a given document is stored and since most hypertext documents are not available online anyway, these services cannot substitute for traditional libraries.

It is very likely, however, that the medium term future will see established publishers and sales channels for hypertext documents. Whether they will be the same as the current system for printed books remains to be seen and would depend on the level of conservatism in the management of publishers and major booksellers. Libraries will certainly have to handle electronic documents, and many of the better and larger libraries are already now starting to invite hypertext specialists to consult on ways to deal with these issues.

Long Term Future: Ten to Twenty Years

What will happen in the *really* long term future, more than twenty years from now? That is for the science fiction authors to tell, and I recommend that you look at the references listed under "Far Out Stuff" at the end of the bibliography in Appendix B.

In the computer business, ten to twenty years counts as long term future indeed, so I will restrict myself to that horizon in the following comments.

Some people like Ted Nelson expect to see the appearance of the global hypertext (e.g. Xanadu) as what has been called the *docuverse* (universe of documents). I don't really expect this to happen completely, but we will very likely see the emergence of very large hypertexts and shared information spaces at universities and certain larger companies.

Already we are seeing small shared information spaces in teaching applications of Intermedia, but they are restricted to the students taking a single class. In the future we might expect students at large numbers of universities to be connected together. Another example of a shared information space is a project to connect case workers at branch offices of a certain large organization with specialists at the main office. The staff at the branch office does not follow the detailed legal developments in the domain that is to be supported by the system since they also have other responsibilities. Therefore the specialists would maintain a hypertext structure of laws, court decisions, commentaries, etc., which would be made available to the case workers at the branches. Also, these local people would describe any cases falling within this domain in the system itself with pointers to the relevant hypertext nodes. In this way they would in turn help the specialists build an understanding of practice and they would also be able to get more pointed help from the specialists regarding, for instance any misapplication of legal theory.

So given these examples which are already near implementation, I would certainly expect to see the growth of shared information spaces in future hypertext systems. There are several social problems inherent in such shared spaces, however. If thousands or even millions of people add information to a hypertext, then it is likely that some of the links will be "perverted" and not be useful for other readers. As a simple example, think of somebody who has inserted a link from every occurrence of the term "Federal Reserve Bank" to a picture of Uncle Scrooge's money bin. You may think that it is funny to see that cartoon come up the first time you click on the Bank's name, but pretty soon you would be discouraged from the free browsing that is the heartblood of hypertext because the frequency of actually getting to some useful information would be too low due to the many spurious links.

These perverted links might have been inserted simply as jokes or by actual vandals. In any case, the "structure" of the resulting hypertext would end up being what Jef Raskin has compared to New York City subway cars painted over by graffiti in multiple uncoordinated layers.

Even without malicious tampering with the hypertext, just the fact that so many people add to it will cause it to overflow with junk information. Of course the problem is that something I consider to be junk may be considered to be art or a profound commentary by you, so it might not be possible to delete just the "junk."

A likely development to reduce these problems will be the establishment of hypertext "journals" consisting of "official" nodes and links that have been recommended by some trusted set of editors. This approach is of course exactly the way paper publishing has always been structured.

An example of such a development can be seen at Carnegie Mellon University where they have a very lively flow of electronic information on their Andrew electronic message system. Most people don't have the time to read all the messages and instead subscribe to electronic magazines [Borenstein and Thyberg 1988], which are put out by human editors who read through the mass of messages to find those of interest for whatever is the topic of their magazine.

It would also be possible to utilize the hypertext mechanism itself to build up records of reader "votes" on the relevance of the individual hypertext nodes and links. Every time users followed a hypertext link, they would indicate whether it lead them somewhere relevant in relation to their point of departure. The averages of these votes could then be used as a filter by future readers to determine whether it would be worthwhile to follow the link.

Another potential social problem is the long term effects of nonsequentiality. Large parts of our culture have the built-in assumption that people read things in a linear order and that it makes sense to ask people to read "from page 100 to 150." For example, that is how one gives reading assignments to students. With a hypertext-based syllabus students may show up at exam time and complain about one of the questions because they never found any information about it in the assigned reading. The professor may claim that there was a hypertext link to the information in question, but the students may be justified in their counter-claim that the link was almost invisible and not likely to be found by a person who was not already an expert in the subject matter.

The reverse problem would occur when the professor was grading the students' essays, which would of course be turned in in hypertext form. What happens if the professor misses the single hypertext link leading to the part of the paper with all the goodies and then fails the student? Actually the solution to this problem would be to consider hypertext design part of the skills being tested in the assignment. If students cannot build information structures that clearly put forward their position, then they *deserve* to fail even though the information may be in there in some obscure way.

A further problem in the learning process is that novices do not know in which order they need to read the material or how much they should read. They don't know what they don't know. Therefore learners might be sidetracked into some obscure corner of the information space instead of covering the important basic information. To avoid this problem, it might be necessary to include an AI monitoring system that could nudge the student in the right direction at times.

There is also the potential problem that the non-linear structure of hypertext as being split into multitudes of small distinct nodes could have the long term effect of giving people a fragmented world view. We simply do not know about this one, and we probably will not know until it is too late if there is such an effect from, say, twenty years of reading hypertext. On the other hand it could just as well be true that the cross-linking inherent in hypertext encourages people to see the connections among different aspects of the world so that they will get *less* fragmented knowledge. Current experience with the use of Intermedia to teach English literature at Brown University [Landow 1989b] did indicate that students were several times as active in class after the introduction of hypertext. They were able to discover new connections and raise new questions.

A Summary: Hypertext versus the Competition

As can be seen from the discussion of the empirical usability research in Chapter 9, there is no clear evidence for whether hypertext is in fact superior to paper. For some applications hypertext tested better, but for other applications paper tested better than the current

	Compared with paper	**Compared with traditional computer systems**
Advantages of Hypertext	Can show moving images, animations, film	Data structures have user-oriented semantics
	Easier to update—can permit automatic downloading of changes	A single framework to handle unstructured data (free text), semi-structured data (semantic nets etc.), and structured data (tables etc.)
	May be shipped over networks	
	Making single copies is easy	
	Takes up less physical storage space	
	Can be shared by several people	Does not require "programming" skills to be able to construct complex structures
	User-oriented reading	
	Potentially: The whole world's literature a click away	
Disadvantages of Hypertext	30% slower reading speed on current displays	Possible spaghetti structure
	Lower resolution graphics	
	Not portable	No central definition of the structure of the data, and therefore no easy way to specify general actions or computations on the data
	Overhead in having to learn system and setting up computer	
	No user interface standard	
	No standard for data transfer	
	No regular publishing channels, bookshops, libraries, ISBN, etc.	
	No "romance"—first editions, leather binding, etc.	
	Computer text "homogenized"	

Table 12.1. *Summary of the advantages and disadvantages of hypertext compared with the competition.*

generation of hypertext. It seems clear that hypertext is indeed superior in some cases even now. But for many other applications we will have to wait for better technology and better user interface designs to get any hope of replacing paper.

Furthermore, we have almost no experience with really big hypertexts. Almost all the hypertexts that have been tested in formal usability experiments have been very small and have contained only about a hundred nodes or less. Only a few larger hypertexts have been constructed, such as *The Electronic Whole Earth Catalog* with its approximately ten thousand nodes (see Chapter 4), and even they can only be considered as medium-large.

A really large hypertext would contain at least a hundred thousand nodes, and we should expect to see some hypertexts with millions of nodes in the future. It may well be that many of the major advantages of hypertext will not become apparent until we have such great hypertexts integrating major fields of human knowledge. But we are guaranteed to discover new usability and implementation problems as we move to such huge information structures.

Table 12.1 gives a summary of the advantages and disadvantages of hypertext. Obviously hypertext has enough advantages to ensure it a bright future if we can design sufficiently usable interfaces to at least partly overcome those disadvantages that have the largest negative impact on our users. But just as obviously, hypertext is not the single answer to all our problems.

Appendix A. Some Hypertext Products and Vendors

Disclaimer: The listing of a product does not imply any kind of endorsement and the non-listing of a product does not imply that it is bad. The names of products and vendors and the addresses and telephone numbers are believed to be correct, but no guarantee of correctness can be given since this kind of information changes rapidly and is not always widely announced.

Hypertext Systems

Guide (Mac and PC versions) *and* **IDEX**
Office Workstations Limited
Rosebank House
144 Broughton Road
Edinburgh EH7 4LE
United Kingdom
Tel. +44-31-557-5720, Fax +44-31-557-5721
or
OWL International
14218 Northeast 21st St.
Bellevue, WA 98007
USA
Tel. +1-800-344-9737 or Tel. +1-206-747-3203, Fax +1-206-641-9367

Guide research version for Unix workstations
Judith Farmer
The Computing Laboratory
The University of Kent at Canterbury
Kent CT2 7NF
United Kingdom
electronic mail to: Mark Wheadon, mcw@ukc.ac.uk

HyperCard
Apple Computer
Sold through authorized Apple dealers and many other outlets.

Hypergate
Eastgate Systems
P.O. Box 1307
Cambridge, MA 02238
USA
Tel. +1-617-924-9044

Hyperties
Cognetics Corporation
55 Princeton-Hightstown Road
Princeton Jct., NJ 08550
USA
Tel. +1-609-799-5505, Fax +1-609-799-8555

Intermedia
Apple Programmers and Developers Association, APDA
c/o Apple Computer
20525 Mariani Avenue, MS 33G
Cupertino, CA 95014-6299
USA
Tel. +1-800-282-2732, Fax +1-408-562-3971
or

IRIS (orders from USA and Canada only)
Brown University
Box 1946
Providence, RI 02912
USA
Tel. +1-401-863-3438 or +1-401-863-2001

KMS
Scribe Systems
Commerce Court, Suite 240
4 Station Square
Pittsburgh, PA 15219
USA
Tel. +1-412-281-5959

NoteCards
Enquire at your local Xerox branch office.

Plus
Spinnaker Software
One Kendall Square
Cambridge, MA 02139
USA
Tel. +1-617-494-1200

SuperCard
Silicon Beach Software
9770 Carroll Center Rd., Suite J.
San Diego, CA 92126
USA
Tel. +1-619-695-6956

Symbolics Document Examiner
Symbolics
8 New England Executive Park East
Burlington, MA 01803
USA

Xanadu
Xanadu Operating Co.
550 California Ave., Suite 101
Palo Alto, CA 94306
USA
Tel. +1-415-856-4112, Fax +1-415-856-2251

Other Products and Contacts

Déjà Vu II
– and other hypermedia-like adventure games
ICOM Simulations, Inc.
648 S. Wheeling Road
Wheeling, IL 60090
USA
Tel. +1-312-520-4440, Fax +1-312-459-3418

DRUID Dynamic Rules for User Interface Design
Jeffrey A. Fox
The MITRE Corporation
Bedford, MA 01730
USA
Tel. +1-617-271-2000, Fax +1-617-271-5255

The Electronic Whole Earth Catalog
Brøderbund Software
17 Paul Drive
San Rafael, CA 94903-2101
USA
Tel. +1-800-521-6263 or +1-415-492-3500

Inigo Gets Out
– and other AmandaStories
ComputerWare
490 California Avenuè
Palo Alto, CA 94306
USA
Tel. +1-415-496-1003, Fax +1-415-855-9440
Applelink: X0996

Lotus Multimedia Demo CD
Lotus
55 Cambridge Parkway
Cambridge, MA 02142
USA

The Manhole
Activision
P.O. Box 3048
Menlo Park, CA 94025-3047
USA
Tel. +1-415-329-7699

Perseus Project
Perseus Project
Department of the Classics
Harvard University
Cambridge, MA 02138
USA

SmartBook
James Hardie Industries Limited
65 York Street
Sydney, NSW 2000
Australia
Tel. +61-2-290 5333, Fax +61-2-290-2215

SoftAd Electronic Advertising
The SoftAd Group
207 Second St.
Sausalito, CA 94965
USA
Tel. +1-415-332-4704, Fax. +1-415-332-1635

Appendix B. Annotated Bibliography

The literature on hypertext and hypermedia is very scattered, reflecting the fact that these concepts have not been subjected to a focused research effort until recently. It is thus almost impossible for any individual to get an overview of the literature, and this bibliography is certainly not intended as a complete listing of every paper ever published on hypertext. It includes the papers and books that I have read and found useful and it also reflects my personal research interest in specifically the user interface aspect of hypertext.

Other Bibliographies

Leggett, J., Kacmar, C.J., and Schnase, J.L. (1989): "Working bibliography of hypertext," *Technical Report* **TAMU 89-005**, February, Hypertext Research Lab, Computer Science Department, Texas A&M University, College Station, TX 77843-3112, USA. The focus in this bibliography is on implementation and system issues in hypertext and not so much on user interface issues. In addition to a large main bibliography, the report contains a shortlist of 22 recommended readings.

A very extensive hypertext bibliography is maintained at the **Institute for Research in Information and Scholarship** (IRIS) at Brown University by Nicole Yankelovich and Paul Kahn.[1] They originally had the goal "to gather references to every published book, article and technical report on the topic of hypertext or hypermedia," but because of the explosion of work in the hypertext field they have now restricted their collection efforts to literature specifically about hypertext. To have

---

[1] An abbreviated version of this bibliography appeared as an appendix to the *Proceedings of the Hypertext Standardization Workshop* (National Institute of Standards and Technology, 16–18 January 1990) which is discussed further below in the section on conferences.

new references added to the data base or to enquire about availability
of the bibliography, please contact:

> Nicole Yankelovich
> IRIS, Box 1946
> Brown University
> Providence, RI 02912
> USA
> email: ny@iris.bitnet or ny@iris.brown.edu

Surveys

For an overview of hypertext, the reader should turn to the
excellent review paper by Jeff Conklin from MCC: "Hypertext: An
introduction and survey," *IEEE Computer* **20**, 9 (September 1987), pp.
17-41. This paper contains examples and comparisons of most
hypertext systems known in 1987. For a briefer and less conceptually
profound survey, see the October 1988 issue of *BYTE* (especially
[Fiderio 1988]) which also includes a list of vendors (with addresses
and telephone numbers) of popular hypertext products.

*"Hypertext Hands-On! An Introduction to a New Way of Organizing
and Accessing Information"* by Ben Shneiderman and Greg Kearsley
(Addison-Wesley 1989) is a short and quickly read book. It is written
like a hypertext with lots of cross-references between sections, and does
indeed include a true hypertext version of the text on two IBM PC
diskettes in Hyperties format.

Conferences

For more in-depth information, the most interesting references on
hypertext at the moment are the proceedings from the ACM series of
hypertext conferences that started with the **Hypertext'87 Workshop**
held at Chapel Hill, NC, 13–15 November 1987. The proceedings from
Hypertext'87 contains all the papers presented at the workshop as well
as position papers by most of the participants. This workshop was the
first formal meeting on hypertext and attracted almost all the people
active in the field.

The proceedings were out of print for a long time but can now be
obtained for $35.00 as ACM Order No. 608892 from:

> ACM Order Department
> P.O. Box 64145

Baltimore, MD 21264

USA

Selected papers from the Hypertext'87 workshop have been published in the July 1988 issue of the *Communications of the ACM*. This issue is also available in various hypertext formats as *Hypertext on Hypertext* in versions for the IBM PC and Macintosh (about $30 each), and Unix workstations such as Sun (rather expensive). It is worth getting hold of several of the versions to compare how different designers convert the same basic information into hypertext.[2] Order information is available from:

Marketing Manager Electronics Products

Association for Computing Machinery

11 W. 42 St.

New York, NY 10036

USA

It may be quite natural to have reports on the Hypertext'87 workshop appear in a hypertext format. I am aware of three such reports: one by Lynda Hardman from the Scottish HCI Centre in Edinburgh written in Guide, one from Mark Bernstein from Eastgate Systems written in their own Hypergate system, and one written by myself[3] in a homemade format (described in [Nielsen 1990b]) running under HyperCard. All three reports run on the Macintosh. Generally, the problem with electronic publications at the moment is that there is no organized way of getting hold of them in the way there is with traditional books, so you may want to read the traditional version of my own report, which is printed in the April 1988 issue of the ACM *SIGCHI Bulletin* (vol. 19, no. 4, pp. 27–35). A good workshop report by Esther Dyson appeared in issue 87-11 of her newsletter *Release 1.0*, dated 25 November 1987.

---

[2] See [Alschuler 1989] for a comparative review of three versions of the ACM *Hypertext on Hypertext*. Some of the versions have been "colorized" (prettied-up after the fact by somebody other than the author) to some extent by adding new information that was not present in the original publication: The HyperCard version for the Macintosh contains scanned photographs of the authors, the HyperTies version for the IBM PC contains added commentary articles, and the KMS workstation version contains new levels of hierarchical subheadings to better structure the text.

[3] The last section of Chapter 2 describes how you may acquire a copy of this hypertext.

The second ACM hypertext conference was **Hypertext'89** (Pittsburgh, PA, 5–8 November 1989). The proceedings from this conference cost $30.00 from the ACM Order Dept. (address above), Order No. 608891.[4] See [Nielsen 1990c] and [Jacques 1990] for conference reports.

The third ACM hypertext conference, **Hypertext'91**, is planned for 15–18 December 1991 in San Antonio, TX. For further information, contact ACM, 11 West 42nd Street, New York, NY 10036, USA.

The Alvey[5] HCI Club sponsored a U.K. workshop on hypertext in Aberdeen 17–18 March 1988. It was not nearly as widely announced as the North Carolina workshop and the proceedings are considerably thinner, but they give a nice overview of the fairly large hypertext activity in the U.K. The proceedings are published as Ray McAleese (ed.): *"Hypertext: Theory into Practice,"* Ablex, 1989.

The second U.K. conference on hypertext, **Hypertext 2**, was held at the University of York on 29–30 June 1989. The proceedings are published as Ray McAleese and Catherine Green (eds.): *"Hypertext: State of the Art,"* Ablex, 1990. See [Nielsen 1989d] for a conference report.

This conference came close to being a true European conference but the first "official" European hypertext conference will be **ECHT'90** (European Conference on Hypertext) in Paris, France, November 28–30, 1990.[6] The ECHT proceedings are published by Cambridge University Press in the U.K. Because of ECHT's role as the major European hypertext conference, Hypertext'3 (Enschede, The Netherlands, 10–12 April 1991) is organized as a special interest workshop on educational use of hypertext.

Proceedings from the annual Microsoft **CD-ROM conference** are published by Microsoft Press. They contain a lot of material of

---

[4] A hypertext version of the Hypertext'89 proceedings is currently being produced as a part of the *ACM Hypertext Compendium* edited by Robert Akscyn. The initial version will be produced in KMS by Knowledge Workshop, and a version will later be made available in some hypertext interchange format to enable other hypertext systems to read it. When complete, the *Compendium* will contain interlinked papers on hypertext from several ACM conferences (including Hypertext'87 and Hypertext'89) and journals as well as additional materials like a list of hypertext researchers.

[5] British research program in information technology.

[6] For further information contact the conference secretariat: SCOIR, 2ter rue de Chantilly, F - 75009 Paris, France. Tel. +33-1-428 51790, fax +33-1- 428 05951.

relevance for hypermedia designers. Steve Lambert and Suzanne Ropiequet (eds.): *"CD ROM—The New Papyrus,"* Redmond, WA: Microsoft Press, 1986, is the proceedings of the very first CD-ROM conference and as a special bonus contains a reprint of the famous *"As We May Think"* paper by Vannevar Bush from 1945 (the paper in which he proposed the Memex). Volume Two is somewhat smaller but includes more examples of actual implementations of CD-ROMs: Suzanne Ropiequet (ed.): *"CD ROM Volume Two: Optical Publishing,"* Microsoft Press, 1987. A report on the 1989 Microsoft CD-ROM conference by Larry Press appears in the *Communications of the ACM* **32**, 7 (July 1989), pp. 784–788.

The National Institute of Standards and Technology (NIST) (formerly known as the National Bureau of Standards) sponsors a series of **Hypertext Standardization Workshops**. The first workshop took place in Gaithersburg, MD, 16–18 January 1990 and is documented in Moline, J., Benigni, D. and Baronas, J. (ed.) (1990): *"Proceedings of the Hypertext Standardization Workshop January 16–18, 1990,"* National Institute of Standards **Special Publication 500-178**. This book is for sale at

> Superintendent of Documents
> U.S. Government Printing Office
> Washington, DC 20402
> USA
> Tel. +1-202-783-3238

and

> National Technical Information Service
> 5285 Port Royal Road
> Springfield, VA 22161
> USA
> Tel. +1-703-487-4600

For information about future standardization workshops contact:

> Hypermedia Standardization Workshops
> attn: Daniel R. Benigni
> National Institute of Standards and Technology
> Hypertext Competence Project
> Technology Bldg. 225, Room A-266
> Gaithersburg, MD 20899
> USA
> email: benigni@ise.ncsl.nist.gov; fax +1-301-590-0932

Other conferences that sometimes have papers on hypertext include:

- IFIP **INTERACT** (Human-Computer Interaction) [September 1984 in London, U.K., September 1987 in Stuttgart, Germany, 1990 in Cambridge, U.K., and 1993 in Amsterdam, the Netherlands]
- ACM **CHI** (Computer-Human Interaction) [every year]
- ACM **SIGIR** (Information Retrieval) [every year]
- ACM **COIS** (Office Information Systems) [every year]
- the British Computer Society **HCI** (Human-Computer Interaction); proceedings published by Cambridge University Press under the title *People and Computers* [every year]
- the ACM conference on **Document Processing Systems** [December 1988 in Santa Fe, NM]
- the **CSCW** (Computer-Supported Cooperative Work) conferences [December 1986 in Austin, TX, September 1988 in Portland, OR, and October 1990 in Los Angeles, CA]
- **International Online Information Meetings** (proceedings published by Learned Information Ltd.)

Journals and Magazines

The only scientific journal specifically dedicated to hypertext is *Hypermedia*, which was started in 1989.

For subscription information (£45/$85 per year) or a free sample copy, contact

> Taylor Graham
> 500 Chesham House
> 150 Regent Street
> London W1R 5FA
> United Kingdom

or

> Taylor Graham
> 12021 Wilshire Boulevard, suite 187
> Los Angeles, CA 90025
> USA

To submit a paper to *Hypermedia*, contact the editor,

Patricia M. Baird
Strathclyde Business School
26 Richmond Street
Glasgow, G1 1XH
United Kingdom
Tel. +44-41-552 4400, ext. 3700
email: ches01@vaxe.strathclyde.ac.uk
In addition to at the conferences listed above, papers on hypertext are also published in several journals in the computer science/user interface/information retrieval area. Wiley is publishing the journal *Electronic Publishing—Origination, Dissemination and Design (EP-ODD)*, which started in 1988 and has hypertext as one of its core subjects. Subscription information (£80/$144 per year) and a free sample copy may be obtained by writing to

Dept. AC
John Wiley & Sons Ltd.
Baffins Lane, Chichester
W. Sussex PO19 1UD
United Kingdom

or

Subscription Dept. C
John Wiley & Sons Inc.
605 Third Avenue
New York, NY 10158
USA

The *Journal of the American Society for Information Science* (JASIS) also covers hypertext to some extent, especially with regard to the search problem and information retrieval issues. The May 1989 issue was a special issue on hypertext.

The special issue of *IEEE Computer* (vol. **21**, no. 1, January 1988) on "Electronic Publishing Technologies" included several papers on hypertext. In addition to the special issue on the Hypertext'87 conference discussed above, the *Communications of the ACM* has also had a special issue on "interactive technology." (July 1989) with emphasis on such hypertext-related issues as interactive video, DVI, and optical disks. The *ACM Transactions on Information Systems* had a special issue on hypertext in January 1989 (vol. **7**, no. 1).

Following the introduction and rapid popularity of Apple's HyperCard, several magazines dedicated to this specific product have appeared. *HyperLink* magazine contains some hypertext information but is focused mostly on tips for programming in the HyperTalk language (the *BASIC* of graphic interaction styles?) and not on the real issues in hypertext design. Subscription information ($25 per year) is available from

> HyperLink Magazine
> P.O. Box 7723
> Eugene, OR 97401
> USA

The various personal computer magazines sometimes have coverage of hypertext and related issues such as multimedia developments. *BYTE* magazine has traditionally had the best general coverage. The June 1982 issue of *BYTE* was an early special issue on interactive videodisks, the November 1986 issue was a special issue on optical storage media, and the October 1988 issue was a special issue on hypertext itself. Magazines such as *PC World, MacWorld* and *MacUser* (U.S. and U.K. editions)[7] cover more platform-oriented developments. *Verbum* magazine (self-styled "journal of personal computer œsthetics") also often has good coverage of hypertext, new computer media, and various forms of interactivity. Subscription information ($24 per year) is available from

> VERBUM Subscriptions
> P.O. Box 15439
> San Diego, CA 92115
> USA

An electronic mailing list, *IF* ("The Journal of Interactive Fiction and Creative Hypertext") is moderated by Gordon Howell of the Scottish HCI Centre. Send contributions to `IF@cs.hw.ac.uk` and requests to be added to the mailing list to `if-request@cs.hw.ac.uk`.

No special professional society exists for hypertext researchers and designers. The Boston Computer Society, however, has a special interest group on hypermedia and optical disk publishing (CD-ROMs etc.), which publishes the *New Media News* newsletter. This group and newsletter are recommended even to people who for geographical

---

[7] Because hypertext and multimedia on personal computers has been most highly developed on the Macintosh, the Macintosh-specific magazines are a good place to look for coverage of new commercial hardware and software.

reasons may not participate in many of the actual meetings. Membership information ($40 per year) is available from

> Boston Computer Society
> One Center Plaza
> Boston, MA 02108
> USA

Videotapes

Since hypertext systems are dynamic by nature, they can often be explained better on a videotape than in a printed article. A highly recommended tape is the ACM's *Interactive Digital Video*, which costs $50 for members and $75 for nonmembers. This tape covers Palenque, the Carnegie Mellon University intelligent meeting simulation, the Intel DVI (Digital Video Interactive) technology, a system from the Getty Museum for access to medieval manuscripts, VideoWindows, samples from the MIT Media Lab (including the *Aspen Movie Map*), and systems from several other companies and universities. Ordering information (order no. 217890 for VHS and 217891 for U-Matic) is available from

> ACM Press Database and Electronic Product Series
> Association for Computing Machinery
> 11 West 42nd Street
> New York, NY 10036
> USA

ACM also has a continuing series of videotapes called the *SIGGRAPH Video Review*, which as the name implies is mostly focused on traditional rendering work in computer graphics and computer animation. But some of the videos in this series are hypermedia-related, including especially issues 13 (the *Movie Manual*), 19 (the Symbolics Document Examiner), 48 (the MIT *Illustrated Neuroanatomy Glossary* and other multimedia applications), and 58 (the Apple MacWorld tradeshow information kiosk). The SIGGRAPH Video Review is available from

SVR Order Department
c/o First Priority
PO Box 576
Itasca, IL 60143-0576
USA
Tel. (24 hr.) +1-800-523-5503 or +1-708-250-0807
Fax +1-708-250-0038

Apple has produced some nice videotapes showing ideas for future hypertext systems. They are discussed further in the section below on "Far Out Stuff."

Classics

Bush, V. (1945): "As we may think," *Atlantic Monthly,* July, pp. 101–108. This was the original paper in which Vannevar Bush proposed his "Memex" device, which is now regarded as the first hypertext system (even though it was never implemented). The paper is reprinted both in the proceedings from the first Microsoft CD-ROM conference (as mentioned in section 3) and in A. Goldberg (ed.) (1988): *A History of Personal Workstations,* Addison-Wesley. It also exists in a hypertext form on a Guide demo disk called "The Guide to Hypertext" available from OWL. Nyce and Kahn [1989] discuss Bush's early essays in which he developed the Memex idea and reprint two illustrations showing how the Memex would have looked had it been built.

Engelbart, D.C. and English, W.K. (1968): "A research center for augmenting human intellect," *AFIPS Conference Proceedings* 33, 1. Engelbart was an early pioneer in actually implementing the hypertext ideas.

Kay, A. and Goldberg, A. (1977): "Personal dynamic media," *IEEE Computer* 10, 3 (March), pp. 31–41. A very influential early paper on multimedia personal computing. Reprinted in A. Goldberg (ed.): *A History of Personal Workstations,* Addison-Wesley 1988.

Lippman, A. (1980): "Movie-Maps: An application of the optical videodisk to computer graphics," *Computer Graphics* 14, 3, pp. 32–42. Paper on the *Aspen* system, which was very likely the first hypermedia system.

Nelson, T. (1974): "*Computer Lib/Dream Machines,*" first edition self-published by Nelson in 1974, revised edition published by Microsoft Press in 1987. The part called "Computer Lib" was probably the first book published on the subject of personal computing. The other half of the book, "Dream Machines," is to a great extent about hypertext.

Nelson, T.: *"Literary Machines,"* Mindful Press, 3020 Bridgeway #295, Sausalito, CA 94965, USA ($25 postpaid in the US, $30 rest of world). An abridged version of *Literary Machines* in hypertext form (on a demo disk for the Guide system) was issued by OWL International, Inc., in 1987. This book has been published in several versions, starting in 1981. It describes Nelson's Xanadu system and many of his other original and pioneering ideas in the hypertext area.

Biographies of several of the hypertext pioneers appear in the following popular book: Rheingold, H. (1985): *"Tools for Thought: The People and Ideas behind the Next Computer Revolution,"* Simon & Schuster, New York.

Alphabetical Listing of Papers and Books

Akscyn, R., and Halasz, F. (eds.) (1991): *"Topics on Hypertext,"* Addison-Wesley.
> Revised versions of selected papers from the ACM Hypertext'89 conference as well as supplementary material such as a survey of existing research and commercial hypertext systems.

Akscyn, R., McCracken, D., and Yoder, E. (1988): "KMS: A distributed hypermedia system for managing knowledge in organizations," *Communications of the ACM* **31**, 7 (July), pp. 820–835.
> KMS is a commercial hypertext system for Unix workstations (e.g. Suns) that was designed as a follow-up to ZOG [Robertson et al. 1981]. Its nodes are called workspaces and take up exactly half a screen or a full screen, and since links point to an entire workspace, the system is highly frame-based.

Akscyn, R., Yoder, E., and McCracken, D. (1988): "The data model is the heart of interface design," *Proc. ACM CHI'88* (Washington, DC, 15–19 May), pp. 115–120.
> A discussion of how the choice of fixed-size frames as the basic data/node structure influenced the design of the KMS system.

Alschuler, L. (1989): "Hand-crafted hypertext: Lessons from the ACM experiment," in Barrett, E. (ed.): *The Society of Text*, MIT Press, Cambridge, MA, pp. 343–361.
> A comparative review of three versions of the same underlying text (the *Communications of the ACM* special issue on hypertext) in HyperCard, Hyperties, and KMS. The review is of a fairly non-conceptual nature, mainly listing various usability problems and inconsistencies without analyzing why they occur. Main conclusions are that there are vast differences in the way the same information can be structured and that there are difficulties in converting linear material to hypertext form.

Ambron, S., and Hooper, K. (eds.) (1988): *"Interactive Multimedia: Visions of Multimedia for Developers, Educators, & Information Providers,"* Microsoft Press.

Very nice book containing the proceedings of a conference on *Multimedia in Education* sponsored by Apple. Most of the systems described run on Apple computers (mostly the Macintosh). A good feature of the book is that many of the papers are highly illustrated, almost to the extent of storyboarding interactions with the systems described (the second best thing to actually trying them out).

Andersen, M.H., Nielsen, J., and Rasmussen, H. (1989): "A similarity-based hypertext browser for reading the Unix network news," *Hypermedia* **1**, 3, pp. 255–265.

The HyperNews system for providing hypertext access to a world-wide bulletin board system in form of the Unix netnews.

Apple Computer (1989): *"HyperCard Stack Design Guidelines,"* Addison-Wesley.

Recommendations for the usability engineering process to be followed in the design of HyperCard stacks. Contains a summary of the general Apple human interface guidelines and specific advice for the use of graphics, buttons, and sound in HyperCard interfaces and for the navigational structure of stacks. Also includes a good annotated bibliography of graphic design, animation, and related issues.

Baird, P. (1990): "Hypertext—towards the single intellectual market," in Nielsen, J. (ed.): *Designing User Interfaces for International Use*, Elsevier Science Publishers, Amsterdam, pp. 111–121.

On the problems associated with producing hypertexts for international use.

Baird, P., Mac Morrow, N., and Hardman, L. (1988): "Cognitive aspects of constructing non-linear documents: HyperCard and Glasgow Online," *Proc. Online Information 88* (London, U.K., 6–8 December), pp. 207–218.

An introduction to the *Glasgow Online* tourist information project and some observations from a field study of the system. Older people tended to look at the system without using it and when using it tended to proceed cautiously through the hyperspace, reading everything on the screen before making a choice. Children, on the other hand, took a much less focused approach and sometimes seemed to click on a random basis.

Baird, P., and Percival, M. (1989): "Glasgow Online: Database development using Apple's HyperCard," in McAleese, R. (ed.): *Hypertext: Theory into Practice*, Ablex, pp. 75–92.

An introduction to the *Glasgow Online* tourist information system and its development process.

Barrett, E. (ed.) (1988): *"Text, Context, and Hypertext: Writing with and for the Computer,"* The MIT Press, Cambridge, MA.

An edited collection of papers from a conference on *Writing for the Computer Industry* at MIT in 1987. Readers should be warned that this book is mostly about general skills for technical writers and has only a few papers about hypertext.

Barrett, E. (ed.) (1989): *"The Society of Text: Hypertext, Hypermedia, and the Social Construction of Information,"* The MIT Press, Cambridge, MA.
More about hypertext than Barrett's 1988 book, this book contains several interesting chapters on various aspects of hypertext as well as some general chapters on online help and technical writing. A few of the chapters are reprints from earlier journal papers.

Barron, D.W. (1989): "Why use SGML?," *Electronic Publishing— Origination, Dissemination and Design* **2**, 1 (April), pp. 3–24.
A nice introduction to the SGML Standard Generalized Markup Language, which is used by some systems for automatic conversion of flat text files to hypertext. This paper does not address hypertext issues in the use of markup languages, however.

Bärtschi, M. (1985): "An overview of information retrieval subjects," *IEEE Computer* **18**, 5 (May), pp. 67–84.
A short tutorial paper introducing the most important information retrieval concepts and models (vector spaces, fuzzy sets, and probabilistic models).

Bechtel, B. (1990): "Inside Macintosh as hypertext," *Proc. ECHT'90 European Conf. Hypertext* (Paris, France, 28–30 November), Cambridge University Press.
The five volumes of the *Inside Macintosh* manual for Macintosh programmers were converted to a hypertext form called *SpInside Macintosh* and were further interlinked with a hypertext version of 265 Apple Technical Notes and a tutorial list of 207 questions (with answers) often asked of Apple's technical support staff. The author claims that his experience from this project confirms Glushko's [1989b] recommendation for the design of multi-document hypertexts, even though the Apple team were not aware of Glushko's paper when they created their product.

Beeman, W.O., Anderson, K.T., Bader, G., Larkin, J., McClard, A.P., McQuillan, P., and Shields, M. (1987): "Hypertext and pluralism: From lineal to non-lineal thinking," *Proc. ACM Hypertext'87 Conf.* (Chapel Hill, NC, 13–15 November), pp. 67–88.
Report on the learning effects from two field studies of educational use of Intermedia. Students were much more active in the English literature class after the introduction of the hypertext system (but note the possibility that this could partly be due to the Hawthorne effect of people working better when they know they are being studied) and were better able to connect concepts in a non-linear way.

Begeman, M.L., and Conklin, J (1988): "The right tool for the job," *BYTE* **13**, 10 (October), pp. 255–266.
The gIBIS hypertext system (graphical Issue-Based Information System). This article is practically a subset (edited for slightly higher readability) of the more complete paper [Conklin and Begeman 1988].

Bernstein, M. (1988): "The bookmark and the compass: Orientation tools for hypertext users," *ACM SIGOIS Bulletin* **9**, 4 (October), pp. 34–45.

Rationale for the design of the Hypergate user interface, including "breadcrumbs" marking the user's footprints, user-defined bookmarks, and author-defined thumb tabs (permanently visible links to landmark nodes). The author advocates use of hand-drawn overview maps instead of automatically generated maps.

Bernstein, M. (1990): "An apprentice that discovers hypertext links," *Proc. ECHT'90 European Conf. Hypertext* (Paris, France, 28–30 November), Cambridge University Press.
A semi-intelligent program that suggests likely hypertext links on the basis of similarity matches between the contents of nodes. The author has the ultimate responsibility for deciding which of the apprentice's suggestions to follow. The apprentice provides the author with easy access to a list of possible nodes to link to the current node and may point out potential links that would otherwise have been overlooked.

Bigelow, J. (1988): "Hypertext and CASE," *IEEE Software* 5, 2 (March), pp. 23–27.
On the use of the Tektronix Neptune system for Computer Aided Software Engineering (CASE): The system interconnects specifications, design documents, user and program documentation, and the source code.

Bigelow, J., and Riley, V. (1987): "Manipulating source code in DynamicDesign," *Proc. ACM Hypertext'87 Conf.* (Chapel Hill, NC, 13–15 November), pp. 397–408.
The DynamicDesign system and its associated GraphBuild utility can automatically construct a hypertext structure from a C source code file. It then allows the software developer to click on a variable, for instance, and see its definition or to utilize bidirectional links in the reverse direction from a variable to the locations where it is used.

Bolt, R.A. (1984): *"The Human Interface: Where People and Computers Meet,"* Lifetime Learning Publications, Belmont, CA. (The book is now distributed by Van Nostrand Reinhold).
A brief but good book on the work done at the MIT Architecture Machine Group (now part of the Media Lab). Much of this work can be classified as hypermedia.

Bolter, J.D., and Joyce, M. (1987): "Hypertext and creative writing," *Proc. ACM Hypertext'87 Conf.* (Chapel Hill, NC, 13–15 November), pp. 41–50.
On interactive fiction and the Storyspace system.

Borenstein, N.S., and Thyberg, C.A. (1988): "Cooperative work in the Andrew message system," *Proc. 2nd Conf. Computer-Supported Cooperative Work* (Portland, OR, 26–28 September), pp. 306–323.
A system for electronic mail and bulletin boards with several advanced features: Users can put together edited *magazines* of selected articles from other bulletin boards, users can vote on messages, and the system can automatically filter incoming messages for them.

Borgman, C.L. (1987): "The study of user behavior on information retrieval systems," *ACM SIGCUE Outlook* 19, 2–3 (Spring/Summer), pp. 35–48.

A survey of research on user difficulties in the use of traditional bibliographic databases.

Brand, S. (1987): *"The Media Lab: Inventing the Future at MIT,"* Viking Penguin.
A perhaps somewhat too popularistic survey of the work at the MIT Media Lab and its predecessor, the Architecture Machine Group, including interviews with several of the main researchers.

Brown, H. (ed.) (1990): *"HyperMEDIA / HyperTEXT and Object Oriented Databases,"* Unicom Seminars Ltd., Brunel Science Park, Uxbridge, U.K.
The proceedings from a seminar with speakers mostly from the U.K. but also some from other countries.

Brown, P.J. (1987): *"Turning ideas into products: The Guide system,"* *Proc. ACM Hypertext'87 Conf.* (Chapel Hill, NC, 13–15 November), pp. 33–40.
The basic principles behind the design of Guide and their relation to previous research ideas. Brown mentions that he did not have a goto link in his original design even though it has been introduced in the commercial version of Guide.

Brown, P.J. (1988): *"Linking and searching within hypertext,"* *Electronic Publishing—Origination, Dissemination and Design* 1, 1 (April), pp. 45–53.
A discussion of how a "find" command (viewed as an unstructured linking mechanism) can be integrated into a hypertext system.

Brown, P.J. (1989a): *"Do we need maps to navigate round hypertext documents?,"* *Electronic Publishing—Origination, Dissemination and Design* 2, 2 (July), pp. 91–100.
Peter Brown restates his argument in favor of hierarchically organized hypertexts with a minimum of "goto-like" cross-references.

Brown, P.J. (1989b): *"Hypertext: Dreams and reality,"* *Proc. Hypermedia / Hypertext and Object Oriented Databases Seminar* (Brunel University, London, 5–7 December). Reprinted in [Brown, H. 1990].
A description of the use of a specially tailored version of Unix Guide at ICL for the diagnosis of hardware problems reported by customer (so-called "laundering"). The paper also discusses seven issues facing hypertext: integration, authorship, testing, large documents, getting lost (including avoiding gotos), abstractions, and the cost of projects.

Brown, P.J., and Russell, M.T. (1988): *"Converting help systems to hypertext,"* *Software—Practice and Experience* 18, 2 (February 1988), pp. 163–165.
The Unix man (manual) help information for the fs program was converted to a Guide hypertext by adding button tags to the nroff file. The same underlying help text could then be accessed both as a hypertext (through Guide) and as a traditionally formatted linear text (through man and nroff—because nroff just throws away those tags that it does not recognize).

Brøndmo, H.P., and Davenport, G. (1990): *"Creating and viewing the Elastic Charles—a hypermedia journal,"* in McAleese, R., and Green, C. (eds.) *Hypertext: State of the Art,* Ablex, pp. 43–51.

The *Elastic Charles* is a hyperfilm combination of video recordings of the River Charles made by 15 people. Links between film clips are anchored on the screen by so-called *micons*, which are miniature moving clips of the destination film.

Bruillard, E., and Weidenfeld, G. (1990): "Some examples of hypertext's applications," in Jonassen, D.H., and Mandl, H. (eds.): *"Designing Hypertext/Hypermedia for Learning,"* Springer-Verlag, Heidelberg, Germany, chapter 21.

Examples of several French hypertext systems, including the LYRE system for teaching poetry (from the authors' company, SOFTIA).

Bush, V.: "Memex revisited," in Bush, V. (ed.) (1967): *Science is not Enough,* William Morrow and Co.

Campagnoni, F.R., and Ehrlich, K. (1989): "Information Retrieval using a hypertext-based help system," *ACM Trans. Information Systems* **7**, 3 (July), pp. 271–291. Also in *Proc. ACM SIGIR'89* (Cambridge, MA, 25–28 June 1989), pp. 212–220.

About the Sun Help Viewer online help system for the Sun386i and the usability testing of this hypertext system. Most test subjects were found to prefer a browsing search strategy over using the index. The subjects were given a standard test of spatial visualization ability, which showed that users with higher visualization scores needed less time to locate the answers to the questions, mostly because they had less need to return to the top level table of contents. This result indicates that users with good visualization abilities were better able to construct a conceptual model of the structure of the information space.

Campbell, B., and Goodman, J.M. (1988): "HAM: A general purpose hypertext abstract machine," *Communications of the ACM* **31**, 7 (July), pp. 856–861.

Discussion of a generalized storage medium for hypertext networks, which are seen as collections of contexts, nodes, links, and attributes. The paper shows how HAM can be used to describe the underlying data structures for many different hypertext systems, including Guide buttons, Intermedia webs, and NoteCards FileBoxes.

Canter, D., Rivers, R., and Storrs, G. (1985): "Characterizing user navigation through complex data structures," *Behaviour and Information Technology* **4**, 2 (April–June), pp. 93–102.

The authors define four graph theory-like classes of user navigation behavior: *paths* (a route that does not cross any node twice), *rings* (a route that returns to the node where it starts, this node being called the base node of the ring), *loops* (a ring that does not contain any ring as part of itself, i.e., it was a path until the user returned to the base node), and *spikes* (a route where the return journey retraces [i.e. backtracks] exactly the route taken on the outward journey). Based on these elementary structures, the authors characterize five different user navigation strategies: *scanning* (mixture of deep spikes and short loops), *browsing* (many large loops and a few large rings), *searching* (ever-increasing spikes with a few loops), *exploring* (many different paths), and *wandering* (many medium-sized rings). The authors compared users navigating a data set by hypertext and by direct command selection of desired nodes (a combination of `goto` and information retrieval) and found that the hypertext users had many more rings and spikes than the direct access users but had about the same number of paths and loops. The authors also discuss a comparison between their studies of real users and a so-called "random user" in the form of a computer simulation that follows links randomly with equal probability for activating any anchor at a given node.

Canter, D., Powell, J., Wishart, J., and Roderick, C. (1986): "User navigation in complex database systems," *Behaviour and Information Technology* **5**, 3 (July–September), pp. 249–257.
Three different access methods were tested for a videotex-like system: direct addressing (command control), linked addressing (hypertext-like links between pages with similar information), and natural language search. Novice users performed best with linked addressing (experts were not tested).

Caplinger, M. (1986): "Graphical database browsing," *Proc. 3rd ACM SIGOIS Conf. Office Information Systems* (Providence, RI, 6–8 October), pp. 113–121.
A graphic browser to a 45,000 item information space. A 3D flyby browser was implemented but did not seem useful without hardware support for depth cues.

Carey, T.T., Hunt, W.T., and Lopez-Suarez, A. (1990): "Roles for tables of contents as hypertext overviews," *Proc. INTERACT'90 Third IFIP Conf. Human–Computer Interaction* (Cambridge, U.K., 27–31 August), pp. 581-586.

Catano, J.V. (1979): "Poetry and computers: Experimenting with the communal text," *Computers and the Humanities* **13** , pp. 269–275.
An early experiment in online poetry used with shared hypertextual annotations by students taking a poetry class.

Catlin, T.J.O., and Smith, K.E. (1988): "Anchors for shifting tides: Designing a 'seaworthy' hypermedia system," *Proc. Online Information 88* (London, U.K., 6–8 December), pp. 15–25.
Intermedia [Yankelovich et al. 1988] was extended to accommodate two new types of hypermedia: *InterAudio* for access to CD-audio sound bites and *InterBrowse* for access to information retrieved from external (and heterogeneous) databases. These new media involved some problems with respect to the established Intermedia model for hypertext anchors: e.g. how does one select a piece of sound, and how can the computer highlight a selection (one option might be to play it louder than the rest of the sound, but the option chosen was to play only the selection and then provide users with a command to also play the rest of the context of the selection). For this new kind of media, it was necessary to extend the Intermedia paradigm to include *proxies* which graphically represent what would otherwise be non-graphic or conceptual, thereby allowing users to make tangible selections.

Catlin, T., Bush, P., and Yankelovich, N. (1989): "InterNote: Extending a hypermedia framework to support annotative collaboration," *Proc. ACM Hypertext'89 Conf.* (Pittsburgh, PA, 5–8 November), pp. 365–378.
InterNote provides a general facility for reader annotation in Intermedia.

Chen, P. P-S. (1986): "The compact disk ROM: how it works," *IEEE Spectrum* **23**, 4 (April), pp. 44–49.

A popular overview of the technology behind CD-ROMs.

Coffman, D.R. (ed.) (1987): *"The Guide to Hypertext,"* Macintosh diskette, OWL International.
A demo of the Guide system containing interlinked articles on hypertext by several authors.

Collier, G.H. (1987): "Thoth-II: Hypertext with explicit semantics," *Proc. ACM Hypertext'87 Conf.* (Chapel Hill, NC, 13–15 November), pp. 269–289.
A system that has a main mode of browsing a graphic representation of a semantic net. From this graph, the user can select a node and enter a special text-reading mode to see its text in a window.

Conklin, J., and Begeman, M.L. (1988): "gIBIS: A hypertext tool for exploratory policy discussion," *ACM Trans. Office Information Systems* **6**, 4 (October 1988), pp. 303–331. Also in *Proc. 2nd Conf. Computer-Supported Cooperative Work* (Portland, OR, 26–28 September), pp. 140–152.
Describes the gIBIS system (graphical Issue-Based Information System). gIBIS is used in the MCC *Design Journal* project to provide a computerized record of a software design process with special emphasis on capturing the rationale behind the design decisions through hypertext links among issues, positions and arguments. gIBIS is designed for color workstations and uses color to indicate node and link status (for a color screen shot, see [Begeman and Conklin 1988]). Preliminary empirical observations indicated that users had a greater tendency to add supporting comments than to add objecting ones. Some users complained about the danger of premature segmentation of new ideas and would have liked a "proto-node" simply to record ideas before structuring them. The first half of this paper (describing the system itself but not the empirical evidence about its actual use) can also be found in [Begeman and Conklin 1988].

Consens, M.P., and Mendelzon, A.O. (1989): "Expressing structural hypertext queries in GraphLog," *Proc. ACM Hypertext'89 Conf.* (Pittsburgh, PA, 5–8 November), pp. 269–292.
GraphLog is a visual query language for finding hypertext subnets that satisfy specified structural properties.

Cook, P. (1988): "Multimedia technology: An encyclopedia publisher's perspective," in Ambron, S., and Hooper, K. (eds.): *"Interactive Multimedia: Visions of Multimedia for Developers, Educators, & Information Providers,"* Microsoft Press, 1988, pp. 217–240.
A discussion of several prototype ideas for enhancing the electronic version of Grolier's *Academic American Encyclopedia* from its 1986 text-only CD-ROM to a future multimedia system.

Cooke, P., and Williams, I. (1989): "Design issues in large hypertext systems for technical documentation," in McAleese, R. (ed.): *Hypertext: Theory into Practice,* Ablex, pp. 93–104.
On OWL's IDEX system to automatically display large databases of existing text encoded in SGML in a hypertext format. Besides SGML, the product also relies heavily on other standards: SQL for the underlying database, Ethernet for LAN, and the Microsoft Windows and Presentation Manager for the user interface.

Crane, G. (1987): "From the old to the new: Integrating hypertext into traditional scholarship," *Proc. ACM Hypertext'87 Conf.* (Chapel Hill, NC, 13–15 November), pp. 51–55.
Converting classical Greek literature to hypertext in the Perseus Project.

Crane, G. (1988): "Redefining the book: Some preliminary problems," *Academic Computing* (February), pp. 6–11 and 36–41.
About the Perseus Project for hypertext representation of classic Greek literature and history. Also discusses specific problems in the representation of Greek text and online dictionaries. Some of the associated issues are whether the existence of automatic hypertext dictionary lookup will keep students from really learning Greek, and the need for affordable platforms such as HyperCard and the Macintosh to ensure decentralized development: only the researchers actually engaged in various forms of study of ancient history will be able to imagine the tools needed.

Crane, G. (1990): "Standards for a hypermedia database: Diachronic vs. synchronic concerns," *Proc. NIST Hypertext Standardization Workshop* (Gaithersburg, MD, 16-18 January), pp. 71–81.
Synchronic standards allow all hypertext systems at any given time to exchange materials, whereas diachronic standards allow a hypertext document to be equally usable now and with future systems many years from now. Crane views diachronic standards as essential for projects like his own Perseus and finds short-lived systems destructive for disciplines where scholars cannot afford to lavish time on creating documents that will not last at least thirty years.

Davis, H. (1990): "Platform wars and the quest for value in interactive entertainment," *Boston Computer Society New Media News* **4**, 1 (Winter), pp. 22-24.
Trip report from the InterTainment'89 conference (New York, 30 October–1 November 1989).

Delisle, N., and Schwartz, M. (1986): "Neptune: A hypertext system for CAD applications," *Proc. ACM SIGMOD'86* (Washington, DC, 28–30 May), pp. 132–142.
The Tektronix Neptune system for working with program code.

Delisle, N., and Schwartz, M. (1987): "Contexts—A partitioning concept for hypertext," *ACM Trans. Office Information Systems* **5**, 2 (April), pp. 168–186.
Version control in a hypertext system to support collaborative writing of large software systems.

DeRose, S.J. (1989): "Expanding the notion of links," *Proc. ACM Hypertext'89 Conf.* (Pittsburgh, PA, 5–8 November 1989), pp. 249–257.
A taxonomy of twelve kinds of links with examples from the CDWord hypertext version of the Bible.

De Young, L. (1989): "Hypertext challenges in the auditing domain," *Proc. ACM Hypertext'89 Conf.* (Pittsburgh, PA, 5–8 November), pp. 169–180.
Auditing is well suited for hypertext because it basically consists of interrelating documents. The links are so important that auditors who define a link take personal responsibility for it by authenticating it with their initials. The paper

describes a prototype system at Price Waterhouse called EWP (Electronic Working Papers) giving several screen dumps. They estimate that auditors spend 30% of their time preparing, maintaining, and reviewing these working papers in the current paper-based procedures.

De Young, L. (1990): "Linking considered harmful," *Proc. ECHT'90 European Conf. Hypertext* (Paris, France, 28–30 November), Cambridge University Press.

The EWP (Electronic Working Papers) project uses structured hypertext in the form of sets of links, relational links, and finite state sequences.

Dillon, A., McKnight, C., and Richardson, J. (1990): "Navigation in hypertext: A critical review of the concept," *Proc. INTERACT'90 Third IFIP Conf. Human–Computer Interaction* (Cambridge, U.K., 27–31 August), pp. 587-592.

An analysis of hypertext navigation using psychological research results from studies of geographical maps and route finding.

Dillon, A., Richardson, J., and McKnight, C. (1989): "Human factors of journal usage and design of electronic texts," *Interacting with Computers* **1**, 2 (August), 183–189.

A study of how scientists read paper journals and some loose thoughts about the design of hypertext journals. The scientists always started by scanning the table of contents of a new journal issue and they expressed a strong preference for having the table of contents on the cover of the journal so that they did not have to open the journal. In other words, an extremely low overhead is desired for the initial process of scanning to find relevant information.

Dixon, D.F. (1989): "Life before the chips: Simulating Digital Video Interactive technology," *Communications of the ACM* **32**, 7 (July), pp. 824–831.

Describes how DVI was simulated before the actual DVI hardware was designed and produced, giving several examples of applications (e.g. the "Galactic Challenge." game) built to test the ideas and provide requirements for the hardware. Interesting both for the historical record and because of the general principle of simulating interactive systems before they are built.

Dumais, S.T., Furnas, G.W., Landauer, T.K., Deerwester, S., and Harshman, R. (1988): "Using latent semantic indexing to improve access to textual information," *Proc. ACM CHI'88* (Washington, DC, 15–19 May), pp. 281–285.

Latent semantic indexing is a method for organizing text nodes into a semantic structure on the basis of the overlap of the words used in those nodes.

Egan, D.E., Remde, J.R., Landauer, T.K., Lochbaum, C.C., and Gomez, L.M. (1989a): "Acquiring information in books and SuperBooks," *Proc. Annual Meeting American Educational Research Assoc.* (San Francisco, CA, 27–30 March).

This is a more in-depth report of the SuperBook experiments described in [Egan et al. 1989b]. This paper also includes logging data of the usage patterns of the SuperBook readers and videotape data of how the readers of the conventional book used it. A comparison showed that readers used the table of contents (overview) much more in SuperBook than in the printed book and that they read about the same number of sections of the text even though they solved the problems in less time. One reason users performed better with SuperBook was that the typographical display of the information was customized to their current needs. The printed page always looked the same, but the SuperBook display highlighted the terms the user had used in the search, thus drawing attention to paragraphs of special importance for the task at hand.

Egan, D.E., Remde, J.R., Landauer, T.K., Lochbaum, C.C., and Gomez, L.M. (1989b): "Behavioral evaluation and analysis of a hypertext browser," *Proc. ACM CHI'89 Conf. Human Factors in Computing Systems* (Austin, TX, 30 April–4 May), pp. 205–210.
A SuperBook hypertext version of a statistics manual was compared with a 562 page paper version. Subjects with a background in statistics were able to locate information in SuperBook significantly faster than in the paper book (4.3 min. vs. 7.5 min.) when questions were phrased using words that were present in the running text but not in the section headings. For questions using words taken from section headings, paper was slightly (non-significantly) faster. The authors conclude that their system help users dealing with questions that are not anticipated by an author's organization of a document.

Egan, D.E., Remde, J.R., Gomez, L.M., Landauer, T.K., Eberhardt, J., and Lochbaum, C.C. (1989c): "Formative design-evaluation of 'SuperBook'," *ACM Transactions on Information Systems* 7, 1 (January), pp. 30–57.
SuperBook is a hypertext system using rich indexing and fisheye views integrated such that aggregated hit rates for word searches show up in the fisheye view. The paper describes two stages in the iterative design of the system: Two main improvements were to speed up search time by a factor of ten and to change the interface to make the *word lookup* function more attractive to use as the first part of a search. When compared with paper in two experiments, the revised version performed better whereas the original version performed worse.

Egido, C., and Patterson, J. (1988): "Pictures and category labels as navigational aids for catalog browsing," *Proc. AC; CHI'88* (Washington, DC, 15–19 May), pp. 127–132.
Pictures *plus* textual labels are better than either alone.

Eisenhart, D.M. (1989): "1-2-3 goes TV: Interactive multimedia at Lotus," Boston Computer Society *BCS Update* (September), pp. 14–17.
An interview with Rob Lippincott who is the director of market development for Lotus's Information Services Group on their current hypertext-like products and future directions. Contains several screen shots from the 1-2-3 Multimedia Release 3.0 Demo.

Embley, D.W., and Nagy, G. (1981): "Behavioral aspects of text editors," *ACM Computing Surveys* 13, 1 (March), pp. 33–70.
Review of much of the early research on the human factors of interactive text.

Engelbart, D. (1988): "The augmented knowledge workshop," in Goldberg, A. (ed.): *A History of Personal Workstations*, Addison-Wesley, pp. 187–236.

Historical review of Engelbart's work at SRI in the period 1963 to 1976, including a discussion of the NLS/Augment system and several photos from the 1968 FJCC real-time demonstration of online structured text.

Evenson, S., Rheinfrank, J., and Wulff, W. (1989): "Towards a design language for representing hypermedia cues," *Proc. ACM Hypertext'89 Conf.* (Pittsburgh, PA, 5–8 November), pp. 83–92.
On the graphic design of hypertexts and the typographical notation needed to indicate anchors and links.

Ewing, J., Mehrabanzad, S., Sheck, S., Ostroff, D., and Shneiderman, B. (1986): "An experimental comparison of a mouse and arrow-jump keys for an interactive encyclopedia," *Intl. J. Man-Machine Studies* **24**, 1 (January), pp. 29–45.
An evaluation of two interaction techniques for Hyperties (then called simply TIES). It turned out that arrow-jump keys were slightly faster for selecting anchors for hypertext jumps (arrow-jump keys are traditional arrow keys that are used to jump the cursor to the next possible anchor instead of just moving the cursor one position).

Fairchild, K. M., and Poltrock, S. (1986): "Soaring through knowledge space: SemNet 2.1" [Videotape]. *Technical Report* **HI-104-86**, Microelectronics and Computer Technology Corporation (MCC), Austin, TX.
Because of the extremely dynamic nature of the three dimensional user interface, the SemNet browser is best understood by watching this videotape before reading the scientific paper [Fairchild et al. 1988].

Fairchild, K.M., Poltrock, S.E., and Furnas, G.W. (1988): "SemNet: Three-dimensional graphic representations of large knowledge bases," in Guindon, R. (ed.): *"Cognitive Science and its Applications for Human-Computer Interaction,"* Lawrence Erlbaum Associates, pp. 201-233.
A graphical interface representing an overview diagram of interlinked pieces of information in three dimensions. The user can move among the nodes using a "helicopter metaphor."

Feiner, S. (1988): "Seeing the forest for the trees: Hierarchical display of hypertext structure," *Proc. ACM Conf. Office Information Systems* (Palo Alto, CA, 23–25 March), pp. 205–212.
A discussion of the use of hierarchical structures in the IGD system (Interactive Graphical Documents). This paper relates IGD somewhat more to the rest of the hypertext tradition than the earlier paper on the same system [Feiner, Nagy, and van Dam 1982].

Feiner, S., Nagy, S., and van Dam, A. (1982): "An experimental system for creating and presenting interactive graphical documents," *ACM Trans. Graphics* **1**, 1 (January), pp. 59–77.
Describes the Electronic Document System, an early hypermedia system. This system has also been known as the Brown Browser and as IGD (Interactive Graphical Documents).

Fiderio, J. (1988): "A grand vision," *BYTE* **13**, 10 (October), pp. 237–244 and p. 268.

Brief popular introduction to the hypertext concept. This issue of *BYTE* has a list of vendors of popular hypertext products (as of medio 1988) on p. 268.

Fischer, G., McCall, R., and Morch, A. (1989a): "Design environments for constructive and argumentative design," *Proc. ACM CHI'89* (Austin, TX, 30 April–4 May), pp. 269–275.
A proposal for a design integrating an AI system that advises on design issues with a hypertext system containing the rationale for the advice given by the AI system. The hypertext system uses an alternative implementation of the IBIS Issue-Based Information System method made famous by the gIBIS system [Conklin and Begeman 1988] to structure the arguments for and against the various design options, and the AI system can then dump the user at the location in this hypertext that corresponds to the user's current undecided design problem.

Fischer, G., McCall, R., and Morch, A. (1989b): "JANUS: Integrating hypertext with a knowledge-based design environment," *Proc. ACM Hypertext'89 Conf.* (Pittsburgh, PA, 5–8 November), pp. 105–117.
A follow-up article to [Fischer et al. 1989a].

Flores, F., Graves, M., Hartfield, B., and Winograd, T. (1988): "Computer systems and the design of organizational interaction," *ACM Trans. Office Information Systems* **6**, 2 (April), pp. 153–172.
On The Coordinator system for electronic mail, which has slightly hypertext-like typed links. The authors discuss how this kind of structured communication can fit with the organization of work and its social environment.

Florin, F. (1988): "Creating interactive video programs with HyperCard," *HyperAge Magazine* (May–June), pp. 38–43.
On the structure of the WorldView prototype electronic atlas and on the practical details of producing interactive videodisks.

Foss, C.L. (1988): "Effective browsing in hypertext systems," *Proc. RIAO'88 Conf. User-Oriented Context-Based Text and Image Handling* (MIT, Cambridge, MA, 21–24 March), pp. 82–98.
A critique of the browsing paradigm, which the author claims leads to two problems: The *embedded digression problem* of multiple sidetracks and redefinitions of current interests, leading users to forget the digressions they wanted to make, and the *art museum phenomenon* where you can spend a whole day in a large art museum and not be able to remember any particular painting in detail. To alleviate these problems, the author has implemented four new kinds of browsing support in NoteCards where she did not believe that the original overview diagram mechanism was sufficient.: graphic history lists, history trees, summary boxes, and summary trees.

Fox, E.A. (1988): "Optical disks and CD-ROM: Publishing and access," in Williams, M.E. (ed.): *Annual Review of Information Science and Technology (ARIST)* **23**, Elsevier Science Publishers, pp. 85–124.
A general survey of CD-ROM: hardware technology, data storage, authoring, and access mechanisms as well as applications. Includes an extensive bibliography. Recommended for getting an overview of the area.

Franklin, C. (1989): "Mapping hypertext structures with ArchiText," *DATABASE The Magazine of Database Reference and Review* **12**, 4 (August), pp. 50–61.
A review of the ArchiText hypertext program from BrainPower, Inc. with an illustrated walkthrough of its use.

Frenkel, K.A. (1989): "The next generation of interactive technologies," *Communications of the ACM* **32**, 7 (July), pp. 872–881.
Survey of the potential for future "intertainment." (interactive entertainment) products and of various current videodisk products such as the Getty Museum disk and the ABC *The '88 Vote*. Also contains a comparison of the competing CD-ROM formats DVI, CD-I, and CD-ROM XA (Extended Architecture) with special emphasis on the last. The reader should note that the comparisons are based on the original specifications for moving video in CD-I and not on the new, considerably improved algorithm, which allows full-quality video and will be used in the final product.

Friedlander, L. (1988): "The Shakespeare project," in Ambron, S., and Hooper, K.: *"Interactive Multimedia: Visions of Multimedia for Developers, Educators, & Information Providers,"* Microsoft Press, pp. 115–141.
A prototype hypertext for teaching drama theory and Shakespeare through the use of linked film clips of real performances and simulations of the students' own design and staging choices.

Frisse, M.E. (1988a): "Searching for information in a hypertext medical handbook," *Communications of the ACM* **31**, 7 (July), pp. 880–886.
On automatically generating a hypertext structure from a popular medical reference book. Also includes discussion of information retrieval techniques that would help physicians find the relevant nodes in the network.

Frisse, M. (1988b): "From text to hypertext," *BYTE* **13**, 10 (October 1988), pp. 247–253.
A discussion of some of the issues involved in transforming existing machine readable text to hypertext form.

Frisse, M.E., and Cousins, S.B. (1989): "Information retrieval from hypertext: Update on the dynamic medical handbook project," *Proc. ACM Hypertext'89 Conf.* (Pittsburgh, PA, 5–8 November), pp. 199–212.
How to use various forms of indexes in combination with belief networks and other information retrieval models for hypertext.

Frye, D., and Carroll, J.M. (eds.) (1990): *"Human Factors in Computer Systems: A SIGCHI Perspective,"* Addison-Wesley.
Reprints of several important papers from the user interface field, including some papers on hypertext user interfaces.

Furnas, G.W. (1986): "Generalized fisheye views," *Proc. ACM CHI'86* (Boston, MA, 13–17 April), pp. 16–23.
Fisheye views show the context immediately surrounding the information of interest in greater detail while information farther away is elided. This idea is similar to the poster from *The New Yorker* showing midtown Manhattan in great

detail while the rest of the U.S. is shown disappearing into the distance with an island marked "Japan" in the background.

Furuta, R., Plaisant, C., and Shneiderman, B. (1989): "A spectrum of automatic hypertext constructions," *Hypermedia* 1, 2, pp. 179–195.
A discussion of four projects on converting existing text to hypertext, including the Hyperties version of the ACM *Hypertext on Hypertext*, a course catalog, and two bibliographic listings of technical reports. The authors conclude that some of the projects were suited for automatic conversion while others required manual massaging. Even in cases like the course catalog where much conversion can be done automatically, the authors believe that manual addition of further contextual structure to the hypertext can be beneficial.

Garg, P.K., and Scacchi, W. (1990): "A hypertext system to manage software life-cycle documents," *IEEE Software* 7, 3 (May), pp. 90–98.
A hypertext system called Documents Integration Facility (DIF) to interrelate the various documents (requirements, specifications, design, source code, testing, and manuals) in the "Software Factory" software engineering research project.

Garrett, L.N., and Smith K.E. (1986): "Building a timeline editor from prefab parts: The architecture of an object-oriented application," *Proc. OOPSLA'86 Conf. Object-Oriented Programming Systems, Languages, and Applications* (Portland, OR, 29 September–2 October), pp. 202–213.
The *InterVal* editor is a part of Intermedia designed for the specialized purpose of generating dynamic hypertext timelines.

Garrett, L.N., Smith, K.E., and Meyrowitz, N. (1986): "Intermedia: Issues, strategies, and tactics in the design of a hypermedia document system," *Proc. 1st Conf. Computer-Supported Cooperative Work* (Austin, TX, 3–5 December), pp. 163–174.
Careful and well-illustrated discussion of some of the user interface issues in hypertexts with overlapping and/or changing link anchors and/or destinations. Also a discussion of other multi-user issues. This paper is substantially the same as some of the sections in [Yankelovich et al. 1988], which has more and better illustrations.

Giguere, E. (1989): "Electronic Oxford," *BYTE* 14, 13 (December), pp. 371–374.
Brief description of the project to convert the *Oxford English Dictionary* to an online format.

Gloor, P., and Norbert Streitz, N. (eds.) (1990): *"Hypertext und Hypermedia: Von theoretischen Konzepten zu praktischen Anwendungen,"* Springer-Verlag, Heidelberg, Germany.
The proceedings from the first German conference on hypertext.

Glushko, R.J. (1989a): "Transforming text into hypertext for a compact disc encyclopedia," *Proc. ACM CHI'89* (Austin, TX, 30 April–4 May), pp. 293–298.
Another paper about the project discussed in [Glushko et al. 1988].

Glushko, R.J. (1989b): "Design issues for multi-document hypertexts," *Proc. ACM Hypertext'89 Conf.* (Pittsburgh, PA, 5–8 November), pp. 51–60.
Issues in converting multiple existing documents to a single integrated hypertext.

Glushko, R.J., Weaver, M.D., Coonan, T.A., and Lincoln, J.E. (1988): "Hypertext engineering: Practical methods for creating a compact disc encyclopedia," *Proc. ACM Conf. Document Processing Systems* (Santa Fe, NM, 5–9 December), pp. 11–19.
Design tradeoffs involved in converting a multi-volume engineering encyclopedia to hypertext. The authors advocate the use of an index constructed by humans rather than one constructed automatically.

Gonzalez, S. (1988): *"Hypertext for Beginners."* Disk with HyperCard stacks, InteliBooks, San Francisco, CA. ISBN 0-932367-10-0.
Yet another "hypertext on hypertext"—it is a good illustration of the more wildly creative use of graphic layout and hyperlinks to form an intertwined and rather undisciplined information base (somewhat in the style of Ted Nelson's *Computer Lib/Dream Machines*). This document surveys the definition of hypertext, its history, and some of its advantages and disadvantages and does so in a typical hypertext manner with lots of literature references and citations. Most of this information will be known to people who have read other works on hypertext. The document also includes short descriptions of about 50 hypertext systems (including some systems that are only "semi-hypertext") as well as addresses of the vendors of most of these systems.

Gordon, S., Gustavel, J., Moore, J., and Hankey, J. (1988): "The effects of hypertext on reader knowledge representation," *Proc. Human Factors Society 32nd Annual Meeting*, pp. 296–300.
Subjects reading hypertext versions of 1,000-word articles did worse than subjects reading linear versions in tests of free recall of the contents of the articles even though they had spent the same time reading them. Subjects also subjectively preferred the linear articles. When reading articles of general interest, subjects after reading hypertext generated only about 60% of the terms generated after reading linear text. When reading articles with a more technically oriented content, however, subjects performed as well after hypertexts as after linear texts. One reason for the result in this paper may be just that the novice subjects used in the experiment had not yet learnt how to use hypertexts, but another reason may be that hypertext is less suited for small articles that are to be read in their entirety.

Gould, J.D. (1988): "How to design usable systems," in Helander, M. (ed.): *Handbook of Human-Computer Interaction*, Elsevier Science Publishers, pp. 757–789.
Good general checklist of methods for testing and improving usability.

Gould, J.D., and Grischkowsky, N. (1984): "Doing the same work with hard copy and with cathode ray tube (CRT) computer terminals," *Human Factors* 26, pp. 323–337.
Reading was 22% slower from screens than from paper.

Gould, J.D., Alfaro, L., Finn, R., Haupt, B., Minuto, A., and Salaun, J. (1987): "Why reading was slower from CRT displays than from paper," *Proc. ACM CHI+GI'87* (Toronto, Canada, 5–9 April), pp. 7–11.
While most studies find that reading from a screen is about 30% slower than reading from paper, the studies discussed in this paper identified certain conditions under which reading speeds were identical: high resolution, dark characters on light background, and use of an anti-aliased font.

Guillemette, R.A. (1989): "Development and validation of a reader-based documentation measure," *Int.J. Man-Machine Studies* **30**, 5 (May), pp. 551–574.
A factor analysis of users' subjective evaluation of documentation found seven factors that explained 65% of the variability: *credibility* (correct, reliable, believable), *demonstrative* (precise, conclusive, strong, complete), *fitness* (relevant, meaningful, appropriate), *personal affect* (varied, interesting, active), *systematic arrangement* (organized, orderly, structured), *task relevance* (useful, informative, valuable), and *understandability* (clear, understandable, readable).

Haas, C. (1989): "Does the medium make a difference? Two studies of writing with pen and paper and with computers," *Human-Computer Interaction* **4**, 2, pp. 149–169.
A comparison of text editing on paper and with computers. Users wrote more words when they used a workstation with large screen and a mouse-based editor than when they used a personal computer with a keyboard-based editor or when using pen and paper. The quality of the writings was about the same on the workstation and paper but was significantly worse on personal computers. Finally, when users who revised their works were asked to think aloud, the proportion of their utterances that referred to the editing medium itself rather than to the text being edited was only 3% when they used paper but 8% on the mouse-based workstation and a whopping 21% on the keyboard-based personal computer, thus indicating that the use of pen and paper was significantly more transparent (even though the test users all had at least 4 years of computer experience).

Hahn, U., and Reimer, U. (1988): "Automatic generation of hypertext knowledge bases," *Proc. ACM Conf. Office Information Systems* (Palo Alto, CA, 23–25 March), pp. 182–188.
By natural language parsing/semi-recognition, full-text bases are supplied with an abstraction hierarchy of so-called text graph concept browsers with hypertextual links.

Halasz, F.G. (1988): "Reflections on NoteCards: Seven issues for the next generation of hypermedia systems," *Communications of the ACM* **31**, 7 (July), pp. 836–852.
Important paper discussing interface and conceptual challenges for designers of future hypertext systems.

Halasz, F.G., and Schwartz, M. (1990): "The Dexter hypertext reference model," *Proc. NIST Hypertext Standardization Workshop* (Gaithersburg, MD, 16-18 January), pp. 95–133.
The general architecture of hypertext systems is described according to a three-layer model. The reference model is formalized in the Z specification language.

This is intended to be a general model for the description of all hypertext systems and the background for implementing a standardized hypertext interchange format. The paper presents a simple, preliminary example of such an interchange format.

Halasz, F.G., Moran, T.P., and Trigg, R.H. (1987): "NoteCards in a nutshell," *Proc. ACM CHI+GI'87* (Toronto, Canada, 5–9 April), pp. 45–52.
On the basic design of NoteCards and how it can be used as an idea organizer.

Hammond, N., and Allinson, L. (1988): "Travels around a learning support environment: Rambling, orienteering or touring?," *Proc. ACM CHI'88* (Washington, DC, 15–19 May), pp. 269–273.
Use of metaphors such as guided tours to aid navigation.

Hammond, N., and Allinson, L. (1989): "Extending hypertext for learning: An investigation of access and guidance tools," in Sutcliffe, A. and Macaulay, L. (eds.): *People and Computers V*, Cambridge University Press, pp. 293–304.
An information system that provided several different access methods was tested with users having either an exploratory task (asked to study for an unspecified subsequent test) or a directed task (had to answer specific questions). In both task conditions, hypertext links accounted for slightly more than half of the transitions between screens, and the overview map accounted for 12–16% of the transitions, whereas the index was used much more for directed search (17% vs. 6% in the exploratory case) and a guided tour facility was used more for exploratory search (28% vs. 8% in the directed case). Some subjects were tested with a system which only contained hypertext links and contained none of the other access mechanisms. Those users visited fewer screens during the experiment and had a significantly lower ratio of different screens to total screens seen, indicating that use of other facilities to supplement hypertext links resulted in wider coverage of the materials and more efficient access to new information.

Hansen, W.J., and Haas, C. (1988): "Reading and writing with computers: A framework for explaining differences in performance," *Communications of the ACM* **31**, 9 (September), pp. 1080–1089.
Discussion of the factors that impact throughput and quality in reading and writing online text, including reports of several empirical studies indicating the importance of having large screens.

Hardman, L. (1988): "Hypertext tips: Experiences in developing a hypertext tutorial," in Jones, D.M., and Winder R. (eds.): *People and Computers IV*, Cambridge University Press, pp. 437–451.
Experience from the development of a tutorial on the structure of the brain for physiology students and some general comments on hypertext style. As a practical comment, the reader should note that the pictures shown in Figures 1 and 2 in the paper have accidentally been swapped.

Hardman, L. (1989a): "Transcripts of observations of readers using the Glasgow Online hypertext," *Technical Report AMU8835/01H*, Scottish HCI Centre, Edinburgh, February.

Detailed notes on a series of user experiments with *Glasgow Online*. For a conceptual discussion of the actual results of this study, see Hardman's 1989 *Hypermedia* paper.

Hardman, L. (1989b): "Evaluating the readability of the Glasgow Online hypertext," *Hypermedia* **1**, 1, 34–63.
Findings from a laboratory study of novice users interacting with a hypertext tourist information system. Most of the usability problems observed seemed to have more to do with traditional user interface issues such as screen design than with hypertext linkage or network navigation. Exceptions were things such as a confused linking paradigm for a "next" button and the lack of a general backtrack command.

Hardman, L., and Sharratt, B. (1990): "User-centred hypertext design: The application of HCI design principles and guidelines," in McAleese, R., and Green, C. (eds.) *Hypertext: State of the Art*, Ablex, pp. 252–259.
On the basis of five general usability principles, the authors derive guidelines for hypertext user interfaces: user action (2 guidelines); information display (6 guidelines); dialogue (5 guidelines); online assistance (2 guidelines). Many of the guidelines are fairly general in nature (e.g. "ordering of lists should be designed to assist readers' tasks") and hard to follow without further analysis. They do provide insights into the special nature of hypertext interfaces (e.g. the matching of list ordering to users' tasks "can be enhanced by having multiple orderings of the same information").

Harmon, J.E. (1989): "The structure of scientific and engineering papers: A historical perspective," *IEEE Trans. Professional Communication* **32**, 3 (September), pp. 132–138.
Brief overview of the development leading to the current rather strict structure of the typical scientific paper. Early papers from the 17th century often were very short (a few paragraphs or so), had no clearly delimited sections (introduction, method, conclusion, etc.), and were written as a personal discourse.

Hewett, T.T. (1987): "The Drexel Disk: An electronic 'guidebook'," in Diaper, D., and Winder, R. (eds.): *People and Computers III*, Cambridge University Press, pp. 115–129.
A custom application to introduce new students to campus. Includes among other things a hypertextually active campus map.

Hitch, G.J., Sutcliffe, A.G., Bowers, J.M., and Eccles, L.M. (1986): "Empirical evaluation of map interfaces: A preliminary study," in Harrison, M.D., and Monk, A.F. (eds.): *People and Computers: Designing for Usability*, Cambridge University Press, pp. 565–585.
On the use of spatially laid out maps as menu interfaces.

Hodges, M.E., Sasnett, R.M., and Ackerman, M.S. (1989): "A construction set for multimedia applications," *IEEE Software* **6**, 1 (January), pp. 37–43.
Describes the software platform for the Athena Muse project and includes screen shots from the Philippe system for teaching French.

Hoekema, J. (1990): "HyperCard as a development tool for CD-I," *Boston Computer Society New Media News* 4, 2 (Spring), p. 1 & pp. 14–20.
HyperCard was used to develop storyboards before the implementation of the CD-I product *Treasures of the Smithsonian*. The author gives examples of preliminary screen designs and discusses the advantages and disadvantages of HyperCard for prototyping CD-I's with their somewhat different interaction techniques.

Houghton, R.C. (1984): "Online help systems: A conspectus," *Communications of the ACM* 27, 2 (February), pp. 126–133.
An overview of traditional computer mainframe online help systems.

Howell, G. (1990): "Hypertext meets interactive fiction: New vistas in creative writing," in McAleese, R., and Green, C. (eds.) *Hypertext: State of the Art*, Ablex, pp. 136–141.
An introduction to the concept of interactive fiction with references to some printed works by traditional authors having hypertext-like characteristics.

Hubert, L.J. (1978): "Generalized proximity function comparisons," *British J. Mathematical and Statistical Psychology* 31, pp. 179–192.

Hubert, L.J. (1979): "Generalized concordance," *Psychometrika* 44, pp. 135–142.
Methods that can be used to measure the proximity of two hierarchical structures and that can be applied to the problem of measuring how far the structure of the user's conceptual model is from a hypertext's structure (see [Gordon et al. 1988]).

Irven, J.H., Nilson, M.E., Judd, T.H., Patterson, J.F., and Shibata, Y. (1988): "Multi-media information services: A laboratory study," *IEEE Communications Magazine* 26, 6 (June), pp. 27–44.
Survey of a number of research projects at Bellcore, including a video browser with different organizations of images, the Movie Browser which can automatically build a hypertext from a conventional database of move titles, and a telesophy (remote access to multiple sources of information) system with a quarter of a million nodes taken from wire services, Usenet News, etc. The "laboratory study" referred to in the title of the paper is only discussed in a small part of the paper and mainly addresses performance issues of response times in relation to network transmission speeds.

Jacques, W. (1990): "The ACM Hypertext'89 conference," *Boston Computer Society New Media News* 4, 1 (Winter), pp. 1 and 17-20.
Trip report from Hypertext'89, including an extensive summary of discussions of links and anchors for temporal data like movies.

Jonassen, D.H., and Mandl, H. (eds.) (1990): *"Designing Hypertext / Hypermedia for Learning,"* Springer-Verlag, Heidelberg, Germany.
The proceedings of the NATO advanced research workshop on hypertext in Rottenburg, Germany, 3–7 July 1989. Includes several chapters on various usability issues relating to hypertext as well as many examples of European hypertext projects. Several of the chapters grapple with the issue of assessing the actual impact of hypertext on learning (if any).

Jones, H.W., III (1987a): "Developing and distributing hypertext tools: Legal inputs and parameters," *Proc. ACM Hypertext'87 Conf.* (Chapel Hill, NC, 13–15 November), pp. 367–374.
Mostly about the copyright problem but also some discussion of liability, royalties, antitrust matters, and problems with international law and certain Latin American countries.

Jones, W.P. (1987b): "How do we distinguish the hyper from the hype in non-linear text?," *Proc. IFIP INTERACT'87* (Stuttgart, Germany, 1–4 September), pp. 1107–1113.
Selectivity of access is seen as a major potential advantage of hypertext and the author presents various approaches to achieving greater selectivity.

Jones, W.P., and Dumais, S.T. (1986): "The spatial metaphor for user interfaces: Experimental tests of reference by location versus name," *ACM Trans. Office Inf. Syst.* 4, 1 (January), pp. 42–63.
Retrieval of objects was more accurate by name than by location in situations with large number of objects, but retrieval by the combination of name and location was better than either method in isolation. The authors conclude that purely spatial filing may be most useful in temporary situations involving a small number of recently encountered objects.

Jordan, D.S., Russell, D.M., Jensen, A-M.S., and Rogers, R.A. (1989): "Facilitating the development of representations in hypertext with IDE," *Proc. ACM Hypertext'89 Conf.* (Pittsburgh, PA, 5–8 November), pp. 93–104.
The *Instructional Design Environment* (IDE) contains several authoring tools, including "structure accelerators" that speed up the construction of entire hypertext structures from templates.

Joseph, B., Steinberg, E.R., and Jones, A.R. (1989): "User perceptions and expectations of an information retrieval system," *Behaviour and Information Technology* 8, 2 (March–April), pp. 77–88.
A hypertext-like implementation of a bridge engineering manual on the PLATO system. Users selecting chapters from a table of contents made the wrong choices 80% of the time because the table of contents displayed only chapter names and not the section listings that are found in the printed manual's table of contents. Chapters were organized by engineering activity and not by type of bridge, so going by the names of the chapters alone, information about arch bridges could have been in at least three of the chapters listed. Use of the table of contents dropped from being 20% of the information access on the first day of the experiment to about 5% on the third day of the experiment.

Kacmar, C., Leggett, J., Schnase, J.L., and Boyle, C. (1988): "Data management facilities of existing hypertext systems," *Technical Report TAMU 88-018*, Texas A&M University, September.
A comparison of the data models and operations provided by 11 hypertext systems. The hypertext systems only provided about 60%–70% of the database functions found in standard database systems. The focus of this report is on back-end issues rather than on user interface issues.

Kaehler, C. (1988): "Authoring with hypermedia," in Ambron S., and Hooper K. (eds.): "*Interactive Multimedia: Visions of Multimedia for*

Developers, Educators, & Information Providers," Microsoft Press, pp. 307–311.
An extremely short article (only a single page of actual text) on the ideas behind the online help package in HyperCard by its designer.

Kahn, P. (1989a): "Webs, trees, and stacks: How hypermedia system design effect hypermedia content," in Salvendy, G., and Smith, M.J. (eds.): *Designing and Using Human-Computer Interfaces and Knowledge Based Systems,* Elsevier Science Publishers, pp. 443–449.
A comparative study of Guide, HyperCard, KMS, and Intermedia from an authoring perspective. The following four issues are discussed: Is the meaning located primarily in the links or in the nodes? What is the relationship between documents, nodes, and visible screen units? Will following a link replace the current node or supplement it? What is the distinction between author and reader? As an example, Kahn gives further detail of an Intermedia web on Lunar geology, "Exploring the Moon."

Kahn, P. (1989b): "Linking together books: Experiments in adapting published material into hypertext," *Hypermedia* 1, 2, pp. 111–145.
Describes the conversion of a set of books on Chinese poetry into Intermedia format, giving plenty of screen shots. One interesting illustration is an overview diagram of the translators of the poet Tu Fu, which are ordered in two dimensions: Chronologically on the on the y-axis and according to the translator's emphasis on sinology or poetry on the x-axis. The author distinguishes between *objective links* (those present in the text being converted such as explicit literature references) and *subjective links* (those added because the converter or other hypertext user sees a connection between two items).

Kain, H., and Nielsen, J. (1991): "Estimating the market diffusion curve for hypertext," *Impact Assessment Bulletin.*
A model for the growth in hypertext use over time is developed based on the Bass curve for product innovation diffusion. The market penetration of hypertext is expected to grow slowly but steadily in the period 1990–2000 and to grow rapidly from the year 2000.

Kerr, S.T. (1989): "Efficiency and satisfaction in videotex database production," *Behaviour and Information Technology* 8, 1 (January–February), pp. 57–63.
A field study of the working style of designers doing everyday production of videotex frames. Over time, designers tend to be bored since most routine frame creation work is not very interesting. The study revealed a conflict over the place of individual creativity in videotex work where the designers chafe at restrictions imposed by managers because using the hardware and software in unusual and exploratory ways is a principal motivation in designers' daily work.

Kibby, M.R., and Mayes, J.T. (1989): "Towards intelligent hypertext," in McAleese, R. (ed.): *Hypertext Theory into Practice,* Ablex, pp. 164–172.
The StrathTutor hypertext system tries to eliminate the need to rely on exclusively manual methods for creating links between hypertext nodes by generating links based on its knowledge of the connection between the nodes as the user browses .

Knuth, D.E. (1984): "Literate programming," *Computer Journal* 27, 2 (May), pp. 97–111.

A proposal for an intertwined representation of program code and descriptive text.

Koved, L., and Shneiderman, B. (1986): "Embedded menus: Selecting items in context," *Communications of the ACM* **29**, 4 (April), pp. 312–318.
Shows that users work faster when selecting items that are embedded in surrounding contextual information.

Kreitzberg, C.B. (1989): "Designing the electronic book: Human psychology and information structures for hypermedia," *Proc. 3rd Intl. Conf. on Human-Computer Interaction* (Boston, MA, 18–22 September).

Kreitzberg, C.B., and Shneiderman, B. (1988): "Restructuring knowledge for an electronic encyclopedia," *Proc. Intl. Ergonomics Association 10th Congress* (Sydney, Australia, 1–5 August), pp. 615–620.
Design issues for writing the content of a hypertext structure.

Lai, K.-Y., Malone, T.W., and Yu, K.-C. (1988): "Object Lens: A 'spreadsheet' for cooperative work," *ACM Trans. Office Information Systems* **6**, 4 (October), pp. 332–353.
Object Lens is the second generation of the Information Lens system for information filtering in electronic mail and online communication. It integrates hypertext, object-oriented databases, and the rule-based agents used to classify incoming messages automatically.

Landauer, T.K. (1988): "Research methods in human-computer interaction," in Helander, M. (ed.): *Handbook of Human-Computer Interaction*, Elsevier Science Publishers, pp. 905–928.
A good introduction to quantitative and statistical methods used to study usability.

Landow, G.P. (1987): "Relationally encoded links and the rhetoric of hypertext," *Proc. ACM Hypertext'87 Conf.* (Chapel Hill, NC, 13–15 November), pp. 331–343.
The rhetoric of hypertext involves establishing conventions for the use of links between nodes: Readers may form expectations for how these links work (e.g. if there is a link, then readers will expect it to have some significance).

Landow, G.P. (1989a): "The rhetoric of hypertext: Some rules for authors," *Journal of Computing in Higher Education* **1**, 1 (Spring), pp. 39–64.
A set of 19 rules for the design of hypertext with coherent, purposeful, and useful relationships. These rules are called the *rhetoric* of hypertext and aim at providing conventions for what to expect with regard to links and anchors. The "rhetoric of departure" gives rules for how to show outgoing links from a node, and the "rhetoric of arrival" gives rules for how to orient a reader upon arrival at a new node.

Landow, G.P. (1989b): "Hypertext in literary education, criticism, and scholarship," *Computers and the Humanities* **23**, pp. 173–198.

The most complete paper on the use of the Intermedia hypertext system for the teaching of English literature at Brown University. The information base is called *Context32* and originally contained 1000 documents and 1300 links, but more are being added. The use of Intermedia for an introductory course proved successful and even improved the quality of the class sessions where the computers were not being used (an ethnographer who observed the course both before and after the introduction of hypertext found that the number of student comments increased by 300% and that the number of students making comments also increased by 300%). The paper also includes the reading list for the course and a complete listing of the first assignment students get when starting to use Intermedia for the study of English literature.

Landow, G.P. (1990): "Popular fallacies about hypertext," in Jonassen, D.H., and Mandl, H. (eds.): *"Designing Hypertext/Hypermedia for Learning,"* Springer-Verlag, Heidelberg, Germany, chapter 3.
The author argues against several current hypertext research directions: He does not believe that one can study the nature and effect of hypertext with small document sets (several of his own problems did not appear until his Context32 hypertext grew large), he does not believe that analogies of navigation, narration, and space will help us think accurately about hypertext (neither temporal nor spatial metaphors tell the entire truth about hypertext), and he does not believe that navigation and orientation poses a serious problem (author-generated overview diagrams normally help point the reader in the right direction). Landow also presents an interesting critique of the analogy between hypertext and traditional publishing.

Lansdale, M.W., Young, D.R., and Bass, C.A. (1989): "MEMOIRS: A personal multimedia information system," in Sutcliffe, A. and Macaulay, L. (eds.): *People and Computers V,* Cambridge University Press, pp. 315–327.
MEMOIRS (Memory Enhanced Management for Office Information Systems) is a personal information system where the traditional concept of files is replaced with interlinked information nodes tied to a timeline (called a "timebase").

Laurel, B. (1989): "A taxonomy of interactive movies," *Boston Computer Society New Media News* 3, 1 (Winter), pp. 5–8.
After a brief survey of the "projections" for future interactive media in various science fiction films, Laurel presents a number of dimensions for interactivity: frequency (how often does the user get to make a choice), range (number of options available to choose from), significance (effect of the choice), and personness (1st, 2nd, or 3rd person experiences). Based on these dimensions, interactive movies are classified as navigational, narrative, or dramatic.

Laurel, B., Oren, T., and Don, A. (1990): "Issues in multimedia interface design: Media integration and interface agents," *Proc. ACM CHI'90 Conf. Human Factors in Computing Systems* (Seattle, WA, 1–5 April), pp. 133–139.
Agents provide an interface to a hypertext by giving the user suggestions for where to go next in a manner similar to guided tours but with the opportunity for more dynamic calculation of the path. The authors also discuss issues in integrating video and other media in a hypertext while avoiding "media ghettoes" with few links between pieces of information of different media types.

Leggett, J., Schnase, J.L., and Kacmar, C.J. (1989): "A short course on hypertext," *Technical Report* **TAMU 89-004**, Computer Science Department, Texas A&M University, College Station, TX 77843-3112, January.
The overheads from what may have been the first university level course on hypertext.

Leggett, J., Schnase, J.L., and Kacmar, C.J. (1990): "Hypertext and learning," in Jonassen, D.H., and Mandl, H. (eds.): *"Designing Hypertext / Hypermedia for Learning,"* Springer-Verlag, Heidelberg, Germany, chapter 2.
Brief reports from the use of hypertext to teach three courses, including summaries of student feedback. In all cases, the students wanted annotations, bookmarks, and the ability to integrate hypertext into their normal computing environment.

Lesk, M. (1989): "What to do when there's too much information," *Proc. ACM Hypertext'89 Conf.* (Pittsburgh, PA, 5–8 November), pp. 305–318.
Approaches to providing overview diagrams and interactive information retrieval mechanisms to a catalog of 800,000 items.

Lippman, A., Bender, W., Solomon, G., and Saito, M. (1985): "Color word processing," *IEEE Computer Graphics and Applications* **5**, 6 (June), pp. 41–46.
A prototype word processor that shows the changes made by users in different colors depending on when those changes were made.

Luther, A.C. (1988): "You are there... and in control," *IEEE Spectrum* **25**, 9 (September), pp. 45–50.
A reasonably popular description of the technology behind DVI (Digital Video Interactive), including some discussion of possible hypermedia applications. The article has some nice color pictures of DVI screens, including a four-frame sequence from Palenque (a surrogate travel application, see [Wilson 1988]).

Mackay, W.E., and Davenport, G. (1989): "Virtual video editing in interactive multimedia applications," *Communications of the ACM* **32**, 7 (July), pp. 802–810.
A discussion of several multimedia projects at MIT (the Media Lab and Project Athena), including the Athena Muse and the Pygmalion multimedia message system with special emphasis on the tools used to build the designs.

MacTech Quarterly **1**, 4 (Winter 1990), pp. 8–26 and 112–124.
Special section on *SuperCard* with reasonably detailed technical articles by Andrew Himes, Chris Van Hamersveld and Tony Myles about SuperCard in general, using SuperCard to build stand-alone applications, and the SuperCard runtime editor.

Mahajan, V., Muller, E., and Bass, F.M. (1990): "New product diffusion models in marketing: A review and directions for research," *Journal of Marketing* **54**, 1 (January), pp. 1–26.
This article is not specifically about hypertext but reviews marketing models for the market penetration of product innovation, and as such contains background material for the estimation of the spread of hypertext ideas and products.

Marchionini, G. (1989): "Making the transition from print to electronic encyclopedia: Adaptation of mental models," *Int.J. Man-Machine Studies* **30**, 6 (June), pp. 591–618.
Sixteen high school students used the *Grolier's Academic American Encyclopedia* in both print form and electronic form and used the two versions in about the same way. This result should not be used to conclude that users in general will use hypertext the same way as they use printed books, however, since the subjects in this study used the electronic book only for a very limited amount of time and since the version of *Grolier's* tested had only very limited hypertext capabilities. An interesting side result from this study came from asking the subjects to compare the print and electronic encyclopedias. Half said that the electronic version was faster, three said that it contained more information than the printed version, and one said that it was more up to date. This result was in spite of the facts that the two versions of the encyclopedia actually contained the *same* text and that the subjects were measured to be slower with the electronic version. This experiment indicates some of the problems with subjective evaluations and the seductive qualities of novel technology.

Marchionini, G. (1990): "Evaluating hypermedia-based learning," in Jonassen, D.H., and Mandl, H. (eds.): *"Designing Hypertext/Hypermedia for Learning,"* Springer-Verlag, Heidelberg, Germany, chapter 20.
A discussion of usability evaluation methods with a bias in favor of very careful (but difficult) methods.

Marchionini, G., and Shneiderman, B. (1988): "Finding facts vs. browsing knowledge in hypertext systems," *IEEE Computer* **21**, 1 (January), pp. 70–80.
The authors present an information seeking model . As examples of how concrete systems fit their model, the authors discuss Hyperties showing an example of the research version with a two-frame display, and the *Grolier's Electronic Encyclopedia* on CD-ROM.

Marshall, C.C., and Irish, P.M. (1989): "Guided tours and on-line presentations: How authors make existing hypertext intelligible for readers," *Proc. ACM Hypertext'89 Conf.* (Pittsburgh, PA, 5–8 November), pp. 15–26.
How to use guided tours and narrative structures such as arrows as *meta-information* to make the main information understandable.

Mayes, T., Kibby, M., and Anderson, T. (1990): "Learning about learning from hypertext," in Jonassen, D.H., and Mandl, H. (eds.): *"Designing Hypertext/Hypermedia for Learning,"* Springer-Verlag, Heidelberg, Germany, chapter 3.
Reports from studies of learners using StrathTutor. The most revealing results came from *constructive interaction* studies observing two users constructively helping each other understand the system.

McCracken, D., and Akscyn, R.M. (1984): "Experience with the ZOG human-computer interface system," *Int.J. Man-Machine Studies* **21**, pp. 293–310.
A frame-based hypertext system developed at Carnegie Mellon University.

McKnight, C., Dillon, A., and Richardson, J. (1989): "Problems in hyperland? A human factors perspective," *Hypermedia* 1, 2, pp. 167–178.
A review of some human factors studies of relevance for hypertext user interfaces.

McKnight, C., Richardson, J., and Dillon, A. (1990): "Journal articles as learning resource: What can hypertext offer?," in Jonassen, D.H., and Mandl, H. (eds.): *"Designing Hypertext/Hypermedia for Learning,"* Springer-Verlag, Heidelberg, Germany, chapter 16.
A project to convert eight volumes of the journal *Behaviour and Information Technology* to hypertext.

Meyrowitz, N. (1986): "Intermedia: The architecture and construction of an object-oriented hypermedia system and applications framework," *Proc. OOPSLA'86 Conf. Object-Oriented Programming Systems, Languages, and Applications* (Portland, OR, 29 September–2 October), pp. 186–201.
A discussion of many of the programming issues involved in implementing a hypermedia system using the object-oriented MacApp programming system.

Meyrowitz, N. (1989a): "The missing link: Why we're all doing hypertext wrong," in Barrett, E. (ed.): *The Society of Text*, MIT Press, Cambridge, MA, pp. 107–114.
According to the author, the reason hypertext has not caught on is that existing systems are not integrated with the rest of the user's computing environment. Intermedia has a linking protocol architecture which allows the integration of third party applications if they would implement it. But to see really widespread use, the hypertext linking protocol must be part of the standard system software on the computer (e.g. part of the Macintosh Toolbox or the IBM Presentation Manager).

Meyrowitz, N. (1989b): "Hypertext—does it reduce cholesterol, too?" *Technical Report* **89-9**, Institute for Research in Information and Scholarship (IRIS), Brown University, Providence, RI, November.
The keynote address from the Hypertext'89 conference. Meyrowitz gives his views on various hypertext design issues and also presents a comparison between Vannevar Bush's original Memex vision and our current technical capabilities.

Meyrowitz, N., and van Dam, A. (1982): "Interactive editing systems" parts I and II, *ACM Computing Surveys* **14**, 3 (September), pp. 321–352 and 353–415.
Only a very small part of these papers is about hypertext, but they give the best survey available of more traditional techniques for interacting with textual structures on a computer and also include some coverage of principles for structure editing.

Mills, C.B., and Weldon, L.J. (1987): "Reading text from computer screens," *Computing Surveys* **19**, 4 (December), pp. 329–358.
A review of an extensive body of empirical evidence on low-level issues in physically presenting text on video displays (e.g. lower case vs. upper case, line spacing, color, scrolling speed, etc.).

Monk, A. (1989): "The personal browser: A tool for directed navigation in hypertext systems," *Interacting with Computers* **1**, 2 (August), pp. 190–196.

An idea for customizing the interface to a hypertext by constructing a table of contents listing exactly those nodes that the user has asked to have added to it. The difference between the personal browser and traditional bookmarks is that the system monitors the user's navigation behavior and in an activist manner interrupts the user to ask whether it should add a node to the browser when it has been accessed frequently.

Monk, A.F., Walsh, P., and Dix, A.J. (1988): "A comparison of hypertext, scrolling and folding mechanisms for program browsing," in Jones D.M., and Winder, R. (eds.): *People and Computers IV*, Cambridge University Press, pp. 421–435.

A study of browsing a quite small "literate program" (i.e. program code intertwined with extensive comments). A hypertext interface without a structural map led subjects to significantly worse performance than a hypertext interface with a structural map or more traditional scrolling and folding (holophrast-based) interfaces.

Monty, M.L. (1986): "Temporal context and memory for notes stored in the computer," *ACM SIGCHI Bulletin* **18**, 2 (October), pp. 50–51.

NoteCards users had trouble due to premature structuring of information and the homogeneous appearance of the text on the screen.

Monty, M.L., and Moran, T.P. (1986): "A longitudinal study of authoring using NoteCards," *ACM SIGCHI Bulletin* **18**, 2 (October), pp. 59–60.

Summary of a study of a graduate student writing a research paper using NoteCards over a period of seven months.

Moulthrop, S. (1989): "Hypertext and 'the hyperreal'," *Proc. ACM Hypertext'89 Conf.* (Pittsburgh, PA, 5–8 November), pp. 259–267.

A literary analysis of interactive fictions with special emphasis on Michael Joyce's "Afternoon" and the Storyspace system.

Nanard, J., Richy, H., and Nanard, M. (1988): "Conceptual documents: A mechanism for specifying active views in hypertext," *Proc. ACM Conf. Document Processing Systems* (Santa Fe, NM, 5–9 December), pp. 37–42.

How to synthesize a document from an underlying information base.

Nelson, T. (1980): "Replacing the printed word: A complete literary system," in Lavington, S.H. (ed): *Proc. IFIP Congress 1980,* North-Holland, pp. 1013–1023.

A paper that is perhaps slightly easier to get hold of (from the World Computer Conference) than the publications which Nelson has self-published. It describes his ideas for a universal hypertext repository containing everything anybody ever has written and will write.

Nelson, T. (1988): "Unifying tomorrow's hypermedia," *Proc. Online Information 88* (London, U.K., 6–8 December), pp. 1–7.

A warning against the current trend towards "balkanized" hypertext existing in lots of incompatible systems. Instead of these closed hypermedia systems, Nelson advocates a more general scheme for open hypermedia.

Nicol, A. (1988): "Interface design for hyperdata: Models, maps and cues," *Proc. Human Factors Society 32nd Annual Meeting*, pp. 308–312.
In a study of designers of HyperCard stacks, most said that they tend not to do much systematic planning but instead construct their designs "button-up."[8] The paper contains several guidelines for more organized designs based on metaphors and navigational conventions.

Nielsen, J. (1986): "Online documentation and reader annotation," *Proc. 1st Conf. Work With Display Units* (Stockholm, Sweden, 12–15 May), pp. 526–529.
Empirical study of which kinds of annotation are used the most.

Nielsen, J. (1988): "Trip report: Hypertext'87," *ACM SIGCHI Bulletin* **19**, 4 (April), pp. 27–35.
Report on events at the first scientific conference on hypertext, held in Chapel Hill, NC, 13–15 November 1987. This report also exists in a hypertext form.

Nielsen, J. (1989a): "Prototyping user interfaces using an object-oriented hypertext programming system," *Proc. NordDATA'89 Joint Scandinavian Computer Conference* (Copenhagen, Denmark, 19–22 June), pp. 485–490.
Technical issues in the use of HyperCard to build user interfaces. Two examples are discussed: a hypertext system with a user interface building on individualized user history and a videotex system.

Nielsen, J. (1989b): "Mini trip report: HyperHyper: Developments across the field of hypermedia," *ACM SIGCHI Bulletin* **21**, 1 (July), pp. 65–67.
A report on events at the British Computer Society meeting in London 23 February 1989, including discussions of the cognitive ergonomics of hypertext and the *Glasgow Online* system.

Nielsen, J. (1989c): "Usability engineering at a discount," in Salvendy, G. and Smith, M.J. (eds.): *Designing and Using Human-Computer Interfaces and Knowledge Based Systems*, Elsevier Science Publishers, Amsterdam, pp. 394–401.
Usability engineering methods that have low complexity and cost.

Nielsen, J. (1989d): "Trip Report: Hypertext II," *ACM SIGCHI Bulletin* **21**, 2 (October), pp. 41–47.
Report on events at the second British conference on hypertext, held in York, U.K., 29–30 June 1989.

Nielsen, J. (1989e): "The matters that really matter for hypertext usability," *Proc. ACM Hypertext'89 Conf.* (Pittsburgh, PA, 5–8 November), pp. 239–248.
A review of 92 quantitative results from 30 research papers comparing various approaches to online text and hypertext. The conclusions are that the three

---

[8] "Button-up" is my term; the paper uses the less humorous "bottom-up."

factors with the largest effects on usability are individual variability among users, variations in users' tasks, and the difference between the way users use hypertext and the way they use printed text or non-hypertext computer systems. Because of the two first factors, the paper also concludes that no single hypertext system is likely to have universal usability.

Nielsen, J. (1990a): "Three medium sized hypertexts on CD-ROM," *ACM SIGIR Forum* 24, 1–2, pp. 2–10.
A review of *The Manhole* (an interactive fiction), the *Time Table of History*, and *The Electronic Whole Earth Catalog*, all of which are hypertext structures implemented in HyperCard and distributed on CD-ROM because of their size. The review evaluates the usability of the systems by using various usability heuristics such as the need for consistent backtracking, history facilities, and support for navigational dimensions.

Nielsen, J. (1990b): "The art of navigating through hypertext," *Communications of the ACM* 33, 3 (March), pp. 296–310.
A description of the design of a hypertext system using the individual user's personal interaction history to provide a greater sense of context in the navigation space and a discussion of human factors problems found in usability testing of earlier versions of the system. The article is illustrated with a large number of screen dumps forming a guided tour of the system.

Nielsen, J. (1990c): "Trip report: Hypertext'89," *ACM SIGCHI Bulletin* 21, 4 (April), pp. 52–61.
Report on events at the second ACM conference on hypertext, held in Pittsburgh, PA, November 5–8, 1989.

Nielsen, J. (1990d): "Evaluating hypertext usability," in Jonassen, D.H., and Mandl, H. (eds.): *"Designing Hypertext/Hypermedia for Learning,"* Springer-Verlag, Heidelberg, Germany, chapter 9.
Methods for measuring or estimating the usability of hypertexts, including a discussion of the usability parameters for hypertext and test plans.

Nielsen, J. (1990e): "Review of BBC Interactive Television Unit's Ecodisc," *Hypermedia* 2, 2.
A CD-ROM from the BBC to teach ecology through the simulation of a nature preserve. From a hypertext perspective, the system is interesting because it includes a section providing surrogate travel through the preserve using a technique similar to that of the MIT *Aspen Movie Map*—complete with a "season knob" to travel in the summer or winter. The disk contains the complete user interface in nine different languages (English, French, German, Spanish, Italian, Danish, Swedish, Norwegian, and Dutch).

Nielsen, J. (1990f): "Miniatures versus icons as a visual cache for videotex browsing," *Behaviour and Information Technology* 9.
Miniatures (graphically reduced images of the nodes) and icons can be used to display a short history list of the previously seen nodes such that the user can easily return to the last few navigational locations.

Nielsen, J., and Lyngbæk, U. (1990): "Two field studies of hypermedia usability," in McAleese, R., and Green, C. (eds.) *Hypertext: State of the Art*, Ablex, pp 64– 72.
A general discussion of using field study methodologies to assess the usability of hypermedia systems, and results from two such studies: a study of professionals

reading a Guide scientific report and a study of kindergarten children "reading" a non-verbal interactive story about the adventures of the cat Inigo.

Nievergelt, J., and Weydert, J. (1980): "Sites, modes and trails: Telling the user of an interactive system where he is, what he can do, and how to get to places," in Guedj, R.A., ten Hagen, P.J.W., Hopgood, F.R.A., Tucker, H.A., and Duce, D.A. (eds.): *Methodology of Interaction*, North Holland Publishing Company, pp. 327–338.
An early paper about usability issues in navigation.

Nyce, J.M., and Kahn, P. (1989): "Innovation, pragmaticism, and technological continuity: Vannevar Bush's Memex," *Journal of the American Society for Information Science* **40**, 3 (May), pp. 214–221.
A historical review of how Vannevar Bush arrived at his ideas for the "Memex," which is normally viewed as the first expression of the hypertext concept. The paper contains excerpts from Bush's unpublished writings from the period where he developed the Memex idea as well as a brief discussion of later work. The paper reprints two original illustrations of the proposed Memex.

Oberlin, S., and Cox, J. (eds.) (1989): "*Microsoft CD-ROM Yearbook 1989–1990*," Microsoft Press.
A 935-page monster of a book containing a comprehensive dictionary of available CD-ROM titles and CD mastering and other services. About 650 pages of the book are filled with short articles (about five pages each) on almost all aspects of CD-ROMs, electronic publishing, and hypertext by a lot of people who are mainly practitioners. Many of the articles are reprints from various sources over the last five years, but since the original sources are extremely scattered and often hard to locate, the reprinting should be seen as a service.

Oren, T. (1987): "The architectures of static hypertexts," *Proc. ACM Hypertext '87 Conf.* (Chapel Hill, NC, 13–15 November), pp. 291–306.
On the special design considerations for hypertexts to be stored on CD-ROMs or other non-changeable storage media. The read-only limitation can even be viewed as an advantage because it ensures the integrity of the original hypertext network while still allowing additions of links, annotations, etc. stored on a magnetic disk and merged by the display front-end at read-time. Most of the paper is really about general user interface issues in hypertext (e.g. overview maps, limiting the connectivity to about 7 ± 2 links per node) and not about CD-ROM-specific issues.

Oren, T. (1988): "The CD-ROM connection," *BYTE* **13**, 13 (December), pp. 315–320.
This is a slightly abridged version of [Oren 1987].

Oren, T., Salomon, G., Kreitman, K., and Don, A. (1990): "Guides: Characterizing the interface," in Laurel, B. (ed.): *The Art of Human-Computer Interface Design*, Addison-Wesley.
Using anthropomorphic and even explicitly human (videotaped) narrators to guide users through a hypertext. These guides are similar to interaction agents but do not show intelligence in the current system. Even so, users often attributed greater sophistication to the guides than their implementation would seem to justify.

Patterson, J.F., and Egido, C. (1987): "Video browsing and system response time," in Diaper, D., and Winder, R. (eds.): *People and Computers III*, Cambridge University Press, U.K., pp. 189–198.
Users retrieved 50% more frames to solve the same problems when system response time was fast (3 sec.) rather than slow (11 sec.).

Pearl, A. (1989): "Sun's link service: A protocol for open linking," *Proc. ACM Hypertext'89 Conf.* (Pittsburgh, PA, 5–8 November), pp. 137–146.
Hypertext as a system service to support links across other applications.

Pejtersen, A.M. (1989): "A library system for information retrieval based on a cognitive task analysis and supported by an icon-based interface," *Proc. SIGIR'89 Twelfth Annual Intl. ACM SIGIR Conf. Research and Development in Information Retrieval* (Cambridge, MA, 25–28 June), pp. 40–47.
The design of the Book House system for finding fiction in a library.

Perlman, G. (1989): "System design and evaluation with hypertext checklists," *Proc. 1989 IEEE Conf. Systems, Man, and Cybernetics* (Cambridge, MA, November).
The NaviText SAM system is a hypertext interface to a large set of user interface guidelines.

Perlman, G., Egan, D., Ehrlich, S., Marchionini, G., Nielsen, J., and Shneiderman, B. (1990): "Evaluating hypermedia systems," *Proc. ACM CHI'90 Conf. Human Factors in Computing Systems* (Seattle, WA, 1–5 April), pp. 387–390.
Several different approaches to usability evaluation are contrasted.

Potter, R.L., Weldon, L.J.., and Shneiderman, B. (1988): "Improving the accuracy of touch screens: An experimental evaluation of three strategies," *Proc. ACM CHI'88* (Washington, DC, 15–19 May), pp. 27–32.

Potter, R., Berman, M., and Shneiderman, B. (1989): "An experimental evaluation of three touch screen strategies within a hypertext database," *Int.J. Human-Computer Interaction* 1, 1, pp. 41–52.
Touch screens were more usable when a take-off strategy rather than a land-on (touch-down) strategy was used for registering user selections.

Potter, W.D., and Trueblood, R.P. (1988): "Traditional, semantic, and hyper-semantic approaches to data modeling" *IEEE Computer* 21, 6 (June 1988), pp. 53–63.
Discusses the difference between computer-oriented data models used in traditional databases and more recent user-oriented hypertext-like database approaches that capture inferential relationships among real-world concepts.

Pullinger, D.J., Maude, T.I., and Parker, J. (1987): "Software for reading text on screen," *Proc. IFIP INTERACT'87* (Stuttgart, Germany, 1–4 September), pp. 899–904.
Readers read text significantly faster when they were allowed to jump through it rather than just scroll or page.

Quick, W.T. (1989): "Bank robbery," *Analog Science Fiction* **109**, 5 (May), pp. 128–143.
Science fiction story about the importance of human editors (and possible AI editorial assistants) in assembling readable sub-information spaces in a future global hypertext system. The protagonist is a editor who creates links to readable material but has his personalized scanning software stolen. This software is used to search the information space for suitable nodes for reference through the editor's recommended links.

Rafeld, M. (1988): "The LaserROM project: A case study in document processing systems," *Proc. ACM Conf. Document Processing Systems* (Santa Fe, NM, 5–9 December 1988), pp. 21–29.
Hewlett-Packard distributes more than 8,000 different publications annually and experiments with putting them on CD-ROM to cut costs. The paper discusses problems in converting existing documents to the new format and integrating illustrations.

Ragland, C. (1988): "Guide 2.0 and HyperCard 1.1: Choices for hypermedia developers," *HyperAge Magazine* (May–June), pp. 49–56.
One of the better comparative reviews of the two leading (as of 1988) popular hypertext products.

Raskin, J. (1987): "The hype in hypertext: A critique," *Proc. ACM Hypertext '87 Conf.* (Chapel Hill, NC, 13–15 November), pp. 325–330.
The author suggests that there may be serious problems with user interfaces to the hypertext principle of linked text, whereas interfaces to linear text can be made excellent and simple.

Raymond, D.R., and Tompa, F. W. (1988): "Hypertext and the Oxford English Dictionary," *Communications of the ACM* **31**, 7 (July), pp. 871–879.
On automatically converting existing documents to hypertext form.

Reisel, J.F., and Shneiderman, B. (1987): "Is bigger better? The effects of display size on program reading," in Salvendy, G. (ed.): *Social, Ergonomic and Stress Aspects of Work with Computers*, Elsevier Science Publishers, pp. 113–122.
Bigger *was* better.

Remde, J.R., Gomez, L.M., and Landauer, T.K. (1987): "SuperBook: An automatic tool for information exploration—hypertext?," *Proc. ACM Hypertext '87 Conf.* (Chapel Hill, NC, 13–15 November), pp. 175–188.
The design of SuperBook was based on principles from human-computer interaction research, including full-text indexing, user-defined aliasing (several terms for the same concept), and dynamic hierarchical views.

Riley, V.A. (1990): "An interchange format for hypertext systems: The Intermedia model," *Proc. NIST Hypertext Standardization Workshop* (Gaithersburg, MD, 16-18 January), pp. 213–222.
An interchange format for Intermedia links.

Ripley, G.D. (1989): "DVI: A digital multimedia technology," *Communications of the ACM* **32**, 7 (July), pp. 811–822.

Well-illustrated article on DVI. Includes both technical information about
hardware architecture and disk capacity for various media, and examples of
several applications (e.g. Palenque and games such as a WWII Spitfire flight
simulator).

Robertson, C.K., McCracken, D., and Newell, A. (1981): "The ZOG
approach to man-machine communication," *Intl. J. Man-Machine
Studies* 14, pp. 461–488.
ZOG was an early and influential system having linked frames of online text.

Russell, D.M. (1990): "Alexandria: A learning resources management
architecture," in Jonassen, D.H., and Mandl, H. (eds.): *"Designing
Hypertext/Hypermedia for Learning,"* Springer-Verlag, Heidelberg,
Germany, chapter 24.
Outline of a project at Xerox PARC to build an integrated learning environment
with many tools and resources (e.g. simulations, tests, a video library, and
linguistic aids such as dictionaries). The architecture is based on a *kernel* to link
many different forms of information and applications. Each of these "resources"
is expected to obey the kernel's hypermedia protocol. Russell gives a brief
analysis of how IDE [Jordan et al. 1989] fits the Alexandria model.

Salomon, G.B. (1990): "Designing casual-use hypertext: The CHI'89
InfoBooth," *Proc. ACM CHI'90 Conf. Human Factors in Computing
Systems* (Seattle, WA, 1–5 April), pp. 451–458.
The design of Apple's information kiosk at the ACM CHI'89 conference,
including screen shots of several stages in the iterative design. During the
conference, attendees entered personal information and digitized photos into the
system, and the complete "yearbook" was later distributed to them on a CD-
ROM.

Salomon, G., Oren, T., and Kreitman, K. (1989): "Using guides to
explore multimedia databases," *Proc. 22nd Hawaii International
Conference on System Sciences* (Kailua-Kona, HI, 3–6 January), pp. 3–
12.
Using anthropomorphic human guides to lead users through a hypertext. See
also [Oren et al. 1990].

Salton, G. (1989): *"Automatic Text Processing: The Transformation,
Analysis, and Retrieval of Information by Computer,"* Addison-Wesley.
Only has three pages specifically on hypertext, but this book is a good
introduction to information retrieval and similar issues of interest for some
hypertext systems.

Savoy, J. (1989): "The electronic book Ebook3," *Int. J. Man-Machine
Studies* 30, 5 (May), pp. 505–523.
Ebook3 is a hypertext system with emphasis on the ability to print the entire
document (which is structured as a strict hierarchy) and on being sufficiently
open to allow the integration of any external system with the text. Executable
programs are typically used for training exercises which may check a student's
understanding of the text, and for simulation models of the concepts discussed
in the text. Experience with the use of Ebook3 for teaching operations research in
Switzerland indicates that students at first print out chapters they want to read
but later turn to a more dynamic reading style, including creating their own

models. Unfortunately this experience is only documented very sporadically at the end of the paper.

Schnase, J.L., and Leggett, J.J. (1989): "Computational hypertext in biological modelling," *Proc. ACM Hypertext'89 Conf.* (Pittsburgh, PA, 5–8 November), pp. 181–197.
Use of hypertext to support biological research by integrating a hypertext structure with raw data and a program to calculate various results from the data.

Schnase, J.L., Leggett, J., Kacmar, C., and Boyle, C. (1988): "A comparison of hypertext systems," *Technical Report* **TAMU 88-017,** Hypertext Research Lab, Texas A&M University, September.
Presents a three-level layered model for hypertext system architecture (front-end, hypertext, back-end) and gives definitions of common hypertext terms. This framework is used to discuss ten of the better-known hypertext systems.

Scragg, G.W. (1985): "Some thoughts on paper notes and electronic messages," *ACM SIGCHI Bulletin* **16**, 3 (January), pp. 41– 44.
Post-It notes have several advantages over current computer systems: They are applicable in a uniform way in many different situations, have very low overhead, and can be added to existing information tools even where no annotation facility has been planned for.

Sculley, J. (1989): "The relationship between business and higher education: A perspective on the 21st century," *Communications of the ACM* **32**, 9 (September), pp. 1056–1061.
A rather broad article by the Apple CEO about possible (and needed) changes in the educational process due to technological progress. Sculley identifies two current core technologies for educational software; hypermedia and simulation, and mentions AI and intelligent "agents" as a future third core technology. The article is illustrated with several color shots from the *Knowledge Navigator* video scenario. It also includes an example of the ALIAS hypertext authoring environment from Stanford for historical simulation.

Seabrook, R.H.C., and Shneiderman, B. (1989): "The user interface in a hypertext, multiwindow program browser," *Interacting with Computers* **1**, 3 (December), pp. 299–337.
The HYBROW system for working with program code. The paper briefly considers various alternative interface designs with respect to windows in hypertext systems such as how to replace earlier windows with new ones. The user can designate a window as "frozen," meaning that it will never be overwritten by new windows.

Shneiderman, B. (1987a): "User interface design and evaluation for an electronic encyclopedia," in Salvendy, G. (ed.): *Cognitive Engineering in the Design of Human-Computer Interaction and Expert Systems,* Elsevier Science Publishers, pp. 207–223.
About TIES (the predecessor of Hyperties), including reports on a number of empirical studies of design details: effect of screen size, embedded vs. explicit menus, and electronic vs. paper versions of the same information.

Shneiderman, B. (1987b): "User interface design for the Hyperties electronic encyclopedia," *Proc. ACM Hypertext'87 Conf.* (Chapel Hill, NC, 13–15 November), pp. 189–194.

Shneiderman, B. (1989): "Reflections on authoring, editing, and managing hypertext," in Barrett, E. (ed.): *The Society of Text*, MIT Press, Cambridge, MA, pp. 115–131.
Surveys several Hyperties applications, including one about the Hubble Space Telescope implemented in a two-frame version on a Sun workstation. The chapter also contains a discussion of the authoring aids in Hyperties. A large part of the chapter is dedicated to the lessons learnt from building more then 30 hypertext structures for Hyperties. One key lesson is that each project was different and had to have its information structured according to a principle that was suited for its specific domain. Experience shows that it is necessary to have a single managing editor to coordinate a project and to copy edit the final result.

Shneiderman, B., Brethauer, D., Plaisant, C., and Potter, R. (1989): "The Hyperties electronic encyclopedia: An evaluation based on three museum installations," *J. American Society for Information Science* **40**, 3 (May), pp. 172–182.
Data from more than 5,000 sessions showed that museum visitors using Hyperties used the hypertext embedded menus far more than they used the traditional index facility also available. On a methodological note, the authors conclude that direct observation and iterative refinement were more useful for improving their hypertext systems than were simple logging data of user navigation behavior. The authors also observe that a user interface that was usable in the laboratory as soon as users had seen a 15-second demo still gave many users problems in the museum environment where they were on their own. To avoid these problems in the field, the user interface was redesigned to have, for instance, larger touchable zones for the selection mechanism.

Slaney, M. (1990): "Interactive signal processing documents," *IEEE Acoustics, Speech, and Signal Processing Magazine* (April).
A discussion of a Mathematica notebook with a signal processing model and the advantages and disadvantages of interactive scientific documents, which are compared to "literate programming."

Stevens, S.M. (1989): "Intelligent interactive video simulation of a code inspection," *Communications of the ACM* **32**, 7 (July), pp. 832–843.
Use of integrated AI techniques and hypermedia presentation to allow users to simulate taking part in a meeting. The system is used to teach the software engineering review technique of code inspection. This is a technique best learnt through practice and participation in inspection meetings so the main teaching approach is to allow the student to act as a meeting participant in a simulated 1–2 hour meeting. The user "participates" in the meeting by assembling sentence fragments from a menu based natural language interface. In addition to the meeting simulation, the DVI disk also contains motivational and instructional films on the importance of software quality and a hypertext library including the NASA Ada style guidelines, about 1,000 traditional course visuals, and 12 important papers on inspection. Finally the system contains two tools to allow the student to see the code that is the topic of the inspection meeting: a traditional source level debugger and a hypertext browser linking code segments and the relevant sections of the specifications. All these various tools and techniques are integrated in a single instructional environment.

Stiegler, M. (1989): "Hypermedia and the singularity," *Analog Science Fiction* **109**, 1 (January), pp. 52–71.
Includes a discussion of "hyperstyle" issues in writing hypertext fiction as well as examples from the hypertext science fiction novel *David's Sling* written by Stiegler.

Stotts, P.D., and Furuta, R. (1988): "Adding browsing semantics to the hypertext model," *Proc. ACM Conf. Document Processing Systems* (Santa Fe, NM, 5–9 December), pp. 43–50.
A model of hypertext based on Petri nets, which includes security possibilities for "enforcing browsing restrictions": Certain links are active or not, depending on a "hypertext state," which again can depend on the individual user's access privileges or interaction history.

Streitz, N.A., Hannemann, J., and Thüring, M. (1989): "From ideas and arguments to hyperdocuments: Travelling through activity spaces," *Proc. ACM Hypertext'89 Conf.* (Pittsburgh, PA, 5–8 November), pp. 343–364.
Hypertext authoring environments should provide active support to the authors' cognitive problem solving. A system based on Toulmin argumentation schemas is described.

Talbert, M.L., and Umphress, D.A. (1989): "Object-oriented text decomposition: A methodology for creating CAI using hypertext," in Maurer, H. (ed.): *Computer Assisted Learning*, Lecture Notes in Computer Science **vol. 360**, Springer-Verlag, Berlin, FGR, pp. 560–578.
A set of principles for partitioning knowledge into hypertext nodes based on looking at the key concepts in the domain as interrelated objects. The authors used the method to convert an existing article on the Ada programming language from linear form to hypertext in the KnowledgePro system and then conducted a test in which computer science students read the article in either hypertext form or as a plain text file. The results showed that the hypertext readers had improved their conceptual understanding of the structure of the article more than the plain text file readers. The paper does not explain the experimental methodology or results in sufficient detail, however, to enable us to evaluate their validity. The authors do report that several of the students were frustrated with problems with the KnowledgePro engine used to display their hypertext structure (e.g. strange inverse video).

Teshiba, K., and Chignell, M. (1988): "Development of a user model evaluation technique for hypermedia based interfaces," *Proc. Human Factors Society 32nd Annual Meeting*, pp. 323–327.
Users sorted cards with terms from the domain described in the hypertext into piles based on their perceptions of the similarity between the terms, and then they sorted the piles into a hierarchy. This procedure provided the experimenters with a way of measuring the structure of the users' conceptual models of the domain knowledge described in the hypertext and to assess the differences between the two structures. The authors use the Hubert gamma measure of proximity between two hierarchies for this comparison and find that the proximity increases slightly with extended use of the hypertext.

Timpka, T., Padgham, L., Hedblom, P., Wallin, S., and Tibblin, G. (1989): "A hypertext knowledge base for primary care—LIMEDS in LINCKS," *Proc. ACM SIGIR'89* (Cambridge, MA, 25–28 June), pp. 221–228.

A hypertext structure for medical general practitioners which is implemented in a distributed architecture with the database residing on a Sun and the user interface running on a Macintosh.

Tombaugh, J., Lickorish, A., and Wright, P. (1987): "Multi-window displays for readers of lengthy texts," *Intl. J. Man-Machine Studies* **26**, 5 (May), pp. 597–615.

Two studies were conducted comparing a single-window system (having the entire text in one big file) and a multi-window system (having the text split into one segment in each window): The first study using untrained users indicated an advantage for the single-window system. In the second study, users were trained in the use of the window-system before their use of it was measured and this experiment indicated some advantage for the multi-window system. An additional insight from this study was that some novices had difficulties in using the mouse (this could be a problem for some hypertext systems in walk up and use situations if they do not use, say, a touch screens instead of a mouse).

Trigg, R.H. (1983): "A Network-Based Approach to Text Handling for the Online Scientific Community," *Ph.D. thesis*, Department of Computer Science, University of Maryland (University Microfilms #8429934).

Probably the first Ph.D. thesis about hypertext. Describes the TEXTNET system, which had a highly developed taxonomy of link types.

Trigg, R.H. (1988): "Guided tours and tabletops: Tools for communicating in a hypertext environment," *ACM Trans. Office Information Systems* **6**, 4 (October), pp. 398–414.

Two tools to allow an author to convey the meaning of hypertext documents to future readers. *Guided tours* are related to the original Vannevar Bush idea of "trails." through a linked medium and provide an author-specified path through the hypertext. Each stop on the tour is a full set of NoteCards cards (rather than just a single hypertext node). The layout of these cards are determined by the *Tabletop* tool, which allows authors to specify an entire screen full of open windows/cards (including the spatial position) as the destination for a hypertext jump. This paper also appears in *Proc. 2nd Conf. Computer-Supported Cooperative Work* (Portland, OR, 26–28 September 1988), pp. 216–226.

Trigg, R.H., and Irish, P.M. (1987): "Hypertext habitats: Experiences of writers in NoteCards," *Proc. ACM Hypertext'87 Conf.* (Chapel Hill, NC, 13–15 November), pp. 89–108.

Observations from 20 writers who used NoteCards to prepare text for later linearizing. The paper includes observations on how authors take notes, structure these notes, and maintain references and bibliographies.

Trigg, R.H., and Weiser, M. (1986): "TEXTNET: A network based approach to text handling," *ACM Trans. Office Inf.Syst.* **4**, 1 (January), pp.1–23.

Trigg, R.H., Suchman, L.A., and Halasz, F.G. (1986): "Supporting collaboration in NoteCards," *Proc. 1st Conf. Computer-Supported Cooperative Work* (Austin, TX, 3–5 December), pp. 153–162.
A discussion of the issues involved when several people want to use a hypertext system to write a collaborative work.

Trigg, R.H., Moran, T.P., and Halasz, F.G. (1987): "Adaptability and tailorability in NoteCards," *Proc. IFIP INTERACT'87* (Stuttgart, FRG, 1–4 September), pp. 723–728.
Examples of how NoteCards has adapted to different users through flexibility, parametrization and integration with other products and how it has been tailored through its programmer's interface and by design of new card types through object-oriented specialization.

Utting, K., and Yankelovich, N. (1989): "Context and orientation in hypermedia networks," *ACM Transactions on Information Systems* 7, 1 (January), pp. 58–84.
An excellent survey of the issues related to various forms of overview diagrams with examples from several hypertext systems and a detailed discussion of the design of the web view mechanism in Intermedia.

Valdez, F., Chignell, M., and Glenn, B. (1988): "Browsing models for hypermedia databases," *Proc. Human Factors Society 32nd Annual Meeting*, pp. 318–322.
Empirical methods for constructing distance measures and indicators of salience (or "landmark quality") for use in the construction of fisheye views. The distance measures were constructed by having subjects sort cards by similarity. Salience indicators were constructed by asking users whether the term being tested would be on the path between two randomly selected nodes. The more times users say that a term associated with a given node would be on the path between two other nodes, the higher "landmark quality" is awarded to the given node. Of the measures that could be derived from non-user testing inspection of the hypertext network, the one having the highest correlation with the empirical landmark quality measure is that of second-order connectivity, i.e. the number of other nodes that can be reached from a given node in two jumps. The correlation between these two measures was r=0.62.

van Dam, A. (1988): "Hypertext'87 keynote address," *Communications of the ACM* **31**, 7 (July), pp. 887–895.
The history of hypertext (especially at Brown University) and a discussion of some of the issues facing designers of future hypertext systems. Contains a description of the Hypertext Editing System from 1967 and the FRESS system from 1968.

Ventura, C.A. (1988): "Why switch from paper to electronic manuals?," *Proc. ACM Conf. Document Processing Systems* (Santa Fe, NM, 5–9 December), pp. 111–116.
A military perspective on the documentation problem. Current fighter aircrafts need 300,000 to 500,000 pages of documentation, and this quantity is impossible to deal with in a paper format. The author details the practical problems of these big piles of paper and hopes that going electronic will solve them (but offers no evidence that it will actually do so).

Walker, J.H. (1987): "Document Examiner: Delivery interface for hypertext documents," *Proc. ACM Hypertext'87 Conf.* (Chapel Hill, NC, 13–15 November), pp. 307–323.
The Symbolics Document Examiner is an online manual that was the first major hypertext system to see real world use.

Walker, J.H. (1988a): "Supporting document development with Concordia," *IEEE Computer* **21**, 1 (January), pp. 48–59.
The authoring interface to documents for the Symbolics Document Examiner.

Walker, J.H. (1988b): "The role of modularity in document authoring systems," *Proc. ACM Conf. Document Processing Systems* (Santa Fe, NM, 5–9 December), pp. 117–124.
Authoring environments viewed as an analogy to software development environments: Support for the writing process should involve support for explicit modularity. Good and recognizable node names are essential for abstraction but at first the writers had difficulties in assigning highly specific names because they were used to standard names like "introduction." Over the years this changed, and the writers actually found that specific node names helped them clarify their writing.

Walker, J.H., Young, E., and Mannes, S. (1990): "A case study of using a manual online," *Machine-Mediated Learning*.
An analysis of the logging of 34,700 user interactions with the Symbolics Document Examiner. 40% of user actions were devoted to finding information (20% keyword search, 19% hypertext jumps from overview diagrams, and 1% jumps from a table of contents) while 60% were devoted to displaying information.

Weyer, S.A. (1982): "The design of a dynamic book for information search," *Int.J. Man-Machine Studies* **17**, 1 (July), pp. 87–107.

Weyer, S.A. (1988): "As we may learn," in Ambron, S., and Hooper, K. (eds.): *Interactive Multimedia: Visions of Multimedia for Developers, Educators, & Information Providers*, Microsoft Press, pp. 87–103.
Advocates a more knowledge-oriented view of hypertext instead of the more widely used book and library metaphors, which according to the author can overshadow the dynamic nature of information and its uses. Instead of being static, information should be adaptable to the learner's preferences, and links should depend on the user's previous actions and current goals.

Weyer, S.A., and Borning, A.H. (1985): "A prototype electronic encyclopedia," *ACM Trans. Office Information Systems* **3**, 1 (January), pp. 63–88.
A knowledge-based system where the text is encoded in a concept network and the actual output to the user is custom generated based on a model of different attributes of the user. Access to the information is through browsing: "navigating through a neighborhood of information and referencing items by pointing or recognizing," i.e., hypertext. Filters control such things as whether metric or English measurement units should be displayed. This work was done at Atari, but they terminated the project before more than a prototype could be built.

Whalen, T., and Patrick, A. (1989): "Conversational hypertext: Information access through natural language dialogues with computers," *Proc. ACM CHI'89* (Austin, TX, 30 April–4 May), pp. 289–292.
A line oriented interface to a hypertext information base. Users move to new hypertext nodes by typing questions in natural language, and the system then interprets these natural language utterances in relation to what would make sense in that location of the hypertext network.

Whiteside, J., Bennett, J., and Holtzblatt, K. (1988): "Usability engineering: Our experience and evolution," in Helander, M. (ed.): *Handbook of Human-Computer Interaction,* Elsevier Science Publishers, pp. 757–789.
Good introduction to generally applicable methods for the lifecycle of usable products.

Wilkinson, R.T., and Robinshaw, H.M. (1987): "Proof-reading: VDU and paper text compared for speed, accuracy and fatigue," *Behaviour and Information Technology* **6**, 2 (April–June), pp. 125–133.
The effect of fatigue on reading speed and errors while proofreading: Over a period of one hour of continued use, the relative performance of screen users dropped even more than the performance of paper users did.

Wilson, E. (1990): "Links and structure in hypertext database for law," *Proc. ECHT'90 European Conf. Hypertext* (Paris, France, 28–30 November), Cambridge University Press.
On the automatic conversion of legal texts into the Justus hypertext system built on top of the Unix version of Guide at the University of Kent. Justus integrates primary law sources with secondary ones, such as a legal dictionary. Unfortunately, some laws use other definitions of terms than the ones in the dictionary, so one has to be careful in making automatic links.

Wilson, K.S. (1988): "Palenque: An interactive multimedia digital video interactive prototype for children," *Proc. ACM CHI'88* (Washington, DC, 15–19 May), pp. 275–279.
A DVI system developed at Bank Street College of Education for teaching Mexican archaeology. Users may move around images and film from Maya ruins and collect a personalized "album" with annotated snapshots. Unfortunately, the paper is not illustrated (a nice videotape of the system was shown at the conference where the paper was presented), but a sequence of four nice color screen shots of Palenque may be found in [Luther 1988].

Wright, P. (1989): "Interface alternatives for hypertext," *Hypermedia* **1**, 2, pp. 146–166.
A classification of hypertext design options from five categories: linking, jumping, visual appearance of the destination, navigation, and reader tasks. For each category, the design options are ordered according to how much they constrain readers, thereby indirectly indicating what user categories they are suited for.

Wright, P., and Lickorish, A. (1983): "Proof-reading texts on screen and paper," *Behaviour and Information Technology* **2**, 3 (July–September), pp. 227–235.

Reading from a computer screen was 27% slower than reading from paper.

Wright, P., and Lickorish, A. (1984): "Ease of annotation in proof-reading tasks," *Behaviour and Information Technology* **3**, 3 (July–September), pp. 185–194.
Proofreaders performed faster when their annotations were integrated with the main text.

Wright, P., and Lickorish, A. (1988): "Colour cues as location aids in lengthy texts on screen and paper," *Behaviour and Information Technology* **7**, 1 (January–March), pp. 11–30.
Color might be a solution to the problems users have in remembering where in lengthy texts they have previously read something. An experiment showed that this was indeed the case when reading a printed document on colored paper, but three additional experiments failed to show any advantage of using different colors of characters on a computer screen. The authors speculate that color might work better as borders or strips or if it was assigned by the readers rather than by the writers (as in highlighting, cf. [Nielsen 1986]).

Wright, P., and Lickorish, A. (1990): "An empirical comparison of two navigation systems for two hypertexts," in McAleese, R., and Green, C. (eds.) *Hypertext: State of the Art*, Ablex, pp. 84–93.
A comparison of so-called page navigation (traditional hypertext with link anchors on the same display as the text) and a so-called index navigation (where users could only jump to new locations in the hypertext by first going to a special display giving an overview of the entire information). These designs were tested on two different hypertexts with the result that index navigation was best for one text while page navigation was best for the other. The general conclusion is that different navigation mechanisms may be needed for different text structures and reader tasks.

Wurman, R.S. (1989): *"Information Anxiety,"* Doubleday.
A famous book designer (creator of the ACCESS guide books) presents his philosophy on how to structure information. If ever a book was suited for hypertext publication, this is it. It is full of sidebars and quotes from other work and the table of contents is an extended abstract of each chapter in outline form. This is a good book, even if he never mentions usability testing (is a good designer always right?).

Yankelovich, N., Meyrowitz, N., and van Dam, A. (1985): "Reading and writing the electronic book," *IEEE Computer* **18**, 10 (October), pp. 15–30.
A discussion of FRESS, Intermedia, and other Brown systems as well as a very good survey of the issues at the point in time just before hypertext hit the market for real.

Yankelovich, N., Landow, G.P., and Cody, D. (1987): "Creating hypermedia materials for English literature students," *ACM SIGCUE Outlook* **19**, 3–4 (Spring/Summer), pp. 12–25.
About the goals for a course on English literature from 1700 to the present taught with the support of the Intermedia hypertext system: Explain historical and cultural context in more depth than possible in a literature class and teach "critical thinking" to let students perceive any phenomenon or event as potentially multidetermined or subject to multi-causation. As their final

assignment, students will add information about an author to system and link it to the existing corpus of information.

Yankelovich, N., Haan, B.J., Meyrowitz, N.K., and Drucker, S.M. (1988a): "Intermedia: The concept and the construction of a seamless information environment," *IEEE Computer* **21**, 1 (January), pp. 81–96.
A good survey article about the major aspects of Intermedia, including a twelve-screen example session and some amount of implementation detail.

Yankelovich, N., Smith, K.E., Garrett, N., and Meyrowitz, N. (1988b): "Issues in designing a hypermedia document system: The Intermedia case study," in Ambron, S., and Hooper, K. (eds.): *Interactive Multimedia: Visions of Multimedia for Developers, Educators, & Information Providers,* Microsoft Press, pp. 33–85.
The chapter starts with a richly illustrated walkthrough of an example session with Intermedia. It continues with a careful and well illustrated discussion of some of the user interface issues in hypertexts with overlapping and/or changing link anchors and/or destinations. Also contains a discussion of other multi-user issues. Most of this chapter is really an edited version of [Garrett et al. 1986] with more illustrations.

Yoder, E., and Wettach, T.C. (1989): "Using hypertext in a law firm," *Proc. ACM Hypertext'89 Conf.* (Pittsburgh, PA, 5–8 November), pp. 159–167.
The HyperLex system used to support work on patent cases and intellectual property law at the largest law firm in Pittsburgh, Reed Smith with 385 attorneys.

Yoder, E., McCracken, D., and Akscyn, R. (1984): "Instrumenting a human-computer interface for development and evaluation," *Proc. IFIP INTERACT'84* (London, U.K., 4–7 September).
Instrumenting the frame-based ZOG system to record user behavior. Data for user time spent at each node was fairly easy to collect because of the frame-based nature of the system.

Yoder, E., Akscyn, R., and McCracken, D. (1989): "Collaboration in KMS: A shared hypermedia system," *Proc. ACM CHI'89* (Austin, TX, 30 April–4 May), pp. 37–42.
The authors advocate using the same system for individual work and collaborative work and claim that KMS is suited for such a role. KMS supports "non-disruptive" annotation by providing a specific annotation-type of link (anchors prefixed with an "@") which is ignored by formatting programs.

Zellweger, P.T. (1988): "Active paths through multimedia documents," in van Vliet, J.C. (ed.): *Document Manipulation and Typography,* Cambridge University Press, U.K., pp. 19–34.
So-called scripts are used to provide a mechanism for guided tours and other predefined directed (but still non-linear) paths (sequences of links) through documents.

Zygmont, J. (1988): "Compact-disc companies test new frontier," *High Technology Business* **8**, 2 (February), pp. 18–23.
Popular introduction to CD-I (Compact Disk Interactive) from both technical and commercial perspectives.

Far Out Stuff

One of the best works of art so far to utilize the principle of parallel story lines is the classic film *Rashomon* (1951) by the famous Japanese director Akira Kurosawa. The film tells four different versions of a violent incident in which a bandit attacks a nobleman in the forests in medieval Japan (one of the versions is told by the ghost of a person who was killed in the incident). The film won the Academy Award for best foreign film. If you cannot find an opportunity to see the film, you can read an English translation of its manuscript together with assorted comments in book form: A. Kurosawa and D. Richie: *Rashomon*, Rutgers University Press, New Brunswick, 1987.

Several of the so-called "cyberpunk" science fiction authors have depicted a future computer system wherein users navigate interlinked highly visual three-dimensional data structures. One of the first and most famous novels in this genre is William Gibson: *Neuromancer*,[9] Ace 1984, which won both the Hugo and Nebula awards for best science fiction novel of 1984. Another relevant science fiction book is Vernor Vinge: *True Names* (Bluejay 1984).

Apple Computer has produced some videotapes narrated by its president, John Sculley, showing scenarios of how future versions of HyperCard and the "Knowledge Navigator" (using intelligent agents in the interface) would look. These very detailed and professionally produced scenarios are very convincing in their demonstrations of how future hypermedia systems might work. There is no substitute for actually watching the video, but you can get at least some idea of the Knowledge Navigator by reading Sculley [1989] and looking at the illustrations in that article.

---

[9] *Neuromancer* is also available in comic book form as a so-called graphic novel by Tom De Haven and Bruce Jensen (Epic Comics, New York 1989, ISBN 0-87135-574-4). It seems to me, however, that Gibson's original written form communicates the cyberspace idea better.

Index

Note: References in square brackets [ ] point to the alphabetical listing in the bibliography in Appendix B. The index does not list the authors of the books and papers mentioned in the alphabetical listing in the bibliography.

Proper indexing is closely related to the hypertext navigation issue. In some cases the number of index entries for a term is large enough to cause disorientation and I have chosen to highlight the one or two most important entries through the use of **bold** page numbers. See for example the entry for "Anchors."